Letts
EDUCATIONAL

ADVANCED
LEVEL

Revise A2
Sociology

Author

Steve Chapman

Contents

Specification lists

AQA Sociology

MODULE	SPECIFICATION TOPIC	CHAPTER REFERENCE	STUDIED IN CLASS	REVISED	PRACTICE QUESTIONS
	Power and politics				
	Explanations of the nature and distribution of power	2.1			
	The role of the modern state	2.1			
	Political parties and ideologies	2.2			
	Voting behaviour	2.2			
UNIT 4	Pressure groups and new social movements	2.3			
	Religion				
	Different theories of religion	3.1			
	The role of religion as a conservative force and as an initiator of change	3.1			
	Cults, sects, denominations and churches	3.2			
UNIT 4 (U4)	The relationship between religious beliefs, religious organisations and social groups	3.3			
	Definitions and explanations of the nature and extent of secularisation	3.4			
	World Sociology				
	Different definitions and explanations of development and under-development	4.1			
	The cultural, political and economic inter-relationships between societies	4.2			
UNIT 5	The role of aid, trade, Trans National Corporations and international agencies in different strategies for development	4.2 4.3			
	Education, health, demographic change and gender as aspects of development	4.4, 4.5, 4.6			
	Theory and methods				
	The relationship between theory and method	1.1			
UNIT 6 UNIT 5 (U5)	Consensus, conflict, structural and social action theories	1.3			
	Modernity and post-modernity	1.3			
	Sociology and science	1.1			
	Objectivity and value freedom	1.2			

MODULE	SPECIFICATION TOPIC	CHAPTER REFERENCE	STUDIED IN CLASS	REVISED	PRACTICE QUESTIONS
	Crime and deviance				
	Different explanations of crime, deviance, social order and social control	8.1 8.3			
	The relationship between deviance, power and social control	8.4			
	The social distribution of crime	8.2			
UNIT 6	The social construction of crime	8.4			
(U6)	Suicide	8.5			
(Synoptic)	**Stratification and differentiation**				
	Measuring social class	9.1			
	Different theories of stratification	9.2			
	Differences in life-chances by social class, ethnicity, gender	9.5 9.6			
	Changes in the class structure	9.3			
	Social mobility	9.4			

Examination analysis

The specification comprises three examinations.

Unit 4	This unit is divided into three sections: Power and politics, Religion, and World Sociology. Each section contains a compulsory short data response question plus two essay questions. Candidates must choose one section and answer the compulsory short data response question and one essay question within the chosen section.	*1 hr 30 min test*	*30%*
Unit 5W	This unit examines Theory and method only. Candidates must answer the compulsory data response question and one essay question from a choice of two. <u>or</u>	*1 hr 30 min test*	*30%*
Unit 5C	Sociological study (not exceeding 3500 words)		*30%*
Unit 6	This unit is divided into two sections: Crime and deviance, and Stratification and differentiation. Candidates must choose one section and answer the three-part synoptic question.	*1 hr 30 min test*	*10%*

OCR Sociology

MODULE	SPECIFICATION TOPIC	CHAPTER REFERENCE	STUDIED IN CLASS	REVISED	PRACTICE QUESTIONS
	Crime and deviance				
	Defining crime and deviance	8.1			
	Measuring crime and victimisation	8.2			
	Patterns of crime by social profile	8.2			
	Victimisation	8.2			
	Theories of crime and deviance	8.3			
	Power, control and the problem of crime	8.4			
	Education				
	Education and socialisation	5.1			
	The hidden curriculum	5.1			
	Streaming and labelling	5.2			
	Patterns of educational inequality	5.2			
	Theories of achievement and under-achievement	5.2			
	Education, training and the economy	5.3			
	The transition from school to work	5.3			
UNIT 2536 (U2536)	**Health**				
	The social construction of health and illness	6.1			
	Mental illness	6.1			
	Disability	6.1			
	Trends and patterns in health and illness	6.2			
	Sociological explanations of health inequalities	6.2			
	Health-care provision	6.2			
	The bio-medical model of health	6.3			
	The medical profession	6.3			
	Medicine and social control	6.3			
	Social policy and welfare				
	Ideologies and theories of welfare	7.1			
	Models of welfare provision	7.1			
	The development of the Welfare State	7.2			
	Community care	7.2			
	Patterns of provision in housing, social security and personal social services	7.2			
	Welfare and control	7.3			

MODULE	SPECIFICATION TOPIC	CHAPTER REFERENCE	STUDIED IN CLASS	REVISED	PRACTICE QUESTIONS
UNIT 2536 (U2536)	**Protest and social movements**				
	Political parties and pressure groups	2.2			
	New social movements	2.3			
	Globalisation, global social movements and nationalism	2.3			
	Direct action	2.3			
	Power	2.1			
UNIT 2537 (U2537)	**Applied sociological research skills**				
	Research design and sociological theory	1.3			
	Reliability, validity, representativeness and generalisability	1.1			
	Techniques of data collection	1.1			
UNIT 2539 (U2539) (Synoptic)	**Social inequality and difference**				
	Class, gender and ethnic inequalities in the workplace	9.3, 9.5, 9.6			
	Changes in the class structure	9.3			
	Poverty				
	Theories of social class inequality	9.1, 9.2			
	Theories of gender inequality	9.6			
	Theories of ethnic inequalities	9.5			

Examination analysis

The specification comprises three examinations.

Unit 2536	Candidates choose one question from a choice of twelve unstructured essay questions, two for each of the six options: Crime and deviance; Education; Health; Social policy and welfare; Protest and social movements and Popular culture.	*1 hr test 30%*
Unit 2537	Candidates must do one compulsory structured questions containing a data response and a research proposal. *or*	*1 hr 30 min test 30%*
Unit 2538	Personal study (between 2000 and 2500 words)	*30%*
Unit 2539	Candidates must do one of two multi-part synoptic data response questions.	*1 hr 30 min test 40%*

AS/A2 Level Sociology courses

AS and A2

All Sociology A Level courses are now in two parts, with three separate modules in each part. Candidates must take and pass three units for the AS (Advanced Subsidiary) course before they can move on to a further three units at A2 (i.e. 50% of the assessment) if they are seeking an A Level in Sociology. AS Sociology is assessed at the standard expected halfway through an A Level course: i.e. between GCSE and Advanced GCE. However A2 candidates will be assessed in line with the expectations that they have covered issues in greater depth and range and demonstrated more highly developed interpretative and critical skills than AS students.

How will you be tested?

Assessment units

For AS Sociology, you will be tested by three assessment units. For the full A Level in Sociology, you will take a further three units. AS Sociology forms 50% of the assessment weighting for the full A Level.

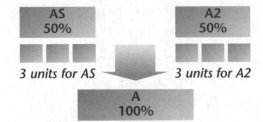

Each unit can normally be taken in either January or June. Alternatively, you can study the whole course before taking any of the unit examinations. There is a lot of flexibility about when exams can be taken and the diagram below shows just some of the ways that the assessment units may be taken for AS and A Level Sociology.

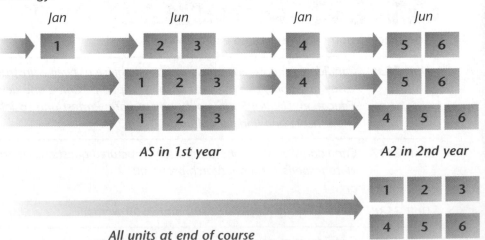

If you are disappointed with a module result, you can resit each module once. You will need to be very careful about when you take up a resit opportunity because you will only have one chance to improve your mark. The higher mark counts.

A2 and Synoptic assessment

The final unit of assessment, both for AQA and OCR Sociology, is called the synoptic assessment and is worth 20% of the total A Level marks (40% of A2). It can only be taken at the end of the course. This unit aims to draw together knowledge, understanding and skills learned in different parts of the A Level course. The questions for this unit will therefore involve the explicit assessment of your understanding of connections between topic areas, and the nature of sociological thought and methods.

Coursework

Coursework may form part of your A2 Sociology course as an alternative to Unit 5 (AQA) and Unit 2537 (OCR).

AQA offers students the option of a Sociological Study at A2. This is an opportunity for candidates to investigate a subject of sociological interest and carry out an analysis of primary and/or secondary data. This study should not exceed 3500 words in length.

OCR offers students the option of a Personal Study at A2. This is an extended piece of work on a sociological topic chosen by the candidate which will involve the analysis of primary and/or secondary data. The study should not exceed 2500 words.

Key skills

It is important that you develop your key skills throughout your AS and A2 courses. These are important skills that you need whatever you do beyond AS and A Levels.

It is a worthwhile qualification, as it demonstrates your ability to put your ideas across to other people, collect data and use up-to-date technology in your work.

What skills will I need?

For A2 Sociology, you will be tested by assessment objectives: these are the skills that you should have acquired by studying the course. The assessment objectives for A2 Sociology are similar to AS Sociology but more emphasis will be put on interpretation and evaluation skills throughout and especially in the synoptic unit.

Knowledge and understanding

- Recall of theories, methods, concepts and various forms of evidence and the links between them.
- Understanding of theories, methods, concepts and evidence and the links between them.
- Clearly and effectively communicating sociological knowledge and understanding.

Interpretation and evaluation

- Identification of facts, opinions and value judgements.
- Analysis and evaluation of the design of a range of investigations.
- Analysis and evaluation of the methods used to collect, select and record relevant evidence accurately.
- Selection and application of a range of relevant concepts and theories.
- Interpretation of quantitative and qualitative data.
- Identification and evaluation of significant social trends.
- Evaluation of different theories, arguments and evidence.

Different types of questions in A2 examinations

In A2 Sociology examinations, different types of questions are used to assess your abilities and skills.

AQA questions

The short data response question (Unit 4)

This will involve one piece of data (Item A) which could take a variety of forms, e.g. text, graphs, charts etc. This particular data response question is only divided into two parts worth 12 and 8 marks respectively. The organisation of these questions is intended to be predictable and the format will generally tend to follow this pattern. If Item A is text-based, it is likely that question (a) will take the following form:

(a) 'Using material from Item A and elsewhere, examine...'

If Item A is based on quantitative data in the form of a graph, chart, table etc. it is likely that question (a) will take the following form:

(a) 'Describe and briefly explain' the patterns, trends, variations etc. in the data in Item A.

Part (b) will focus on the word 'examine' as in 'examine some of the problems involved' in measuring or defining religious belief or voting behaviour or development etc. A possible alternative might be 'Briefly examine two influences on' particular types of behaviour related to the topics.

You should aim to spend about 30 minutes on this section.

Essay questions (Unit 4)

These too will use regular command words and phrases such as 'assess', 'evaluate' and 'compare and contrast'.

You should aim to spend about an hour on this section in terms of planning and writing.

Examples of AQA Unit 4 data responses and essays can be found in chapters 2, 3 and 4. Examples of AQA Unit 5 essays can be found in Chapter 5.

The extended data response questions (Unit 5)

This will involve two pieces of data (Items A and B) which could take a variety of forms, e.g. text, graphs, charts etc. This particular data response question is divided into four parts. It is likely that parts (a) and (b) will relate directly in terms of instructions to Item A whilst parts (c) and (d) will relate to Item B. Questions should take the following format:

(a) 'With reference to Item A, give two reasons' – the Item is likely to focus on a piece of research and the question will therefore focus on how or why that research was organised in a particular way. This question is worth 2 marks.

(b) 'Using the information in Item A, state a suitable hypothesis regarding ... that a sociologist would be able to test'. This question therefore focuses on you interpreting the material in Item A and coming up with a fresh perspective on it. It is worth 4 marks.

(c) This question is likely to ask you to 'briefly describe' how the information in Item B was collected, i.e. what research method was used, and to explain why. It is worth 6 marks.

(d) This question is likely to offer you a hypothesis, i.e. a statement that can be tested, that is suggested by the information in Item B. You will be asked to suggest two ways in which this hypothesis could be tested with justifications for your choice. The question is worth 8 marks.

It is recommended that you spend at least 30 minutes on this section which is worth 20 marks overall.

Examples of AQA Unit 5W data responses can be found in chapter 1.

The synoptic questions

AQA Module 6 is synoptic and candidates are given a choice of two topic areas; Crime and deviance, and Stratification and differentiation, to study. Synoptic assessment of these topics involves the explicit assessment of understanding of the connections between these topics, other areas of Sociology, the nature of sociological thought and methods of sociological enquiry.

In practice, this means a compulsory short data response question plus an essay question worth 60 marks in all for each topic. The data used is aimed at stimulating you to think about a particular sociological issue. However you should be aware that questions (a) and (b) worth 8 and 12 marks respectively which accompany the data will not ask you for responses which can be found in the data as in AS Level data response questions. Rather both questions aim to elicit a synoptic response from you, either by asking you to relate the topic area to other areas of social life (i.e. other units) or by asking you about methodological problems associated with collecting data about crime or stratification. For example, in regard to Crime and deviance, you may be asked about possible influences on criminal behaviour which may allow you to draw on your knowledge from other units (both AS and A2) such as family, poverty, unemployment, peer groups, youth culture, education etc. You may also be asked about problems of reliability and validity in regard to the official collection of statistics about crime or victims of crime. The essay question worth 40 marks will simply focus on the synoptic topic itself although relevant links to other units and theory and method will be rewarded. You will find examples of AQA synoptic questions and specimen answers in Chapters 8 and 9 of this revision guide.

OCR questions

Unstructured essay questions (Unit 2536)

Candidates have to answer one question in one hour. All the questions, which are worth 60 marks, will have the same command phrase 'outline and assess' and will be followed by phrases such as 'sociological explanations', the sociological view', 'the strengths and weaknesses', 'how sociologists might explain', 'theories', 'how recent changes' etc. Examples of these types of question can be found in Chapters 2, 5, 6, 7 and 8 of this book.

Data response questions (Unit 2537)

Candidates have to answer one compulsory data response questions in one hour thirty minutes worth 90 marks in all.

Candidates will be presented with one piece of data (Item A) which could take a variety of forms, e.g. text, graphs, charts etc.

Question (a) worth 10 marks will be a straightforward question asking you to interpret the information in Item A.

Question (b) worth 10 marks will ask you to identify two strengths or weaknesses of a particular method or approach.

Question (c) worth 14 marks will ask you to summarise in your own words what the research findings in Item A tell us about a particular sociological problem.

It is recommended that you spend approximately 45 minutes on this section.
You will then be presented with a practical research problem (Item B). You will be asked to think about the design of a research proposal which might be used to investigate this problem. Questions (d) and (e) aim to assess your proposed solution to the problem.

Question (d) worth 22 marks will ask you to 'outline and explain' how you propose to collect information on the problem.

Question (e) worth 34 marks will ask you to assess potential weaknesses of your proposed methods, 'briefly explaining' how you intend to overcome them.

The synoptic question (Unit 2539)

OCR module 2539 is the synoptic unit and focuses exclusively on Social inequality and difference. This assesses candidates' understanding of the relationship between social inequality, the nature of sociological thought and methods of sociological enquiry. It also revisits candidates' knowledge and understanding of how social inequality impacts on other units studied throughout AS and A2.

In practice, this means doing a data response question from a choice of two. Both questions will ask candidates to examine two pieces of data (Items A and B), one of which is likely to be organised in a quantitative form (tables, graphs, bar-charts etc.) and the other which is likely to be in textual form. There will be a total of five questions in all totalling 120 marks.

Parts (a) and (b) worth 10 marks each will ask candidates to interpret the data in Items A and B. Part (c) worth 18 marks will link Social inequality and difference to methods of sociological enquiry by asking candidates to think about the problems in gathering data relating to this area. Part (d) worth 30 marks will ask candidates to link Social Inequality and Difference to other areas of the specifications, e.g. you may be asked to give examples from 'other areas of social life' of ethnic or gender inequalities. You could draw from your knowledge of education, health etc. to do this. Finally, part (e) worth 52 marks will focus on sociological theories and explanations of particular types of inequality. You will find an example of an OCR synoptic question in Chapter 9 of this revision guide.

Exam technique

Examiners use instructions to help you to decide the length and depth answer. In essays and data response questions the following 'action' or 'trigger' words and phrases are frequently used.

State, define, what is meant by, name

These normally require a short, concise answer and is often recall material that can be learned by rote.

Explain, discuss

Some reasoning or some reference to theory is required. It normally involves reference to both sides of a debate.

Outline, describe

This implies a short response which sums up the major points of one particular theory or approach.

Identify, suggest, illustrate

These words normally require you to apply your knowledge to a particular sociological problem or theory.

Assess, examine, evaluate

These words suggest that you should look at the strengths and weaknesses of an argument or both sides of a particular debate. You should offer judgements based on evidence.

Some dos and don'ts

Dos

Do read the rubric, i.e. the set of instructions at the start of the exam paper.

- You don't want to answer too many questions or not enough or answer from the wrong sections.

Do answer the question set rather than the one you wished was set.

Do spend 5 minutes reading through the Items and the questions.

- It is especially important to read through all the questions before attempting any of them. A common mistake is to use information to answer a question which is more appropriate to another question.

Do plan your response to any question worth over 20 marks.

Do pay special attention to the way marks are divided up between sections of data responses.

- It is wasteful to write more than is required and it will impact negatively on the time left for the bigger questions.

Do always clearly label the part of the question you are answering.

Do use the data provided in the Items whenever it is relevant to do so.

- Respond to the appropriate 'action' words and phrases. Failure to use them could result in you failing to pick up marks.

Do exercise care when it comes to the interpretation of statistics, tables and diagrams especially in regard to scale.

- Marks are easily wasted because the candidate fails to look at how the data is organised (i.e. into percentages, thousands, etc.).

Do take care in how you present sociological thinkers and theory.

- You need to recognise that contributions to sociological debate are a product of a specific time and place. For example, try to avoid suggesting that 19th-century sociologists are still making a regular contribution to modern sociological debate.

Do take notice of 'action' words and phrases such as 'contemporary', 'recently', 'post Second World War', 'last twenty years', etc.

- These words want you to set your response in a modern context. Any reference to studies and debate outside these periods (e.g. 'contemporary' and 'recent' usually mean the last 20 years) will be regarded as largely irrelevant to the question. It is not necessary to know the exact date of a study but do know the decade in which it was produced.

Do make your sociology more valid by being aware of current social and political events.

- Be aware of how sociological theory and methods can be applied to them. Examiners want you to be able to apply your knowledge to the real world and its social problems.

Do take care with regard to grammar and spelling.

- Poor grammatical structure and spelling can impair the intelligibility of a response or weaken the argument used. A coherent and logical presentation of argument and evidence is necessary to achieve a good AS Level standard.

Don'ts

Don't waste time writing out the question.

- This wastes time. The marks are for the answer.

Don't mistake your own opinion for sociology.

- Try and back up what you say with evidence.

Don't over-simplify sociological debate by presenting ideological positions as irreconcilable.

- Examiners are concerned that functionalists and positivists are often presented as 'bad' sociologists whilst Marxists and interpretivists are seen as 'good' sociologists. You need to demonstrate that sociological studies which seem opposed actually share common research problems and theoretical underpinnings. In other words, similarities are just as important as differences. This is comparing and contrasting.

Don't over-rely on pre-prepared 'shopping list' answers.

- Try to avoid writing down all you know about a particular area, regardless of the question asked.

- Be prepared to be flexible and to adapt your knowledge to the question set. Think on your feet. There are no rehearsed or model answers.

Don't be one-sided in your evaluation.

- Don't focus disproportionately on the virtues of a debate, theory or method at the expense of its drawbacks or vice versa. In order to get into the higher mark bands, your evaluation must be balanced.

What grade do you want?

Everyone would like to improve their grades but you will only manage this with a lot of hard work and determination. You should have a fair idea of your natural ability and likely grade in Sociology and the hints below offer advice on improving that grade.

For a Grade A

You will need to be a very good all-rounder.

- You must go into every exam knowing the work extremely well.
- You must be able to apply your knowledge to new, unfamiliar situations.
- You need to have practised many, many exam questions so that you are ready for the type of question that will appear.

The exams test all areas of the syllabus and any weaknesses in your sociology will be found out. There must be no holes in your knowledge and understanding. For a Grade A, you must be competent in all areas.

For a Grade C

You must have a reasonable grasp of Sociology but you may have weaknesses in several areas and you will be unsure of sociological concepts and theories.

- Many Grade C candidates are just as good at answering questions as the Grade A students but holes and weaknesses often show up in just some topics.
- To improve, you will need to master your weaknesses and you must prepare thoroughly for the exam. You must become a better all-rounder.

For a Grade E

You cannot afford to miss the easy marks. Even if you find Sociology difficult to understand and would be happy with a Grade E, there are plenty of questions in which you can gain marks.

- You must memorise all definitions and basic concepts.
- You must practise exam questions to give yourself confidence that you do know some Sociology. In exams, answer the parts of questions that you know first. You must not waste time on the difficult parts. You can always go back to these later.
- The areas of Sociology that you find most difficult are going to be hard to score on in exams. Even in the difficult questions, there are still marks to be gained.

The table below shows how your average mark is translated:

average	80%	70%	60%	50%	40%
grade	A	B	C	D	E

You can always gain some marks if you only partly outline a theory or sociological response to a problem. If it is a data response question, you can pick up marks by fully using the data.

Four steps to successful revision

Step 1: Understand

- Study the topic to be learned slowly. Make sure you understand the logic or important concepts.
- Mark up the text if necessary – underline, highlight and make notes
- Re-read each paragraph slowly.

GO TO STEP 2

Step 2: Summarise

- Now make your own revision note summary:
  What is the main idea, theme or concept to be learned?
  What are the main points? How does the logic develop?
  Ask questions: Why? How? What next?
- Use bullet points, mind maps, patterned notes.
- Link ideas with mnemonics, mind maps, crazy stories.
- Note the title and date of the revision notes
  (e.g. Sociology: Religion, 3rd March).
- Organise your notes carefully and keep them in a file.

This is now in **short-term memory**. You will forget 80% of it if you do not go to Step 3.
GO TO STEP 3, but first take a 10 minute break.

Step 3: Memorise

- Take 25 minute learning 'bites' with 5 minute breaks.
- After each 5 minute break test yourself:
  Cover the original revision note summary
  Write down the main points
  Speak out loud (record on tape)
  Tell someone else
  Repeat many times.

The material is well on its way to **long-term memory**.
You will forget 40% if you do not do step 4. **GO TO STEP 4**

Step 4: Track/Review

- Create a Revision Diary (one A4 page per day).
- Make a revision plan for the topic, e.g. 1 day later, 1 week later, 1 month later.
- Record your revision in your Revision Diary, e.g.
  Sociology: Religion, 3rd March 25 minutes
  Sociology: Gender and religion, 5th March 15 minutes
  Sociology: Religion and social change, 3rd April 15 minutes
  ... and then at monthly intervals.

Chapter 1

Theory and method

The following topics are covered in this chapter:

- *Is sociology a science?*
- *Subjectivity, objectivity and value-freedom*
- *Sociological theories*

1.1 Is sociology a science?

After studying this section you should be able to:

- *debate the nature of science*
- *outline and evaluate the strengths and weaknesses of arguments that suggest sociology is scientific*
- *identify the relationship between positivism, interpretivism and sociological methods*

LEARNING SUMMARY

Defining science

AQA ▶ U5

Lawson argues that science differs from other belief systems because it provides **objective evidence for its propositions using logical and systematic means of collecting data**. In other words, it is **empirical**. Science is an attempt to create knowledge that is 'true' and certain. Other belief systems such as common sense and religion are based upon individual perceptions and beliefs. They are partial and subjective. They depend upon faith or experience rather than fact.

Positivism

Positivists are thinkers who believe that science – and science alone – can provide unbiased knowledge which is generalisable (i.e. it is true in many situations, not just one specific case) and which can solve social and sociological problems.

Auguste Comte

Positivist sociology originated with the work of Auguste **Comte** (1798–1857). He believed that the social world closely resembled the natural physical world. He argued that both were made up of objective facts, which were independent of individuals and waiting to be discovered. Comte believed that behaviour in both the natural and social world was governed by external laws. He argued that sociology could be a 'science of society' engaged in discovering the social laws governing human behaviour.

Comte believed society should be studied using scientific methods of analysis to produce accurate, quantified data. The term **'positivism'** derives from this emphasis upon the positive sciences, on tested and systematic experience. Positivism, then, is closely identified with and its methodology closely modelled on the **traditional scientific world**.

Key points from AS
- **Positivism**
  Revise AS pages 17–18

The aim of positivists, therefore – whether they are natural or social scientists – is to produce **scientific 'laws'** about any phenomena: laws that accurately describe the causes, functioning and consequences of phenomena. Positivists have developed a 'model' scientific approach to research which is known as the **hypothetico-deductive approach**. This involves a number of logical steps in carrying out research:

- **observation** – a phenomenon or problem is observed to exist and needs explanation

- **hypothesis** – a possible explanation is put forward
- **experiment** – the hypothesis is subjected to rigorous testing to see if it holds up
- **theorising** – if confirmed by the experiment, a law is created which explains all identical phenomena or problems.

In the testing of hypotheses, the **laboratory experiment** is the preferred technique of the positivist natural scientist.

Sociological positivism

| AQA | U5 |
| OCR | U2537 |

Key points from AS

- **The experimental method**
  Revise AS page 20
- **The social survey**
  Revise AS pages 20–21
- **Structured interviews**
  Revise AS page 22
- **Official statistics**
  Revise AS page 24

The sociological positivist insists that the methods and techniques applied in research should display certain essential features.

- They must be **objective**, possibly **quantitative** (involving numbers or statistics) and **under the control of the researcher**.
- They should satisfy the criteria of **reliability**, that is, if repeated, the same findings would always emerge.
- The method of collection should be **systematic and standardised**.
- The findings should be **generalisable** so that **social laws** (even if only partial laws) can be established.

Positivists argue that **official statistics** meet these scientific criteria. There is little opportunity for error or subjectivity to affect the 'truth' of hard data such as birth or death statistics. The **social survey** incorporating the use of questionnaires and structured interviews is popular with positivist sociologists because it gathers quantifiable data. It is regarded as **objective and reliable**.

Sir Karl Popper

Karl Popper argued that the most important characteristic of scientific knowledge was that it should be capable of being proved **false**. Popper claimed that there is no such thing as 'objective truth'. He claimed that at the very best only partial truth can be achieved because all knowledge is **provisional** or temporary.

Popper proposed a scientific method which he called the '**Conjecture and Refutation**' model of science which follows the following logic:

- scientists make observations (although these are limited by the fact that they are socialised into particular scientific communities which structure the observation)
- **hypotheses or conjectures are generated by such observations**
- experimentation should apply the '**principle of falsification**' i.e. the scientist should look for evidence that proves the hypothesis wrong because no amount of evidence in support of an hypothesis can ever prove that hypothesis. On the other hand, a single item of evidence which contradicts the hypothesis proves it wrong. Popper argued that we can never be conclusively right, we can only be conclusively wrong.

Popper was particularly critical of Marxism.

Popper therefore concluded that scientists should engage in '**industrious scepticism**'. **Popper was sceptical about the scientific status of sociology** because he argued that it deals in theoretical concepts that are not open to empirical falsification.

Feyerabend and Kaplan

Paul Feyerabend argues that science is not as logical or as rational as the previous two models of science claim. Feyerabend suggests that what scientists say they do is quite different from what they *actually* do. He claims that there is no such thing as a special scientific method good for all times and places – rather, the rule in science is that 'anything goes'.

Kaplan agrees with Feyerabend and notes that when scientists come to write up their findings in scientific journals they fail to account for all the blind alleys, false starts, strokes of **luck** and inspired guesses which are part of their everyday science.

A good example of this is Fleming's discovery of penicillin.

The realist position

Realists, too, believe that positivists and Popper are mistaken about the nature of science. **Sayer** suggests many **sciences are engaged in the study of unobservable phenomena** such as evolution, sub-atomic particles, magnetic fields, continental drift and black holes. Therefore a number of disciplines which are readily accepted as sciences such as seismology, meteorology, astronomy and even physics are based on unobservable structures and processes rather than hard empirical data.

Keat notes that many sciences cannot make precise predictions. For example, the science of medicine cannot predict with any certainty who will become ill, seismologists cannot predict exactly when an earthquake will occur and meteorologists did not predict the 1987 hurricane in the south-east of England. Sayer and Keat call these types of science 'open sciences'. Sociology may be classed as an open science because it, too, is concerned with explaining underlying structures.

Thomas Kuhn

Kuhn also challenged the positivist and Popperian notion that science is a method of collecting data about the world. Kuhn claimed that scientific enquiry is characterised by conservatism because scientists are socialised into basic assumptions called '**paradigms**' that they take for granted and rarely question. A paradigm is a particular way of looking at the natural world. It affects the way a scientist sees the world and his or her choice of research method. All evidence gathered is guided by the paradigm. The method of collecting data is therefore dependent upon the dominant paradigm and its dominance blocks the ability of scientists to see contradictory evidence.

In physics, a Newtonian paradigm was overthrown by one based on Einstein's work.

Scientific progress only occurs when pieces of evidence (**anomalies**) build up which cannot be ignored. The established paradigm then loses its credibility and is overthrown in a period of 'scientific revolution'. Scientists produce a new paradigm that explains what the old paradigm could not and normal science resumes.

Kuhn therefore challenged the view that science is a method. Rather he saw science as a **body of knowledge**, i.e. a paradigm. Scientific method depends upon the dominant paradigm of the time. Scientific method is therefore not free to wander in any direction it wishes. It is constrained by 'taken-for-granted' assumptions about how the world is. **Scientific knowledge is therefore socially produced rather than discovered**.

If we accept Kuhn's definition of science as a body of knowledge, **sociology is probably not scientific**. It is doubtful whether there has been one sociological paradigm dominant at any one time. However, an alternative argument might be that sociology until the 1960s was dominated by a functionalist or positivist paradigm until it was overthrown by a conflict (or interpretivist) paradigm in the 1970s. Sociologists also point out that the natural sciences are characterised by competing paradigms rather than any paradigmatic unity.

Interpretivist sociology

AQA   U5
OCR   U2537

Also known as anti-positivism and phenomenology.

Interpretivist sociology is very sceptical about sociology's claim to scientific status. It argues that the **logic and methods of the natural sciences are inappropriate for sociological enquiry** because the subject matter of sociology and the subject matter of the natural sciences are very different. Human beings are **active, conscious beings**, who are aware of what is going on in a social situation and capable of making **choices** about how to act. Natural phenomena lack this consciousness.

Key points from AS

- **The interpretivist critique of positivism**
  Revise AS page 18
- **The unstructured interview**
  Revise AS page 22
- **Observational studies**
  Revise AS page 23

> **KEY POINT**
>
> Interpretivists believe that social reality is not the product of external social laws. Instead, they suggest that **society is socially constructed**. It is the product of **interaction** and the **interpretations or meanings** that we bring to interaction. People interpret the actions of others and react accordingly. Therefore in order to explain social action we need to see it from the point of view of the participants. The researchers' task is to investigate how the people under scrutiny view the world around them and how they make sense of it in *their terms*. Interpretivist sociology has therefore developed research methods which aim to do this.

Interpretivist methods aim to be **qualitative** in that they aim to reveal the meanings behind social action. Therefore **ethnographic methods**, i.e. those that focus on the everyday life of 'social actors', are preferred such as observation and unstructured interviews. Emphasis is placed upon *verstehen* (**a type of social empathy**) and **validity**, and research findings aim to reflect the reality of those being studied.

Post-modernism

AQA   U5
OCR   U2537

Post-modernists point out that science dominated the modern world as a '**big story' or meta-narrative**. (For a definition of modernism and post-modernism see later in 1.3 Sociological theory.) However, it is argued that in the post-modern world science no longer has the monopoly on truth because knowledge and information are characterised by **diversity**. For example, a range of ideas have appeared that are challenging science's view of the world – including 'new age' movements, environmental and 'green' social movements, alternative medicines and fundamentalist 'back to tradition' beliefs. Moreover, the status of science is in decline as people increasingly distrust it in the light of environmental damage, pollution and anxieties about nuclear power.

Progress check

1 What, according to positivists, is the only belief system capable of producing unbiased knowledge?
2 Which research method is the preferred technique of the positivist natural scientist?
3 Why did Popper believe Sociology to be unscientific?
4 What is a paradigm?
5 How is society socially constructed according to interpretivist sociologists?

5 Through interaction and the interpretations we bring to it.
4 A dominant way of looking at the world and approaching problems which scientists are socialised into.
3 Because it dealt with concepts and theories which were impossible to falsify.
2 The laboratory experiment.
1 Science.

1.2 Subjectivity, objectivity and value-freedom

After studying this section you should be able to:

- *define value-freedom, objectivity and subjectivity*
- *describe and evaluate the debate about whether sociology can or should be value-free*

Positivist sociology and value-freedom

AQA   U5

Objectivity through neutrality

Max Weber

Weber, although not a positivist, argued that objective sociological analysis should proceed via the construction of **ideal types** – logically perfect mental constructs to which reality could be compared. For example, to illustrate his theory of organisations, Weber constructed an ideal type of bureaucracy. Weber argued that a bureaucracy that is working well is one that is achieving its goals. Weber suggested that it should not matter to the sociologist whether those goals are immoral or not. The organisation should be judged solely on the objective criteria of achieving its goals. Moral problems therefore are not the scientist's concern because objectivity excludes moral issues. Social science should not concern itself with value judgements.

Functionalism

It was after World War II that functionalist sociologists argued that sociological research should avoid subjectivity, i.e. being influenced by the personal views and political prejudices of the researcher. They argued that social scientists should not aim to change society. Rather, they should subscribe to **'objectivity through neutrality' or value freedom**. In this sense, objective social scientists were presented as **disinterested and trustworthy pursuers of truth**.

Such benefits allowed some sociologists to work alongside the military in Vietnam in the 1960s.

> In functionalist theory, value-freedom has three dimensions.
>
> - The sociologist should not allow their prejudices or beliefs to influence **the research design or process**. It is important that the research tool, e.g. the questionnaire or interview, does not in any way lead the respondents towards the researcher's own beliefs about an issue.
> - It is also important that research data is interpreted objectively by the researcher. **Selectivity** on the basis of prejudice and belief would invalidate the research findings. Sociologists should aim only to see facts as they *are,* not as they may wish to see them.
> - It is believed that the job of the sociologist is to objectively carry out research and **how the research data is used by social policy makers is not the business of the sociologist**. It is the funcionalist view that it is not the job of the sociologist to solve problems or change society.

The critique of value-freedom

It is argued by some sociologists that the influence of values cannot be avoided in the research process. At the very beginning of research, at the proposal and funding stage, **the choice of research topic depends upon those with power making value judgements about what is interesting and worth while**. These might be university heads of department, government ministers or businesses.

Research which is critical of government or big business is less likely to be funded.

Gomm argues that when academic resources are low (especially when governments are cutting back on university spending), sociological research may be monopolised by the state and big business. This may mean that it only focuses on issues that these groups see as important. For example, corporate business has funded an enormous amount of research in the USA aimed at improving worker productivity (e.g. the Hawthorne experiment conducted by E. Mayo).

The research process

For example, interview bias.

Some sociologists, notably **Derek Phillips**, have argued that data collection is itself a social process so we can expect bias and invalidity to arise out of the effects of **interaction**. Some members of society when they are faced with a questionnaire or interview may seek social approval and may therefore act in ways they feel the sociologist will expect or agree with.

The nature of sociology

> It is argued that **the very nature of sociology means that it is value-laden. Alvin Gouldner** argues that value-free sociology is a myth because it is impossible to separate sociologists from what they observe – knowledge does not exist outside of people. It is a **social product**, the result of human actions and values. According to Gouldner, all researchers possess '**domain assumptions**' – a world-view that is the result of socialisation into a particular culture. As a result, most sociology reflects Western, capitalist and patriarchal values. For example, the work of Rostow and modernisation theory stresses the superiority of US democracy and capitalism. Rostow goes as far as calling communism 'a disease'.
>
> **KEY POINT**

Similarly, Gomm argues that sociology is a **social activity** carried out by real people in a world characterised by **conflicts of interest** between different social groups. Any research therefore must inevitably take one side or the other, whether the researcher admits this or not. Sociological research, according to Gomm, reflects **ideological beliefs**. For example, some sociologists – functionalists, sub-culturalists and cultural deprivationists – believe that society is characterised by a consensus on values. These sociologists tend not to engage in social dissent or criticism. Rather, they support the status quo and thus, unconsciously, the values of the establishment. Examples of such sociological ideas would include:

'**Poverty is the fault of the individual or the culture**'
'**Crime is a working-class phenomenon**'
'**Working-class culture is inferior to middle-class culture**'

Gomm suggests that by presenting facts as 'truth' such sociologists are able to **deny responsibility** for the way in which their research is used by policy-makers. For example, compensatory education (EPAS) introduced in the 1960s was based on the idea that working-class culture was somehow inferior. Such policy distracted from other possible causes – e.g. the role of the school and the 'cultural capital' held by the middle class. Gomm suggests that the most important aspect of sociological research therefore is **what is not investigated**. Such sociology is therefore **ideological** because it helps maintain social inequality.

Marxism

Marxists would agree with these arguments. They argue that the major function of scientific knowledge is **the maintenance and legitimisation of inequality**. In this sense, then, science is not objective or value-free. Instead, it supports powerful **capitalist interests** such as big business or the military.

Prescriptive research

Such sociologists are still committed to ensuring reliability and validity.

KEY POINT

Some sociologists have rejected the concept of value-freedom because they suggest that it is undesirable to pretend to be value-free. This theme has been taken up by critical sociologists who feel that they must take sides. Many **Marxists** (e.g. Corrigan, Willis) feel they should take the side of the working class. **Feminists** obviously take the side of women, whilst many involved in **labelling studies** such as Becker take the side of the deviant.

Such perspectives acknowledge that values do and should enter sociological research. They argue that sociology should not and cannot be morally neutral or indifferent. Rather, **sociology is value-laden**. Moreover sociology *should be* **prescriptive** – it should suggest ways forward in order to create a better society.

Progress check

1 What did both Comte and Durkheim believe should be the main purpose of sociology?

2 What is objectivity through neutrality?

3 What did functionalists argue about the relationship between sociologists and social policy-makers?

4 Why is Gomm critical of functionalist sociology?

5 What are domain assumptions?

6 Why might a value-free sociologist be accused of being ideological?

7 What do sociologists who say that sociology should be prescriptive believe?

7 That sociology should change the world.
6 Because they essentially support the status quo and, therefore, inequality.
5 A world-view that reflects the culture that sociologists are brought up in.
4 Because it claims to be value-free but in reality supports Western, capitalist, white, middle-class values.
3 That what social policy-makers did with the knowledge that sociologists produced was not the concern of the sociologist.
2 The idea that sociologists should not take sides and instead be the disinterested pursuers of truth.
1 To change society for the better.

1.3 Sociological theories

After studying this section you should be able to:

- *compare and contrast structural and social action theories*
- *identify and evaluate consensus theory*
- *identify and assess a range of conflict theories*
- *distinguish between, and explain, the concepts of modernity and post-modernity*

LEARNING SUMMARY

Structural theories

AQA   U5

Structural theories are macro-theories in that they study the effects of social structure on social life.

Structural theories see human behaviour as constrained, and even determined by, **the social organisation of society**, i.e. the **social structure** that is made up of interrelated institutions such as families, schools, religion, the economy, political system, etc. These theories see society as **something that exists externally** to individuals. We are born into a society that already exists and when we die society continues on regardless. We cannot see or touch society but we feel its influence on a daily basis because it **shapes** what we think, feel and do. Structural theories, therefore, argue that we are pushed into courses of action by social structures over which we normally have little or no control. In this sense, then, these theories suggest that **people are the product or puppets of society**.

Structural theorists take a **positivist** approach in terms of research techniques. They generally use scientific methods because their focus on social forces bringing about patterns in human behaviour requires **reliable** techniques of measurement.

Consensus theory – functionalism

Functionalism is a structural theory because it sees society as a social system made up of interrelated and interdependent institutions such as education, work, religion, law, the family, etc. The main function of these institutions is to maintain **social equilibrium or order**. An organic analogy is often employed to illustrate this idea. This suggests society is similar to the human body because our internal organs work together to bring about our physical health – or equilibrium.

Functionalists see suicide as influenced by social structure. See pages 143–145.

Functionalists see individual action as the product of social institutions such as the family and education socialising the young into cultural values and norms. The result of this is **value consensus** – people believe in much the same thing and consequently their actions are patterned and **predictable**. Individuals behave similarly in the same social context because they have been socialised into the same cultural rules and goals. Functionalists also see social institutions such as education and work organisations **allocating people to roles** in which they will make an effective contribution to the day-to-day running of society.

Functionalists, therefore, believe human action is controlled and shaped by social forces (i.e. value consensus and the need to maintain social order) beyond the individual's control. The result of this conformity is **social stability** and the **reproduction of society,** generation by generation. These controls do not exclude the possibility of social change. Functionalists argue that occasionally consensus may break down or be challenged on some issues. However, the likely result of this is gradual change as social institutions adapt to solve the problem and re-establish social order.

Criticism of functionalism

It is argued that functionalists **over-emphasise consensus** and order and play down conflict. They tend to focus on the functions or benefits of social institutions and consequently neglect the **dysfunctions** or harm that institutions can cause individuals. For example, the family is nearly always seen as a harmonious institution by functionalists and consequently social problems such as domestic violence are rarely acknowledged. Finally, functionalist theory has been accused of **ethnocentrism**, meaning that its view of society and its institutions is an attempt to impose a middle-class (and American) view of the world on the rest of us.

Conflict theory – Marxism

Marxism is a **structural** theory because it sees society as being made up of two interlocking parts. The most important part – **the infrastructure** – is the economic system, i.e. the way society produces goods. In capitalist societies, goods are mainly manufactured in factories. This production involves a relationship between two economic groups or **classes**. The bourgeoisie or **capitalist class** (also known as the 'ruling class') owns the means of production (i.e. land, factories, machines, etc.). The proletariat (or **working class**) hires out its labour-power (i.e. its skills, strength, etc.) to the capitalist class for a wage.

The relationship between these two classes is **unequal** and based on **conflict** because the bourgeoisie aim to extract the maximum labour from workers at the lowest possible cost. The result is that the bourgeoisie **exploit** the labour of the working class especially because the value of labour when, for example, sold as a product is worth more than the wage paid. This '**surplus value**' is pocketed by the capitalist class and is the basis of the vast profits made by many employers. These profits are responsible for the great **inequalities in wealth and income** between the ruling class and the working class.

> The superstructure is a product of the infrastructure. It exists in order to help reproduce and legitimate social class inequalities.

The second part of the capitalist social system – **the superstructure** – is made up of social institutions such as the family, education, mass media, and so on. Marxists argue that capitalist societies are inherently unstable because of class conflict. However, the function of the superstructure is to reproduce the values and ideas of the ruling class (i.e. **ideology**) so that the working class are unaware of the conflicts of interest that divide them from the capitalist class. The true nature of their exploitation therefore goes unrecognised by the working class or is accepted as natural and inevitable. This '**false class-consciousness**' ensures that working-class conformity and class inequalities in areas such as income, education and health are reproduced generation by generation. Marxists are therefore suggesting that **working-class behaviour is constrained and shaped by ideology** and ultimately by the class inequality that characterises the infrastructure. Free will and social change can only come about once workers become politically conscious and collectively take action.

Criticisms of Marxism

Marxism may put too much emphasis on conflict. Capitalism has considerably improved the standard of living of the working class. It may be that the working class are aware of inequality and exploitation but they feel that their standard of living compensates for this. They may therefore **actively choose** to go to work despite this knowledge.

Marxism has also been criticised for '**economic reductionism**', i.e. reducing behaviour to class relationships. They may neglect the fact that social behaviour can also be influenced by religious, patriarchal, nationalistic and ethnic structures.

Conflict theory – Feminism

Feminist theory has been very critical of sociological theory and argues that prior to the 1960s sociology was 'malestream' in that it largely excluded women and was rarely interested in their behaviour. In the 1970s feminists set themselves the task of demonstrating how the **patriarchal** (male-dominated) structure and organisation of society kept women as a disadvantaged, subordinate and dominated group in most areas of life. On the whole, feminist theories have subscribed to a conflict perspective in that they generally see men exploiting women and consequently benefiting in various ways from gender inequality. However, feminism has split into various types that analyse gender relationships in different ways.

Liberals tend to be optimistic about social change.

Liberal feminists generally focus on how social institutions such as the family, education and mass media encourage male exploitation of women. They argue that these institutions function to ensure that **gender-role socialisation** shapes men and women's behaviour according to patriarchal culture.

Marxists suggest patriarchy benefits capitalism.

Marxist feminists generally see women's oppression as a product of the economic position of women. It is argued that women occupy a more subordinate position than men in terms of the class relationships that characterise the infrastructure. Women are **semi-proletarianised workers** because they are economically below the working class in that they earn less than men and are mainly responsible for domestic labour in the home – which they perform free of charge.

Radical feminists explain women's oppression by arguing that societies are characterised by **patriarchal structures**. Quite simply, **it is men who exploit and oppress women**. Many radical feminists suggest that patriarchal attitudes and practices are embedded in social institutions that socialise both men and women into male-centred ideas and culture. Some argue that **the family** is the main source of patriarchy. This has led to radical feminists believing that patriarchy permeates the relationship between men and women at two levels. First, it is found in the '**structural and ideological features**' of social institutions and, second, it exists at the **private** level of intimate relations between men and women, i.e. the 'sexual politics' level.

'Men as the enemy'

Dual-systems theory combines Marxist and radical-feminist ideas and acknowledges that both capitalism and patriarchy are the cause and means of women's oppression and subordination.

Social action theory

AQA   U5

Key points from AS

• **Unstructured interviews**
  Revise AS page 22
• **Observation studies**
  Revise AS page 23
• **Mass media reports and documents**
  Revise AS page 24

Social action theory, also known as **phenomenology** or **interpretivism**, takes a **micro** approach to explaining and understanding human behaviour. It stresses the ability of individuals to exert control over their own actions. The individual is not seen as a passive recipient of society's directions but as an **active creator** of social behaviour. In this sense, society does not have an independent existence or objective reality. Social situations are not the product of structural factors. Rather, they are the outcome of human beings making choices to engage in **interaction** with each other and the shared **interpretations or meanings** we bring to those interactions. **The social world is a world of meaning**. In this sense, then, **society is the sum of interaction and interpretation** and people shape society rather than society shaping people.

The research methods of interpretivists are devised to make it possible to get at the individual's consciousness and to spell out the shared world-view. Interpretive researchers exploit to the full the fact that their sociological skills make it possible for them to get inside the heads of others, and see the world as others see it.

Key points from AS

• **Triangulation**
  Revise AS page 26

Structuration theory

In recent years, sociologists such as Giddens, Willis and Steve Taylor have argued that the structural and social action approaches need to be combined. **Structuration theory**, which originated with **Giddens**, stresses that individual action is to some extent shaped by social factors beyond our control, e.g. social class, race and gender. However, Giddens points out that individuals react to these forces in a variety of ways, e.g. some will **negotiate** a path through these external pressures whilst others may attempt to **resist** them altogether. Similarly, people might choose to behave in a certain way but **their choices are limited or shaped by the structure of their society.**

Post-modernism

AQA — U5
OCR — U2537

'**Modernity**' refers to the modern world which is generally seen as beginning with industrial production and associated with:

- urbanisation (i.e. the growth of cities)
- the growth of the bureaucratic state
- the rise in status of scientific thinking.

Many of the classic sociological theories aimed to explain why modern societies had come about (i.e. social change) and/or to describe and explain why they were organised the way they were. This led to the development of 'big stories' or '**meta-narratives**' such as functionalism and Marxism which claimed a monopoly of truth in regard to explaining the way society worked and had come about.

Post-modernist thinkers argue that in the late-20th century society has progressed into a post-modern age. This is characterised by:

- changes in the nature of work (e.g. more flexible working practices)
- the **globalisation** of both production and consumption
- the shrinking of space and time because of developments in communication networks like the Internet, e-mail and satellite television
- the loss of faith in science as seen in the rise of environmental politics
- the emphasis on **consumption of information**
- the emphasis on **style and conspicuous consumption**
- **cultural diversity and pluralism** in a range of social contexts, e.g. the family, media, youth culture, etc.

Know some criticisms of post-modernism.

These changes mean that how we think and how we use knowledge have also changed. Society has become disillusioned with 'big ideas' that claimed to have all the answers because these in reality only created more problems. In a rapidly changing and fragmented world, no theory can lay claim to the truth because of the sheer diversity of experience, institutions and contexts that exist in the world today. Post-modern theories, on the other hand, point out that there are competing theories, many of which will have something valid to offer about the nature of post-modern society.

Progress check

1 What is a structural theory?
2 What do functionalists probably overemphasise?
3 What is the infrastructure?
4 What is *verstehen*?
5 What is the post-modern claim in regard to big stories such as Marxism and functionalism?

5 People have lost faith in them as truth.
4 Empathetic understanding.
3 It is a Marxist concept meaning the economic systems and the unequal class relationships that underpin it.
2 Consensus and social order.
1 One which believes that human behaviour is determined by the organisation of society, i.e. its social structure.

Sample questions and model answers

Item A

A survey of lifestyles and living standards published by the Joseph Rowntree Foundation in 1997 concluded that poverty still exists in Britain today. The survey covered a representative sample of 1239 children. The researchers defined poverty as a situation where families could not afford things that most families treat as part of normal life. Specifically, it was where families could not afford three or more of these basics of normal life that they were deemed to be 'poor'. The list of basics the researchers used included things like three meals a day, each child having a bed of their own, having fresh fruit every day, having a warm coat, having a carpet in the bedroom, having educational games in the house, etc.

Rather than rely on conventional indicators of living standards which are based on the whole household as a unit, the researchers separated the expenditure related to children in the family from the expenditure on the adults. On the basis of this new definition, the researchers arrived at the conclusion that one in ten children in Britain are 'poor' and that lone parent families are the worst affected.

(Extracted from page 12 of Sociology Updates *(1998) by Martyn Denscombe, Olympus Books.)*

Item B

The research centred on the city of Newcastle upon Tyne, where there were 6,593 lone parent households in 1991. The main sample for individual interview consisted of 40 mothers who fitted the criteria of being aged between 16 and 24 years, who had never been married, were not cohabiting and who had given birth to their first child before the age of 20. To get as diverse a sample of mothers as possible, it was decided to recruit the mothers through health visitors wherever possible. Despite their willingness to assist, the health visitors from the more middle-class districts did not come forward with names of young single mothers, whereas those from the inner-city estates had many names to offer. The actual success rate for contacting the mothers was poor. Interviewers often found no one at home when they called.

We found that many of the younger mothers feel excluded from mother and toddler groups because of their age. Jackie said 'I don't go anymore – they look at you like you're a slag … cause I was so young like … 15 when I had her. It's for older mothers, they're all older you know, 20 and that.'

(Adapted from Young single mothers: barriers to independent living *by S. Speak et al., Family Policies Studies Centre, 1995, pages 8–9.)*

1 (a) With reference to **Item A**, state **two** ways in which a representative sample of children in poverty might be obtained. (2 marks)

A suitable sampling frame is required which identifies the children of the poor. Free school dinners are probably a good indicator of poverty – schools could provide a list of pupils claiming these. Another possibility might be to conduct a general survey of living standards and include questions that operationalise and therefore identify poverty. The sub-sample of those who were experiencing poverty could then be followed up. Another possibility might be to approach a local Gingerbread group (a support group for single parent families) and ask for their co-operation.

Don't over-respond. It's only worth 2 marks.

Sample questions and model answers (continued)

verify findings and check its reliability. Fourth, that the research should be mainly quantitative, i.e. statistical, so that it can be converted into tabular or graphical information. Such data can be observed for patterns and cause-and-effect relationships in order to establish 'social facts' or laws about human behaviour.

Illustrating the usefulness of a scientific method.

The survey is the research method most favoured by positivist sociologists. It normally involves the random selection of a sample (which is representative of the population the sociologist is interested in studying). This sample may be sent standardised questionnaires through the post and/or may be asked to take part in structured interviews. This method normally results in the obtaining of large amounts of quantitative data in a relatively short period of time. Positivists see the social survey as scientific because all possible variables are controlled via sampling and questionnaire design. It is seen to have high reliability because it is easily repeated. Other sociologists can verify the data obtained by using the same standardised questionnaire and similar samples. It is seen as objective because the sample population is randomly rather than deliberately selected.

Note the question stresses 'evaluate'. Contrast with interpretivism.

Interpretivist sociologists argue that people choose how to behave rather than being shaped by social factors beyond their control. They accuse positivist sociologists of being over-deterministic, meaning they fail to see that people can resist social forces and structure their own behaviour and outcomes. Instead, interpretivists argue that society is created by people interacting with each other and bringing their own meanings or interpretations to those interactions, e.g. the classroom is a mini-society made up of students and teachers interacting and sharing similar interpretations as to the purpose of lessons.

Evaluating the usefulness of a scientific approach.

Interpretivists go as far as to argue that the scientific approach gets in the way of good sociological research because the positivist concern with collecting hard data or facts may conceal the real meaning behind social behaviour. For example, crime statistics collected in a scientific manner may tell us more about those who collected them than crime or criminality. Scientific method therefore is seen as fairly irrelevant to good sociology.

An alternative approach is outlined.

In practice, interpretivists stress three factors. First, the task of the researcher is to investigate how those being investigated interpret the world around them. In order to succeed in this task, the sociologist has to get inside their heads and see the world through their eyes. This is called 'verstehen' and is an attempt to empathise with those being studied. Second, interpretivists emphasise validity – seeing the world as it really is. Third, cause-and-effect relationships are probably impossible to construct because people socially construct social situations and the interpretations people give to certain situations often vary. Interpretivist sociological research has tended to focus on the use of qualitative methods such as unstructured interviews and observation.

Combining positivism and interpretivism for a conclusion.

In the 1990s sociologists have tended to use a combination of quantitative and qualitative methodology known as triangulation. These are seen as complementing each other. The most important consideration today is not whether we are scientific but whether we are using the best range of methods for the job of studying the social world.

Practice examination questions

Item A

A study of women who choose to be childless found that they hold conventional views about relationships and parenting and that their professional careers were only one factor contributing to their sense of personal fulfilment.

The study, by Fiona McAllister and Lynda Clarke of the Family Policy Studies Centre, combines an analysis of demographic trends with results from a qualitative survey of 45 individuals identified as having chosen not to have children. It finds that relatively few interviewees of either sex had made an early, irrevocable decision not to have children. Their choice of childlessness had come about slowly in the context of their work, personal health, relationships and other life events. The series of in-depth interviews with voluntarily childless women and with some of their partners reveal a high degree of caution about assuming the responsibilities of being a parent. Parenthood is clearly identified with unwanted disruption and change in their lives as well as a heightened risk of financial insecurity.

Item B

This study focused on comparisons between two groups; a group of juvenile offenders and a representative sample of schoolchildren were asked the same questions about their viewing habits and preferences. With the offenders, these questions took the form of a formal interview conducted in the young person's home. The schoolchildren completed a confidential questionnaire containing the same questions, administered in their classrooms by their teachers.

Of the 78 frequent offenders chosen to take part in the research, nine were girls and 69 were boys. They were aged 12 and 18 at the time of the interview. In terms of the schoolchildren, schools were randomly chosen and questionnaires administered to 538 schoolchildren with a sex ratio equal to that of the offender sample. The teachers were instructed not to select special classes, but to choose a representative group. The schoolchildren did not have to put their names on the questionnaires, so neither the teachers nor the research team knew the identity of respondents.

The study found that both groups watched equal amounts of television directly after the 9pm watershed but offenders were more likely than schoolchildren to be watching beyond 11pm at night.

(Adapted from Young offenders and the media: viewing habits and preferences (1994) *by Ann Hagell and Tim Newburn, Policy Studies Institute.)*

1 (a) With reference to **Item A**, give **two** reasons why the sample used might not be representative. (2 marks)

  (b) Using the information in **Item A**, state a suitable hypothesis regarding the reasons why some women are choosing childlessness which a sociologist would be able to test. (4 marks)

  (c) Briefly describe what you see as the strengths and weaknesses of the research design outlined in **Item B**. (6 marks)

  (d) The following statement is a hypothesis suggested by the information in **Item B**: 'Juvenile delinquents are subject to less parental controls than ordinary youth.'

  Suggest **two** ways in which this hypothesis might be tested, giving reasons for your answer. (8 marks)

2 Compare and contrast the contribution of structural and social action theories to an understanding of social life. (40 marks)

Chapter 2

Power and politics

The following topics are covered in this chapter:

- *Power*
- *Political parties and voting behaviour*
- *Defining political action*

2.1 Power

After studying this section you should be able to:

- *compare and contrast different definitions of power*
- *outline and assess pluralist and Marxist accounts of power*
- *examine theories of the modern state*

LEARNING SUMMARY

Defining power

AQA ▶ U4
OCR ▶ U2536

Max Weber defines power as being able to **impose one's will on another, despite resistance**. According to Weber, power comes in different forms.

- **Coercion** is force, the use of violence or physical power.
- **Authority is institutionalised power** and usually depends upon **consent** – that is, people believe that the power is **legitimate**. Legitimacy is found in three types of authority:
  - charismatic authority derives from a powerful personality
  - traditional authority derives from historical precedent, e.g. a line of succession to a throne
  - **Rational–legal authority** derives from formal rules and/or law and is thought to be rational because it is impartially applied to everyone and enforced without bias. Consequently people consent to obey this type of power, which is administered by a hierarchical bureaucracy. The option of force still exists but is used only as a final resort.

Modern states tend to be underpinned by rational–legal authority. Governments and their bureaucratic agents such as the civil service, the secret services, the police, the courts, etc. are generally regarded as being legitimate by the vast majority of the population.

The distribution of power

AQA ▶ U4
OCR ▶ U2536

Pluralism

Robert Dahl defines power as making someone do something that they would not normally do. Dahl carried out an **empirical** study of decision-making in New Haven, USA of three contentious issues and concluded that no one group dominated the decision-making process. He argued from a pluralist perspective that power in modern societies is widely **diffused** and distributed among a variety of community élites. No single group dominates and possesses power because each group serves as a **veto** group on the others, thus preventing monopoly. Such élites are **tied** to specific issues. If one group does succeed in dominating one area of policy, it will fail to dominate others. All élites are **accountable** because they rely on popular support.

However, pluralist methodology has been criticised. **Bachrach and Baratz** note that Dahl only looks at what **Lukes** calls the **first dimension of power**, i.e. decisions that can be seen and observed. He consequently neglects the **second dimension of power** – the ability to prevent issues from coming up for discussion and therefore decision. Power, then, is not just about winning situations but also about **managing** them and confining decision-making to 'safe' issues that do not threaten specific interests.

S. Lukes takes this critique further by identifying a **third dimension of power**. Those that benefit from decision-making may not be the ones making the decision. It is therefore important to identify the '**objective interests**' of groups, i.e. what benefits are derived in the long term from particular decisions. Powerful groups may pursue policies which they genuinely believe will benefit the whole community but which objectively benefit some groups more than others. For example, a shopping precinct may benefit the community but may benefit builders, owners of businesses, transport companies, etc. more. Lukes argues that this is the most potent type of power because it is never questioned or challenged.

Elite theory

Elite theory stresses that power is **concentrated** in the hands of a closed minority group, i.e. an **élite** holds all power. Classical élite theorists such as **Pareto and Mosca** argued that élites are superior to the masses because they have innate ability, talent and moral judgement. Mosca argued that the masses will always be powerless because they don't have the intellectual or moral qualities to run their societies. **Mannheim** argued that 'cultured' and 'rational' élites were essential to the maintenance of civilisation because the masses were '**irrational**'. Mannheim therefore concluded that democracy was the problem rather than élite power.

> An important élite in post-modern society is the entertainment élite made up of film and rock stars.

The power élite

C. Wright Mills was critical of élite rule. Mills argues that three key élites monopolise power in modern societies: the economic or business élite, the political elite and the military élite. Mills argued that the activities of each élite interconnected to form a single ruling minority – '**the power élite**'. The unity and cohesiveness of this group is strengthened by their similarity of social background, i.e. white, male, Protestant, urban and sharing the same educational and social class background. Moreover, there is interchange and overlap between these élites. Such unity means that power élites run Western societies like the USA **in their own interests**.

Marxism

Whilst élite theory does stress sources of power other than social class, e.g. gender, coercion, rational–legal authority etc., it is difficult (as **Milliband** argues) to distinguish the power élite from the Marxist notion of a **ruling class** whose major aim is the preservation of capitalist interests. Milliband argues that this capitalist class rules **directly** when Conservative governments are in power and **indirectly** by manipulating agencies of the state.

The empirical evidence does **support** the view that a capitalist class exists in the UK. Many studies indicate that **wealth is concentrated in few hands**. Most stocks and shares, despite privatisation, are in the hands of a minority whilst over 50% of the top 250 companies are owned and controlled by individuals or families. This economic élite is a **closed** group in that inheritance and public school/Oxbridge are the only means of entry to the group. Lupton and Wilson have noted the internal connections are strengthened by inter-locking directorships of companies and intermarriage.

Milliband argues that **this economic élite is similar enough to the political élite to constitute a ruling class**. Both élites share social class, education and family ties. Moreover, many politicians have extensive commercial interests and élite members often swap roles, e.g. top civil servants and politicians often retire from politics to a top job in business. Prominent business men often sit on government committees. **Scott** refers to this overlap as **'the establishment'** and claims it monopolises the major positions of power and influence within the state. However, pluralists argue that Marxists have only demonstrated *the potential* to control and it is very difficult to **prove** actual control itself.

Structural Marxism

The **instrumental Marxist** theory of Milliband was criticised by **Poulantzas, a structural Marxist** who suggested that the common social background of the ruling class was less important than **the nature of capitalism itself**. It therefore does not matter whether élite groups rule directly or indirectly – objectively the ruling class will always benefit, whoever is in power, from the maintenance of capitalism. Legislation may seem to benefit less-powerful groups but in the long term it will also benefit the capitalist class. For example, health and safety legislation obviously benefits the working class but ultimately benefits the ruling class because it results in a healthy, fit and, possibly, more productive workforce.

Poulantzas argued that the capitalist class will always ultimately benefit unless capitalism is dismantled. The capitalist class does not have to interfere directly in decision-making – the fact that the decision-making process is happening within a capitalist framework will always benefit it.

Hegemonic Marxism

Key points from AS

- Hegemonic Marxism
  Revise AS page 75

Another way to look at power is to look at the work of the hegemonic Marxist, **Antonio Gramsci**. He developed the idea of **hegemony** defined as **cultural domination and intellectual leadership**. He argued the capitalist class does not need to have political control because they control **popular ideas or culture** through the mass media, education system, and so on.

Defining the state

| AQA | U4 |
| OCR | U2536 |

A state can be defined as a **central authority** ruling over a given territory. It can be divided into:

- a **legislature** which passes laws; in a democracy, the legislature is elected by the people
- an **executive** or government which speaks on behalf of the state and is responsible for carrying out the will of the legislature; some argue that if the executive has a huge majority (as is the case with the present Labour government) then the executive can impose its will on the legislature
- a **bureaucracy** (e.g. the civil service and local government) concerned with the management of the state's activities
- a **judiciary** which is mainly concerned with interpreting laws which have been passed
- a **military** machine, which in Western societies is very rarely used internally but may be employed quite often in non-democratic states.

Theories of the modern state

AQA   U4

Pluralists like **Dahl** suggest that the role of the state is to act as an **'honest and neutral broker'** in terms of the distribution of power in society. The state 'distributes' power in the form of resources to 'deserving causes' on the basis of the national interest. In this sense, it **regulates** competing interest groups and operates to make sure that no one group accumulates too much power. However, **Lukes** notes that state policy benefits the objective interests of the ruling class in the long run. For example, the Welfare State has raised the standard of living of the working class and reduced their potential for revolutionary discontent.

Marxism

Marxists like Milliband argue that **'the executive of the state is but a committee for managing the affairs of the whole bourgeoisie'**. In other words, the state is an **instrument** of the ruling class. Marxists claim that there are clear links between the political and the economic élites and they consequently comprise a capitalist ruling class. However, **Poulantzas** argued that the state can be **'relatively autonomous'** from the ruling class. It is consequently able to present itself as neutral because the ruling class is made up of competing power blocs such as manufacturing and finance which may disagree on how to manage capitalism. The state is able to operate independently from these power blocs in the sense that it may mediate between them. However, Poulantzas also noted that state policy will always eventually benefit capitalism because the ultimate responsibility of the state as part of the superstructure is to reproduce the relations of inequality that underpin capitalism.

> **Hegemonic Marxists** argue that the state is able to present itself as autonomous and neutral because it exercises **hegemonic** control. The consent of the people for state activities is achieved by dominating cultural agencies such as the media, and convincing society that the state is operating on behalf of the people. In reality, however, hegemonic control means ruling-class domination.
>
> **KEY POINT**

However, the view that the British state is an instrument of the capitalist class can be criticised because a great deal of economic policy has been unsuccessful. The state has been unable to prevent events such as stockmarket crashes, devaluation of sterling compared with other currencies and the decline of heavy industry and manufacturing. If the state is an agent of the ruling class, it is a very unsuccessful one. Other criticisms suggest that Marxists ignore the fact that the British state is not only capitalist but is also **patriarchal and racist**. The state supports the interests of men and white people. Laws protecting the rights of women and ethnic minorities are weak, whilst departments of the state such as the Home Office and the police have admitted to institutionalised racism.

The future of the state

AQA   U4

Key points from AS

- **Nationalism and identity**
  Revise AS page 69

Recent research into the state suggests that the state (and therefore its power to act in favour of any sectional interest) is under threat from a number of trends including the following.

- **Regionalisation** – the Labour government has devolved some state powers to a Scottish Parliament, Welsh Assembly and Northern Ireland power-sharing assembly. The British State is undergoing fragmentation and this has led in the UK to the emergence of multiple national identities and interests, especially Celtic nationalism.

Post-modernism sees such processes as reducing the importance of the nation-state.

- **Europe** – the European Commission has some legal authority over the British state especially in the fields of economic policy and trade.
- **Internationalisation** – British foreign policy is increasingly tied in with either US foreign policy or Europe.
- **Globalisation** – **Hall** argues that globalisation threatens the very existence of the nation state for four reasons.
  - States find it almost impossible to control the international flow of money, especially digital global trading in currency which can severely affect exchange rates and undermine economies.
  - **Transnational behaviour** can severely disrupt economic policy by shifting investment and, therefore, employment between countries.
  - The global economy means that **recession** in one part of the world can undermine the economy in another part.
  - Global communications and the Internet have made it difficult for states to regulate the flow of information across borders. There are concerns about transnational media influence, cultural imperialism (in which the indigenous culture is weakened by American mass culture) and the use of the Internet to encourage global dissidence.

Progress check

1 Define coercion.
2 Define authority.
3 Which theory argues that power is widely distributed amongst a variety of interest groups?
4 What are the second and third dimensions of power according to Lukes?
5 What does Mills call the ruling minority group in the USA?
6 What does Scott mean by the 'establishment'?
7 What is hegemonic control or power?
8 What is the biggest threat to the nation-state according to Hall?

8 Globalisation.
7 It is the domination of intellectual power and cultural agencies such as the media and education by the middle-classes.
6 This is made up of power blocs or élites related to business, politics, etc. that working together constitute a ruling class.
5 The power élite.
4 The second dimension refers to the ability to prevent issues coming up for decision whilst the third dimension focuses on who benefits in the long term from any decision made.
3 Pluralism.
2 Institutionalised power which is exercised with the consent of the people.
1 Use of physical force.

2.2 Political parties and voting behaviour

After studying this section you should be able to:

- *link political ideologies to political parties*
- *outline and evaluate the role of political parties and the mass media in the political process*
- *describe and evaluate theories of voting behaviour*

LEARNING SUMMARY

Ideology and political parties

AQA   U4
OCR   U2536

Ideology generally refers to **any belief system that binds a group together**. Ideologies can be categorised into five broad political belief systems: fascism, communism, socialism, liberalism and conservatism. These political ideologies are transformed into social policy through political parties. Weber defined political parties as **organisations functioning to turn a communal interest into action**. These interests may be based on social class or status or both.

Political parties

Politics is therefore the site of an **ideological or hegemonic struggle between belief systems** represented by political parties. In the UK, this struggle has generally been between belief systems associated with the **'Left'** at one extreme with their emphasis on equality for all and social change and the **'Right'** at the other extreme associated with individualism, free enterprise and respect for tradition. This is an over-simplified model because in the post-war period **consensus**, rather than ideological struggle, has characterised British politics.

The Conservative Party

Mrs Thatcher promoted New Right thinking.

The right-wing belief system which characterised this party pre-1979 was generally paternalistic and interventionist. However, an ideological struggle amongst the Right led to the emergence and dominance of a **New Right ideology** in the Conservative party which preached minimal state intervention, the promotion of free enterprise and individual choice, and the determination to challenge the power of organisations such as the trade unions. Since the fall of Mrs Thatcher the emphasis has shifted again. Majorite ideology shifted in favour of paternalism although under William Hague, right-wing ideology has become more **populist** by tapping into people's nationalist fears about Europe taking away British sovereignty and the impact of immigration on British identity.

The Labour Party

Left-wing ideology has also undergone radical change since 1979. From 1945 to the 1970s the Labour party was generally seen as the party of the working class and its ideology was predominantly socialist in principle. Nationalisation of key industries such as coal, steel, the railways, etc., the setting up of the Welfare State (especially the NHS and the introduction of the comprehensive system) can all be seen as socialist ideology put into practice. However, the party reacted to the election defeat of 1979 by embarking on a re-evaluation of its ideology and a revamp of its image. This resulted in Labour under Kinnock and later Smith, jettisoning many of the overtly socialist principles embodied in its constitution, especially after 1983, and describing itself as a party aiming to work for all sections of the community, rich and poor. Tony Blair's election to the leadership saw a major shift to the centre in terms of ideology. Labour presents itself today as a social democratic rather than socialist party forging a 'third way' towards a common good and as being trustworthy and competent enough to prudently look after the economy.

Voting behaviour

AQA ▶ U4

Note that there are also deviant middle-class voters who support the Labour party. These were mainly professionals such as teachers.

Forty years ago, most explanations of voting behaviour saw social class as the major influence on the electorate's voting habits. Sixty-five per cent of the working-class vote in the 1960s went to Labour, making up three-quarters of that party's support, whereas approximately 75%–80% of the middle-class vote went to the Conservative party. This class-based voting became known as 'partisan alignment'.

However, the existence of 'deviant voters', i.e. a third of the working class were voting Conservative whilst one-fifth of the middle class were voting Labour, suggested that the relationship between social class and voting behaviour was not so clear cut.

Early explanations of voting behaviour focused on the working-class deviant voter and explanations focused on the possibility of these being:

- **deferential** voters – **McKenzie and Silver** argued that these were likely to be older working-class voters living in rural areas who looked up to high-status individuals.

- **secular or privatised instrumental voters** – young affluent factory workers who, like consumers in a supermarket, **rationally** evaluated the policies of political parties and voted in terms of **individual goals** rather than out of class loyalty.

Explanations focusing on working-class instrumental voters became very popular among sociologists in the light of the Conservative election victories in the 1970s and 1980s. In particular, the 1983 result was Labour's worst defeat since 1931 in terms of total votes cast (i.e. 28%). What was evident was that the traditional working-class vote deserted Labour – little more than half of the manual working class voted for them.

The work of Ivor Crewe

Ivor Crewe identified a number of factors that he claimed were central to Labour's loss.

- The proportion of manual workers in the labour force had declined as older primary industries were hit by recession. Therefore the number of those who traditionally voted Labour had fallen. Crewe called this **'class de-alignment'**.

- The expansion of the service sector and high-technology manufacturing had led to the emergence of a well-paid **'new working-class'**, mainly living in the South, who owned their home because of the sale of council houses. This group no longer automatically identified with the Labour party. Crewe referred to this as **'partisan de-alignment'**.

- Crewe also highlighted **'party image'** as important to voters. The Labour party's organisation was seen as amateurish and divided whilst the image of the Labour party leader (Michael Foot followed by Neil Kinnock) was poor compared with the 'Iron Lady' image of Margaret Thatcher.

Crewe concluded that **the Labour vote in the 1980s remained largely working class but that the working class was no longer largely Labour**. Moreover, people no longer voted along social-class lines but instead on the basis of 'issues'.

However, Crewe's methodology was severely criticised by sociologists such as **Gordon Marshall** – especially in terms of the lack of evidence for the existence of a new working class. Marshall argued that Crewe had exaggerated both class and partisan de-alignment. His research suggested that classes had not withered away and that **class identity was still important** to the working class.

Butler and Kavanagh, too, were sceptical about changes in the class structure. They argued that Conservative election victories in this period were the result of short-term factors such as the Falklands War and the subsequent **agenda-setting** by the mass media. Prior to the War, Mrs Thatcher was at her most unpopular in the opinion polls. Victory led to the media setting a 'national interest' agenda which portrayed the Conservatives taking on the enemy without (i.e. the Argentinians) and the 'enemy within' i.e. the trade unions, Labour, etc. Such support won her the 1983 election.

The evidence suggests that Labour did come under sustained attack from the majority of newspapers throughout the 1980s and 1990s until the *Sun* switched to Tony Blair in 1996. Both the **Glasgow University Media Group and Goldsmiths College Media Group** documented how in the press and on television the Labour party was constantly presented as a 'divided' party dominated by '**left-wing loonies**' who allegedly threatened the national interest.

Heath *et al.* looked at voting behaviour between 1964 and 1987 and argued that Crewe's partisan and class de-alignment theories were wrong. Heath concluded that people in the same classes behaved in much the same way they always had in regard to voting behaviour. Heath argued that the main reason Labour had lost four elections in a row between 1979 and 1992 was their record of **inept political management** in this period. In other words, people saw them as divided and interpreted their leadership as weak. The Liberal Democrats also increased their number of candidates in this period and this competition also took votes away from Labour.

The 1997 Election

The result of this election – a Labour landslide – was out of keeping with previous trends. Most sociologists now agree that structural changes such as class and/or partisan de-alignment had little bearing on this result. Rather, sociologists have focused on the **changing political environment**. The Conservatives were interpreted by the electorate as hopelessly divided over issues such as Europe, as incompetent at economic management and, in some cases, corrupt. On the other hand, the public had greater confidence in Labour. People could see that the party had modernised and that they had distanced themselves from the trade unions. Most importantly, there was public confidence in the leadership of Blair and Brown.

Progress check

1 In regard to political parties, what is an 'ideology'?
2 What belief system became the dominant ideology of the Conservative party during Mrs Thatcher's term in office?
3 In terms of ideology, how does New Labour present itself today?
4 What is partisan alignment?
5 What two structural trends, according to Crewe, were responsible for four straight Labour election defeats between 1979 and 1992?
6 How is Marshall's research critical of Crewe?
7 What does Heath conclude about Crewe's findings?

7 That Crewe neglected short-term factors to do with political management and competence – the political environment is more important than long-term structural changes.
6 He found no evidence for Crewe's 'new working-class'. Manual workers still generally identified mainly with Labour.
5 Class de-alignment meaning the number of manual workers was in decline and partisan de-alignment meaning the number of manual workers automatically identifying with Labour had fallen.
4 Identifying with a particular political party because it represents the interests of the social class to which you belong.
3 As pursuing a social-democratic third way.
2 The New Right.
1 A political belief system.

2.3 Defining political action

After studying this section you should be able to:

- outline and evaluate the role of pressure groups and new social movements
- describe and assess sociological explanations of direct action
- examine the relationship between globalisation, nationalism and post-modernist theory

LEARNING SUMMARY

Pressure groups

| AQA | U4 |
| OCR | U2536 |

Pressure groups exist in order to persuade governments to reform existing policy or to encourage new policy. There are two types:

- **interest or sectional** pressure groups who aim to **protect the interests** of their members, e.g. trade unions and professional associations

- **promotional** pressure groups who focus on specific **issues or causes**, e.g. Greenpeace focuses on environmental issues, Oxfam on debt and Third World poverty and Gingerbread on single-parent families.

These groups mainly aim to influence government and they do this by directly lobbying government and Members of Parliament. They also attempt to put government under pressure by presenting their case to the mass media and generating public opinion in their favour. Their campaigns will therefore involve demonstrations, boycotts, media campaigns (e.g. advertisements), writing to those with influence and giving evidence to government committees. Some pressure groups have gone further than this and either disobeyed the law or challenged the law through the courts.

New social movements

| AQA | U4 |
| OCR | U2536 |

Recent political sociology has moved away from the study of pressure groups to examine social movements. Sociologists generally distinguish between:

- **old social movements (OSM)** which refer to working-class alliances such as trade unions seeking to bring about economic change and which are organised in a formal hierarchical and centralised way

- **new social movements (NSM)** which are defined as broad, middle-class alliances which are less hierarchical, more loose-knit in organisation and concerned with a wider agenda of issues. These issues are often described as **'post-materialist'**, i.e. they are not concerned with economic gain.

NSMs are generally concerned with promoting and **changing cultural values** and with the construction of **identity politics**. A range of theories have emerged to explain this focus.

Touraine

Touraine argues that NSMs are a product of **post-industrial society** which stresses the production and consumption of knowledge rather than manufactured goods. The focus on knowledge has led to a critical evaluation of cultural values.

> NSMs are therefore concerned with the promotion of cultural values which encourage quality of life, concern for the environment and individual freedom of expression and identity.

KEY POINT

Marcuse

Marcuse argues that NSMs are the direct result of the **alienation** caused by the capitalist mode of production and consumption. Marxists like Marcuse argue that capitalism produces a superficial **mass culture** which is devoid of intellectual and moral content in order to maximise its audience and profits. However, the emptiness of this culture has led some middle-class students (whose education has given them critical insight) to reject materialism.

> NSMs are a form of counter-culture which aims to encourage people to focus on emotional and personal needs (e.g. community concern for other people or the environment) which are repressed by capitalism.
>
> **KEY POINT**

Habermas

Habermas argues that NSMs are a **form of resistance** to the rational and rigid systems of **bureaucracy** which have come to characterise the modern world. He distinguishes between two types of NSM:

> - **defensive** NSMs aim to promote the **defence of a natural or social environment or traditional way of life** threatened by modern economic or bureaucratic interests, e.g. environmentalist, anti-nuclear power and animal-rights groups
> - **offensive** NSMs aim to defend or extend **social rights** to particular groups who are denied status, autonomy or identity or who are repressed by the state, e.g. anti-racism, human rights, gay liberation, etc.
>
> **KEY POINT**

Some NSMs will contain both defensive and offensive characteristics. For example, the environmental movement argues for greater public participation in political decision-making in areas such as nuclear power and genetically modified foods. It also retains a traditional concern to protect the environment.

Giddens suggests that NSMs have important **democratic** qualities because they initiate public discussion into issues and events previously monopolised by governments and experts.

Direct action

Many members of NSMs are involved in '**direct action**'. This is a form of political action which operates **outside** the formal political process and may include demonstrations, sit-ins and other obstructive action, e.g. militant disabled groups have chained themselves to the gates of Downing Street and the Reclaim the Streets movement has severely disrupted traffic in the centre of London. In recent years, illegal direct action has become more common. Society has seen symbolic attacks on targets such as politicians (throwing paint or eggs at them), damage to nuclear weapons installations or military hardware, and the destroying of genetically modified crops. Some animal-rights groups have even physically attacked scientists with letter and car bombs.

Global social movements

New social movements are becoming increasingly globalised because:

- there is a growing sense of **risk** – people are increasingly aware of the dangers of the world we live in and more willing to take responsibility

- people have grown increasingly concerned with the activities of transnational companies, especially in the developing world
- there is a growing distrust of experts such as scientists, who are seen as responsible for many of the world's problems
- **increasing reflexivity** – **Giddens** argues that more and more people are taking responsibility for the state of society and the natural world.

Such global movements have led to action such as '**green consumerism**' aimed at protecting the environment or vulnerable peoples in less-developed nations. This involves consumer boycotts of environmentally unfriendly goods, goods produced by child labour or regimes that regularly engage in human-rights abuse. High-profile global NSMs have been able to exert pressure on governments and transnational companies, e.g. Greenpeace, Oxfam, etc.

Urban disorder – riots

OCR U2536

Urban disorder in the form of **riots** may be an expression of protest by those social groups who do not have resort to pressure groups or NSMs. This is seen more clearly when the features of riots are examined.

- Riots tend to occur in **working-class areas** with high levels of **unemployment and deprivation**. These are generally declining inner-city areas or council estates that have experienced a deterioration in their upkeep.
- Many urban riots have involved **ethnic minorities** who may be experiencing **racial discrimination** and who may feel excluded from participating fully in society.
- Younger members of the ethnic-minority community may be in **conflict with the police** because of what they perceive to be harassment. Minor incidents between youth and police may spark riots. Military-style policing has also been blamed.
- **Left realists** suggest that both black and white youth who take part in urban riots may be reacting to a sense of '**relative deprivation**' and frustration at their **powerlessness**.
- **Campbell** believes that young working-class men may be attempting to re-assert their **masculinity** in a social world in which femininity is increasingly valued and the traditional male role is in decline.

Post-modern theories of politics

AQA U4
OCR U2536

Some argue that this type of politics appeals mainly to the young who are cynical about conventional politics.

Jorgensen suggests that there have been three major shifts in the way people view political relationships in the world.

- **Identity politics** have become more important than class-based politics. This is reflected in increased participation in NSMs. People are now interested in politics because they believe they can make a **difference** in bringing about a better world, rather than because they want to change one ideological set of beliefs for another.
- People are more conscious of the **inter-connectedness** of the world and the fact that as a nation the UK is part of a **global order**. There is a growing demand that our society should take a **moral lead** on a range of issues, such as human rights, debt, child labour and environmentalism.
- People have lost faith in the **grand narratives** and **big ideologies** such as capitalism and socialism.

The post-modern political world, then, is seen as highly pluralistic. Political life is becoming more **de-centred** and 'micro' in character. Political goals have been transformed. They are less likely to be materialistic or the product of ideological conflict between grand narratives. They are more likely to reflect local, cultural, ethnic, sexual, and religious issues – in other words, **identity** issues.

Progress check

1 Identify two types of pressure group.
2 What methods do pressure groups use to influence governments?
3 Why do neo-pluralists refer to the UK as a 'deformed polyarchy'?
4 What causes people to join NSMs according to Marcuse?
5 Why have new social movements come about according to Marcuse?
6 What is direct action?
7 What does Left Realism blame for social disorder?
8 What is increasing 'reflexivity'?

8 People feel they should take more responsibility for the state of the world.
7 The relative deprivation experienced by young blacks and whites living in declining inner-city areas and the frustration they feel at being powerless to change their situation.
6 Action that tends to lie outside the law, e.g. sabotaging hunts, terrorism, riots, etc.
5 Because of disillusion with capitalism and especially mass culture.
4 People want to resist aspects of capitalism such as mass culture, alienation, consumerism, materialism, environmental damage, etc.
3 Because some pressure groups have far more power than others.
2 Lobbying; mass media publicity campaigns; advertising; demonstrations; boycotts; writing letters to people with influence; etc.
1 Interest or sectional, and promotional or issue-based.

Sample questions and model answers

Item A

Disillusioned with politics and alienated from the system, young people of today are turning their back on the traditional democratic process according to a report called 'The Kids are Alright?' compiled by London Youth Matters. 24% of young people aged between 18–24 years said they had no interest in politics compared with 8% of the general population. However, individual issues tended to stir young people more than getting involved in politics generally: 73% said they supported help for the homeless and 64% for animal rights. 32% said they had protested. The report concludes that just because they do not participate in mainstream politics does not mean that young people are apathetic.

(Source: The Independent *17/2/97)*

1 (a) Using material from Item A and elsewhere, examine the view that young people are generally apathetic about political issues. **(12 marks)**

> Use Item A first to set a context.

According to a survey conducted in 1997 a substantial minority of young people (24%) have no interest in politics. This has led to concerns that young people are politically apathetic. However, the evidence suggests that young people are more likely to be motivated by issue or identity politics such as homelessness, animal rights and human rights than mainstream party politics.

> Illustrate with material from elsewhere i.e. in this case, new social movements.

Sociologists who study 'new social movements' suggest their membership is mainly composed of young people from middle-class backgrounds who are happy to take direct action in the form of demonstrations, etc. 32% of the sample in Item A said they had protested. Moreover, an increasing number are willing to take more militant action in the form of violence and damage in support of animal rights and environmentalism, e.g. the destroying of genetically modified test crops.

(b) Briefly examine two reasons why people join new social movements.

(8 marks)

> Focus on brief. This response should not be longer than question 1(a).

First, people today are less concerned with material matters such as money and are more concerned with spiritual values. Young people, in particular, are likely to subscribe to belief systems that are in opposition to mainstream or parental belief systems. Second, there is a growing sense of risk – people are aware that the world they live in is in danger from environmental damage, etc. caused by the unethical practices of scientists, transnational companies and governments. People are therefore taking more responsibility for the state of society and the natural world.

2 Evaluate the view that power is widely diffused across a range of competing interest groups in modern societies. **(40 marks)**

> Essay question – aim for two sides at least.

Pluralists maintain that there is no one identifiable group or élite that rules. From a pluralist perspective, power in society is dispersed among a number of interest groups. They believe that society is too complex for everyone to have a say in decision-making and that the best channels for opinion are individual groups such as trade unions, lobby groups, pressure groups, etc.

> Identify the view, i.e. a pluralist one.

Pluralists maintain that this multi-centred power structure creates a democratic society in which all views are represented. They see the government as an 'honest broker' mediating the many different views and interests. This maintains harmony and cohesion within society and is beneficial to all.

Sample questions and model answers *(continued)*

Evaluate the view.

Pluralists have been criticised for neglecting the fact that the specific interests of some powerless groups such as ethnic minorities are not represented by either political parties or pressure groups. Moreover, they neglect the fact that some powerful groups can prevent issues from coming up for debate in the first place.

Evaluate by examining alternative views.

Elite theorists such as Mosca and Pareto argued that it is inevitable that societies divide into the rulers and the ruled. They argued that this is human nature and that rulers are determined by their natural leadership qualities. This minority represent and act in the interests of the majority of citizens who are by nature apathetic or irrational. The majority need the moral guidance and leadership of a unified minority élite. In criticism, Marxists agree that there is a unified power élite but they argue that the political arena and therefore the distribution of power is determined by the economic infrastructure. In other words, those who own the means of production – the bourgeoisie or capitalist class – wield political power.

Another alternative.

Instrumental Marxists such as Milliband argue that the ruling class is made up of an economic élite and a political élite. Unity is maintained through the sharing of similar social background, education (i.e. public schools and Oxbridge), kinship ties especially through intermarriage, membership of clubs and directorships of key companies. Milliband argues that the ruling class rule in their own interest. They rule directly when Conservative governments are in power. This political party is openly protective of the interests of capital. They also take up influential positions in the civil service, judiciary, etc., and rule from within.

The structuralist Marxist Poulantzas disagreed with Milliband. He argued that there may sometimes be conflicts of interests between capitalist power blocs, for example, between financiers and manufacturers. Poulantzas argued that the state has to remain 'relatively autonomous' in order to deal with this conflict. However, because government is conducted within the framework of capitalism, the capitalist ruling class benefits in the long term from any decisions made even if these seem to benefit the working class. For example, the Welfare State has been beneficial for the working class but it has also provided a healthy and fit workforce. Lukes calls this the third dimension of power. This sort of power is not just economic or political. It is also hegemonic in that capitalist ideas culturally dominate institutions such as the media and education and ensure little challenge to the capitalist system.

Your conclusion should attempt to briefly summarise all the arguments raised.

In summary, then, the pluralist idea that power is widely diffused is contradicted by both élite theory and Marxism which suggest that power is concentrated in very few hands. Although there may be some differences between Milliband and Poulantzas on the tactics of the capitalist class, there is agreement that democracy is merely an ideological smokescreen for the fact that power lies in the hands of a capitalist minority.

Practice examination question

Outline and assess the view that new social movements aim to challenge the established cultural, economic and political order of advanced capitalist society.

(60 marks)

Sample questions and model answers *(continued)*

This question will always ask you to think on your feet. Be prepared. Practice.

(b) Using the information in **Item A**, state a suitable hypothesis regarding the effects of poverty on children that a sociologist would be able to test.

(4 marks)

One possible hypothesis might be – There is a strong link between poverty as measured by the lack of three or more basics of normal life such as three meals a day, having a warm coat and having carpets, and rates of ill-health and educational underachievement.

Note this question is asking you to exclusively focus on Item B. Don't include anything else. It will not be rewarded.

(c) Briefly describe, in your own words, the sampling problems apparent in the research in **Item B** and how you would overcome them. (6 marks)

There were problems finding an equal number of working-class and middle-class mothers. Consequently the sample was mainly working class. This problem may simply reflect the facts of the type of single motherhood that the researchers were looking for. There may be a need to adjust the hypothesis or the sample's characteristics. The sample was reduced to 40 because when interviewers turned up at the homes of the single mothers they were not in. The researchers need to make the interview worth while for the single mother in order to motivate her to take part, e.g. through an interview payment perhaps.

A knowledge of research methods is required. Make sure your suggestions are practically possible.

(d) The following statement is a hypothesis suggested by the information in **Item B**: 'Teenage mothers often feel that society negatively labels them.'

Suggest **two** ways in which this hypothesis might be tested, giving reasons for your answer. (8 marks)

There are a number of ways in which this could be done. A large-scale survey of the population could be conducted of family life in general, including questions on teenage mothers which operationalise in various ways positive and negative attitudes towards them. Interviews could be conducted with professionals who come into regular contact with teenage mothers which would measure their attitudes and their perception of social attitudes towards teenage mothers. A longitudinal content analysis could be carried out on newspaper coverage of teenage mothers.

An essay question. Aim for two sides at least.

2 Evaluate the usefulness of the view that the adoption of a scientific approach is the only effective way to study society. (40 marks)

Positivism argues that society and therefore human behaviour (social life) is the product of social laws largely beyond our control. For example, Durkheim saw suicide as the product of such social facts as integration and regulation. Positivists believe that the adoption of the logic and methods of the natural sciences is the only effective way to study society and these social laws. In practice, four factors are stressed.

Identify the view in your opening paragraph, i.e. a positivist view.

First, that research should be carried out under controlled conditions. Natural scientists obviously have the advantage of conducting experiments in laboratories. Social scientists who rarely use laboratory experiments have focused on control through sampling and skilfully designed questionnaires. Second, that research should be objective or value-free. The social scientist should approach research without imposing their own personal beliefs or prejudices on it and interpret all evidence with an open mind. Third, that the research should be open to replication by other social scientists in order to

Elaborate the view.

Chapter 3

Religion

The following topics are covered in this chapter:

- *The role of religion*
- *Religious organisations*
- *Religious beliefs, religious organisations and social groups*
- *The nature and extent of secularisation*

3.1 The role of religion

After studying this section you should be able to:

- *outline and assess the relationship between religion, social conservatism and social change*
- *describe and evaluate the ideological function of religion in relation to preventing social change*
- *evaluate the view that under certain circumstances religion can act as an initiator of change*

LEARNING SUMMARY

The role of religion as a conservative social force

AQA   U4

Functionalism

Emile Durkheim believed that religion is central to the reproduction and maintenance of social order in societies. The major function of religion is to **socialise society's members into value consensus** by the following.

> Religion is a major agent of secondary socialisation.

- **Setting certain values** apart and infusing them with special significance. These values become '**moral codes**' or beliefs which society agrees to revere and socialise children into. Such codes formally and informally **control** our social behaviour. For example, some of the Ten Commandments have become embodied in law (Thou shalt not steal) and some have become part of informal morality (honour thy mother and father).

- **Encouraging collective worship.** Through worship, the individual is encouraged to feel part of a **wider moral community** – for example, a Church of England member may feel part of a larger Christian community. Durkheim strongly believed that **the worship of God symbolised the worship of society** – God and society are the same thing.

This idea has been developed into a theory of '**civil religion**' by other functionalist thinkers. **Shils and Young** argue that it is difficult to separate national identities from religious identities. We can particularly see this in Islamic societies in which every aspect of social, cultural, political and economic life is shaped by religion. In the UK, the Queen is both Head of State and Head of the Church of England. Oaths of allegiance used in the armed forces and the police stress 'God, Queen and Country'. Shils and Young argue that events like the Queen's Coronation affirm both patriotic and moral values.

Some sociologists argue that the **funeral of Princess Diana** performed a religious function in that it brought society together as a **moral collective** and reaffirmed our commitment as a society to Christian values. It also functioned to remind us of our British identity in terms of her position in society and the ceremonial trappings that shaped the funeral service and procession.

Later functionalist thinkers such as **Malinowski** see **religious rites of passage** as functioning to **appease the stress and anxieties created by life crises** such as birth, puberty, marriage and death. The rite of passage usually involves some sort of ceremony or ritual in which the society celebrates or mourns the role of the individual in the greater collective of the family or society, e.g. christenings, bar mitzvahs, confirmations, church weddings and funerals.

Functionalists argue that the role of religion is to preserve the **status quo** rather than to promote social change. **Functionalists agree that religion is a beneficial** conservative force because it maintains consensus, binds people together and promotes social order.

Religion as an inhibitor of change for positive reasons.

Criticisms of functionalism

The following weaknesses have been identified in the functionalist theory of religion.

- It is difficult to see how religion can be functioning to socialise the majority of society's members into morality and social integration if **only a minority of people regularly attend church**.

- There is **little empirical evidence** to support the view that national ceremonies such as the funeral of Diana result in social integration. It is merely *assumed* that they have that effect.

- Functionalists neglect the extent to which religion has been **dysfunctional** for society. For example, in Northern Ireland and Bosnia, religious divisions have caused social disruption and conflict rather than promoted social order.

Marxism

Like Durkheim, **Karl Marx also argued that religion was a conservative force in society**. However, he did not agree that religion is beneficial to society but instead argued that the primary function of religion is to **reproduce, maintain and legitimate class inequality**. In this sense, Marx argues that:

Religion as an inhibitor of change for negative reasons.

> - Religion is an **ideological** apparatus which serves to reflect ruling-class ideas and interests
> - Religion is the '**opium of the people**' because it lulls the working class into a state of **false class-consciousness** by making the true extent of their exploitation by the ruling class invisible.

KEY POINT

Religion is seen by Marx to be ideological in three ways.

- It promotes the idea that **the existing socio-economic hierarchy is God-given** and therefore unchangeable. This can be particularly seen during the feudal period when it was widely believed that kings had a divine right to rule.

- **Religion explains economic and social inequalities in supernatural terms** – in other words, the real causes (i.e. exploitation by the ruling class) are obscured and distorted by religion's insistence that inequality is the product of sin or a sign that people have been chosen by God, etc.

- Some religions even **present suffering and poverty as a virtue to be welcomed** and accepted as normal. Such ideas promote the idea that there is no point in changing the here and now. Rather, people should wait patiently for divine intervention.

Marx therefore argued that religion functions to produce **fatalistic** followers uninterested in changing their world for the better. **Religion is a conservative social force because it inhibits and prevents real social change.** Marx concluded that religion would not be necessary in a classless society – although its survival in communist societies is seen by some as evidence that this prediction was flawed.

There are a number of examples cited as evidence in favour of Marx's arguments.

- **Halevy** claims Methodism in the 19th century distracted workers from their class grievances and encouraged them to see enlightenment in spirituality rather than revolution.
- **Hook's analysis of the Catholic Church** notes that it has a very conservative stance on contraception, abortion, women priests and homosexuality. Hook also suggests that the considerable wealth of the Catholic Church could be used to do more to tackle world poverty.

Criticisms of Marxism

The following weaknesses have been identified in the Marxist theory of religion.

- Like functionalism, Marxism fails to consider **secularisation**. The ideological power of religion is undermined by the fact that less than 10% of people attend church.
- There are examples of religious movements that have brought about radical social change. For example, the **Reverend Martin Luther King and the Southern Baptist Church** were important in dismantling segregation and bringing about political and social rights for black people in the USA in the 1960s. **Liberation theology** (a combination of the teachings of Christ and Marx) has encouraged people to actively change societies in South America.

Religion as an initiator of social change

AQA ▶ U4

Otto Maduro

The Marxist, **Otto Maduro (1982)** recognised that religion in some special circumstances could bring about radical change. He argued that ruling élites sometimes blocked all conventional avenues for change, e.g. politics, trade unions, etc. through force or ideology. Religion therefore may be the **only agency of change** for some oppressed groups. The potential for change through religious avenues is enhanced by the presence of a **charismatic leader** who provides a focus for expressing discontent.

For example, Martin Luther King, Mahatma Gandhi.

Max Weber

Like Marx, Weber subscribed to the idea that religion could be **ideological** in two ways.

Agrees with Marx.

- It gave **assurance to the most fortunate**, i.e. the powerful and wealthy, by stressing that their position was natural or God-given.
- It offered **religious reasons for poverty** and suffering in terms of themes such as wickedness, sins committed in former lives, etc. Weber argued, like Marx, that both these themes legitimate the status quo.

However, Weber believed that **some religious ideas**, specifically Protestant beliefs, **had initiated the economic and social conditions in which capitalism emerged**.

Parts company with Marx.

> From his comparative studies, Weber noted that while similar economic conditions prevailed in China, India and Europe, capitalism only developed in the latter. He noted that capitalism had developed in those parts of Europe where a particular set of Protestant beliefs known as **Calvinism** were dominant. He concluded that Calvinism had brought about the right **cultural climate** for capitalist ideas and practices to develop in two ways.

Weber noted that:

- Calvinists believed in **predestination**, i.e. that they were chosen by God for salvation. They were taught to believe that righteous living was all-important and that their reward for sticking to such religious principles would be economic success.

- Consequently Calvinism encouraged values such as self-discipline, hard work, thrift, modesty and the rejection of self-indulgence, pleasure, idleness and lavish spending: the '**Protestant Work Ethic**'. The adoption of these ideas, Weber argues, led to the rapid accumulation of capital which was invested in industrialisation and the emergence of a Calvinist capitalist class at the end of the feudal era.

Don't make the mistake of using the word 'cause'.

Weber did not say Calvinism 'caused' capitalism, he only suggested that it was the major contributor to a climate of change. Many other pre-conditions needed to be in place. For example, Calvinist beliefs had to be supplemented by a certain level of technology, a skilled and mobile workforce and rational modes of law and bureaucracy. These latter pre-conditions were also present in China and India but Weber claimed that Eastern religions emphasised the spiritual rather than the rational or material – in other words, ideas which were not conducive to sustained economic activity.

Criticisms of Weber

The following weaknesses have been identified in Weber's theory of religion.

- **Sombart** suggests that Weber was mistaken about the beliefs held by Calvinists. Calvinism was against greed and the pursuit of money for its own sake.

- Some countries with large Calvinist populations did not industrialise and this is cited as evidence that Weber's thesis is wrong. However, **Marshall** points out that Weber did not claim that Calvinism was the **sole** pre-condition for the emergence of capitalism. For example, Scotland lacked a skilled technical labour force and capital for investment.

- Some commentators have suggested that slavery, colonialism and piracy were more influential than Calvinist beliefs in accumulating the capital required for industrialisation.

- Marxists have also been critical of Weber. **Kautsky** suggested that capitalism pre-dated Calvinism. Bourgeoise capitalists were attracted to it because it offered convenient justification for the pursuit of economic interests. Thus the Protestant religion was an ideology used to legitimate capitalist interests.

Despite some empirical difficulties in testing Weber's thesis, his ideas remain important because he highlighted the relationship between **social structure** (i.e. the economic and social system) and **social action** (i.e. interaction and interpretation). His point was that if certain structural factors are present, people may **choose to act** upon religious ideas and bring about change.

Progress check

1 Why is religion necessarily a conservative social force according to functionalists?
2 In what way might religion be described as dysfunctional?
3 What is an ideology?
4 What is the role of religious ideology according to Marxists?
5 What does Maduro argue?
6 What Protestant religion helped to bring about capitalism according to Weber?
7 What was the Protestant Work Ethic?
8 Does Weber believe religion to be a conservative social force?

8 Yes and No. Yes, in that it often acts as an ideology which serves the status quo. No, in that under certain circumstances, religious ideas can promote social change.
7 A set of ideas subscribed to by Calvinists which stress hard work, idleness as a sin, thrift, etc.
6 Calvinism.
5 That under certain circumstances, religion can bring about revolutionary change.
4 To reproduce, maintain and legitimate class inequality. To prevent social change.
3 A set of powerful ideas used to justify some type of inequality.
2 It may be the basis of conflict between social groups or nations.
1 Because its function is to ensure people are committed to consensus and social order.

3.2 Religious organisations

After studying this section you should be able to:

- identify the characteristics of religious organisations such as churches, denominations, sects and cults
- outline and assess sociological explanations of the increase in sect and cult membership and activity

LEARNING SUMMARY

Ideal models of religious organisation

AQA ▶ U4

Sociologists have constructed models or 'ideal types' of religious organisation covering the major forms of religious activity.

Church

I.e. the Anglican Church dominates English religion whilst the Catholic Church dominates religious life in Spain, Italy and Eire.

This is a **formal** organisation with a **hierarchy** and **bureaucracy** of paid officials, e.g. the Archbishop of Canterbury leads the Church of England. Its beliefs and values are **widely accepted**, e.g. a substantial part of the population are born 'Anglican'. It tends to have a close relationship with the state and Monarchy, e.g. the Queen is the formal Head of the Church of England. Worship tends to be formal, organised in the form of specific and predictable **rituals** and conducted by ordained clerics. It may be involved in some non-religious activities such as the provision of education, e.g. Church of England and Catholic schools.

Denomination

This organisation also has beliefs and values which are widely accepted, e.g. people may identify themselves as Methodists or Baptists. It has no formal connection with the state. Worship is **less formal** and hierarchy and bureaucracy are less developed. Lay-persons are encouraged to lead worship.

Sect

A sect is an organisation whose members join it of their own **free will**. (People tend on the whole to be 'born' into churches and denominations and will call themselves Anglican, not because they attend church but, because their parents do.) A **charismatic leader** may lead it and sect members tend to believe in the **superiority** of their group. They are the chosen ones who are 'saved', 'enlightened' or have experienced the '**truth**'. Sect beliefs tend to **conflict** with those of society, because they tend not to tolerate the beliefs of others. Sects are generally **insular** and make strong claims on the loyalty of their members, often attempting to **repress individuality**. New members may be encouraged to take on a new name and their contact with family and friends is restricted. Personal responsibility may be surrendered and little opportunity is given for freedom of thought.

> Illustrate with examples i.e. the Unification Church or Moonies, Black Muslims, Rastafarianism.

Cult

There is some sociological **debate** about how cults should be distinguished from sects. **Bruce (1995)** argues that cults lack a coherent and exclusive belief system and they are happy to tolerate other beliefs (unlike sects). Cults do not usually challenge social norms. People normally join in order to achieve some practical end but they are 'customers' rather than disciples. They may have little involvement with the cult on a day-to-day basis once they become familiar with cult beliefs. They usually appeal to the socially privileged who are looking for ways to improve the quality of their spiritual life without sacrificing material comforts.

Stark and Bainbridge (1985) suggest that cults are new religions, whereas sects tend to be the product of disillusion with established religions. They differentiate between three broad types of cult.

- '**Audience cults**' tend to be the product of a general shared interest (e.g. belief in UFOs) and the market-place rather than dominated by any specific organised religious group (e.g. the demand for horoscopes and tarot readings is met by newspapers and phone-lines).

- '**Client cults**' are specifically organised to provide a particular service, e.g. the spiritual fulfillment offered by New Age religions, etc.

- '**Cultic movements**' offer spiritual and material supports to their members, demand exclusive attention and some participation from their followers, e.g. selling books on the street. Some of these demands on followers have led to the suicide of the group, e.g. The Solar Temple cult in France, Switzerland and Canada, and the Heaven's Gate cult.

> Sometimes difficult to differentiate from sects.

New Religious Movements (NRMs)

Roy Wallis claims that NRMs are generally distinct from sects and cults. He argues there are three general types.

- **World-rejecting NRMs reject** the secular world as corrupt and beyond redemption. Such NRMs either **abandon** the world or they attempt to **transform** the world with evangelical zeal. The Children of God and Jesus People are examples of NRMs with evangelical goals whilst the Plymouth Brethren, (who reject modern technology such as televisions, radios and computers) are an example of a NRM which sees the secular world as problematic.

- **World-affirming NRMs accept the values and goals of wider society** but aim to provide a **new means** to achieve these. Human beings are seen to have enormous physical, mental and spiritual potential. These NRMs advertise themselves as an alternative way of achieving economic and social success.

Such sects usually involve some financial investment and their recruits mainly originate in the middle class, e.g. Scientology has a number of high-profile members including John Travolta and Tom Cruise.

- **World-accommodating NRMs** neither fully accept the values and goals of wider society nor do they entirely reject society. These **NRMs exist on the margins of established churches and denominations**. They are thought to be a response to the increasing decline in membership and attendance of the established churches. For example, fundamentalist 'born again' and evangelical Christian groups are good examples of world accommodating sects which have attracted a great number of young people in recent years.

New Age Movements (NAMs)

NAMs are similar to cultic movements but revolve around the selling of specific messages such as opposition to traditional scientific approaches, an emphasis on green issues such as environmentalism and/or vegetarianism, and a focus on spiritual and personal empowerment. For example, many people involved in the anti-road movement and opposed to genetically modified crops subscribe to pagan beliefs such as **Wicca** which believes that all living things have a spirit and need protecting from human progress.

Why people join sects

AQA ▶ U4

Questions on sects tend to focus on how they differ from mainstream religion and their relationship to social charge.

Sects may be evidence of **disillusion with the established churches**. G.K. Nelson argues that the young, in particular, may be 'turned-off' by overly bureaucratic and formal religion. However, Nelson argues that a **religious revival** is underway in evangelical circles. These churches offer a more spontaneous version of religion which is less reliant on ritual and consequently more attractive to the young. Sects therefore may be the product of a search for more genuine and creative ways of satisfying spiritual needs.

Types of deprivation

Max Weber linked sects to **social stratification**. Sects are most likely to emerge amongst **the poor**. Such groups may develop a **'theodicy of disprivilege'** – a religious set of ideas that explain why they are in that position. For example, the group may believe that they are 'God's chosen people'. The promise of 'salvation' is **'compensation'** for their poverty or ill-treatment by the rest of society.

Sects also attract members from the middle classes. **Glock and Stark** use the concept of **relative deprivation** to explain this, suggesting that some members of the middle class may feel relatively deprived compared with other groups.

Glock and Stark identify a number of different types of relative deprivation.

- **Social deprivation** may stem from a **lack of power, prestige and status**. For example, those lacking job satisfaction may find alternative sources of satisfaction in the goals set by sects such as Jehovah's Witnesses, Mormons, etc. These sects are known as **conversionist** sects because they strongly encourage their members to be evangelical in their beliefs and convert non-believers.

- **Organismic deprivation** is experienced by those who suffer physical and mental-health problems, e.g. people may turn to sects in the hope of being **healed** or as an alternative to drugs or alcohol.

- **Ethical deprivation** is the result of people perceiving the world to be in **moral decline**. They may retreat into an **introversionist** sect which believes in cutting itself off from the society that it perceives to be immoral and a threat to its religious integrity. For example, Jim Jones' People's Temple retreated into the jungle of Guyana where its 800 plus members eventually committed mass suicide.

- **Psychic deprivation** refers to those searching for more than the dominant value-system offers. They may wish for some **inner spiritual fulfilment** rather than the materialist goals on offer in capitalist societies. Certain sects, e.g. the Divine Light Mission, Transcendental Meditation (TM), Moonies, etc. claim to offer this. Such cults tend to be attractive to the middle class and the young.

Social change

Closely related to the concept of relative deprivation is the idea that religious sects are the product of **social change**. Such change may create the conditions for various forms of deprivation.

- **Wilson** argues that the popularity of religious sects in the late 18th and early 19th centuries, both in the UK and USA, was a reaction to anxieties created by **industrialisation and urbanisation**.
- Twentieth-century sects may be a response to anxieties created by the dominance of scientific rationalism, materialism and the resulting decline in religious belief in society, i.e. **secularisation**.
- **Robert Bellah** argues that the increase in sect and cult membership seen in the late 1960s in the USA was due to middle-class youth experiencing a **'crisis of meaning'** in regard to the materialistic values of their parents' culture. Anti-materialist and 'free love' values such as the Jesus People and Eastern-influenced NRMs such as Hare Krishna recruited in large numbers from young people in search of spiritual goals.

The future of sects

The **future of sects** is difficult to predict. Some may become extinct when their charismatic leader dies or because children of sect members are not as committed to the belief system. They may destroy themselves (e.g. Jim Jones' People's Temple). They may be destroyed by society because society dislikes and fears the superior attitude of these groups (e.g. David Koresh's Branch Davidian sect in Waco, Texas was wiped out in a fire after the FBI besieged their compound).

Some will flourish. Evidence suggests that world-affirming NRMs attract a great deal of wealth. Some may become so popular that they evolve into denominations and churches, e.g. some of the born-again Christian movements.

Progress check

1 Who argues that sects are a product of young people being turned off by the bureaucratic rituals of the established church?
2 What is a theodicy of disprivilege?
3 What is organismic deprivation?
4 What is ethical deprivation?
5 What was the main cause of sect growth in the 1960s and 1970s?

5 The search for meaning (psychic deprivation) experienced by educated middle-class youth.
4 A feeling that the world is in moral decline. A sect might be joined in order to combat this.
3 Experience of physical or mental problems which may act as a motivation for joining a sect.
2 A set of ideas that rationalises poverty by suggesting that those who experience it are chosen by God.
1 G.K. Nelson.

3.3 Religious beliefs, religious organisations and social groups

After studying this section you should be able to:

- *explain why women are more involved in religious beliefs and practices than men*
- *outline the role and function of religion for ethnic-minority communities*

Religion and ethnicity

AQA ▶ U4

Key points from AS

- **Ethnicity and identity**
  AS Guide pages 68–69

Madood and Berthold's survey (1994) of religious affiliation among ethnic-minority groups indicates that they are more religious than the majority population. Involvement in the religious practices of Islamic, Hindu and Sikh religions is high in the UK. In particular, young Asians are more likely than young whites to regularly practise their religion.

Davie (1994) suggests that religious belief is crucial to South-Asian minorities such as Bangladeshis, Pakistanis and Indians in shaping their cultural identity and family community in an alien or racist environment. **Johal (1998)** notes that religion functions to maintain cultural identity. Consequently ethnic-minority religions may come into conflict with the increasingly secularised majority culture over issues such as worship in schools, the education of females, clothing requirements, etc. **Bird** argues that religion **functions to maintain cultural identity and resist assimilation into a mainly white and Christian society.**

The evidence suggests that religion plays a crucial part in the lives of second- and third-generation Asians in the UK despite having a **dual identity**, i.e. being British and Asian. Surveys suggest that young Asians feel a strong sense of obligation and duty to their parents and extended kin because of religion, compared with their white peers. Most young Asians seem happy to have an arranged marriage with somebody of their own religion. Research by **Jacobson (1997)** found that Islam has a strong impact on young Pakistanis in terms of diet, worship, dress and everyday behaviour.

Research in 1997 indicated that religion was less important than **colour** in shaping Afro-Caribbean identity. However, **Hennels (1997)** notes that many Afro-Caribbean people participate in the Pentecostal tradition which tends to subscribe to fundamentalist Christian values, e.g. it encourages hard work and a strict sexual and family morality. It may therefore attract members of the Afro-Caribbean minority who are experiencing economic, social and ethical deprivation. Marxists have been critical of Pentecostalism because they see its emphasis on religious experience as diverting Afro-Caribbean people from the real cause of their oppression, i.e. a racist capitalist system.

Rastafarianism has proved popular among young Afro-Caribbean men in the UK. There is some evidence that participation in this sect **symbolises protest** at the racial discrimination that young Afro-Caribbean men see as denying them full social and economic status.

Gender and religion

AQA ▶ U4

An increasingly popular topic for exam questions!

Women attend church more often and regularly than men do. **Walker (1990)** argues that women are consequently more religious than men. Religion may be a way of **compensating for a subordinate position in patriarchal societies.** However, it may also be a function of age. Religious belief is more likely in middle and old age. There are more older women in the population than men.

KEY POINT

Almost all the major world religions are **patriarchal** and therefore **view women as subordinate and inferior**. A number of religions see women's bodies and sexuality as threatening because menstruation and childbirth are seen to '**pollute**' the spiritual purity of religious belief and places. Women are therefore **policed by religion**. For example, there is widespread opposition in many religions to females conducting religious rituals.

Traditional ideas about women tend to characterise most **fundamentalist** religions because of the fundamentalist desire to oppose modernity. However, it is important not to stereotype fundamentalist religions in terms of their attitudes towards women. For example, it is often assumed that Islam is oppressive towards women yet evidence from studies by **Anwar and Butler** suggest that Muslim women in the UK play an active rather than passive role in that religion.

Women do seem to play a greater role in NRMs and NAMs, although some NRMs subscribe to what feminists would describe as **oppressive beliefs** about women. For example, the New Evangelical movements and groups such as Rastafarians and the Nation of Islam stress traditional roles for women in the home.

Bird suggests NAMs appeal to women more than men because their emphasis is on healing, co-operation, caring and spirituality (all regarded as feminine characteristics). Women may be more attracted to NAMs because they are more likely to experience social and psychic deprivation.

3.4 The nature and extent of secularisation

LEARNING SUMMARY

After studying this section you should be able to:

- *identify the different definitions of secularisation used by sociologists*
- *outline and assess the extent of the decline of religious belief and practice*

The secularisation debate

AQA   U4

Defining secularisation

KEY POINT

Bryan Wilson argues that **secularisation is the process by which religious institutions, actions and practices lose their social significance**. There are four key elements to his argument.

The statistical argument

Wilson focuses on **statistical evidence** relating to religious institutions and their activity. The strongest evidence for secularisation in the UK comes from church-attendance statistics. According to the 1851 Census approximately 40% of the population attended church in the UK. By 1997 this had dropped to **8.2%**. The only exception is Northern Ireland. Attendance at religious ceremonies such as baptisms, communion and confirmation have also dramatically fallen. The decline in church marriages (down to 50% in 1997), the rising divorce rate, the increase in cohabitation and children born outside of marriage are seen as evidence that religion and its moral value-system exerts little influence today.

This is a useful topic to use to illustrate the problems faced when sociologists use secondary data as part of theory and method.

The critique of religious statistics

However, **interpretivist** sociologists suggest these statistics should be treated with caution for the following reasons.

- Statistics relating to the previous century are probably **unreliable** because sophisticated data-collection practices were not in place.

- Contemporary statistics may not be **reliable** because different religious organisations employ **different counting methods**.

- **Bellah** questions the **validity** of such statistics because people who attend church are not necessarily practising religious belief, whilst those who do believe may not see the need to attend. Religion is a private experience for many and consequently can not be reliably or scientifically measured.

- There is a great deal of **contradictory statistical evidence**. Membership of NRMs has risen substantially in the last ten years especially amongst the young. The number of ethnic-minority religions in the UK has also increased, e.g. there are twice as many Muslims in the UK as Methodists.

In conclusion, then, critics of Wilson point out that the statistical **evidence only measures participation in institutionalised religion not religious belief**.

The growth of rationalism and disenchantment

Sometimes referred to as the 'de-sacrilisation' of religion.

> Wilson suggests that **rational thinking in the shape of science** has replaced religious influence in our lives because scientific progress has resulted in higher living standards. Moreover, science has produced convincing explanations for phenomena that were once the province of religion, e.g. how the world was created, etc. People have therefore become increasingly '**disenchanted**' with religion.
>
> **KEY POINT**

Critics of Wilson argue the following.

- He may be over-emphasising the influence of rationality. There is evidence that people prefer 'religious' explanations for random events like the early death of loved ones, e.g. 'God has taken them', etc.

- Many people subscribe to quasi-religious concepts like 'luck' or 'fate'.

- Social-attitude surveys indicate that 70% of the UK population profess a strong belief in God.

- Decline in religious practices may be part of a more **general decline in people being willing to demonstrate commitment to their beliefs**. In the late 20th century, there has been a general decline in the membership of high-commitment organisations such as trade unions, political parties and churches which demand time and effort from their members. Membership of low-commitment organisations such as the National Trust has increased. The popularity of some sects and cults can be explained by the fact that they do not demand a great deal of commitment.

Disengagement of the church from society

> Wilson argues that the church is no longer involved in important areas of social life such as **politics**. Politicians are no longer interested in ensuring that their policies meet with the approval of religious leaders. People are more likely to take **moral direction from the mass media** than the church. Public apathy to religion now means that it only has **symbolic value** today. People now only enter church for '**hatching, matching and dispatching**' ceremonies. Wilson concludes that the Church has become disengaged from wider society and plays only a **marginal** role in modern society.
>
> **KEY POINT**

Critics of Wilson argue the following.

- Religion is still a major provider of education and welfare for the poor.
- The media still shows a great interest in religious issues such as women priests or the Church of England's attitudes towards homosexuality.
- National religious ceremonies such as the funeral of Diana, Princess of Wales suggest that the sacred might still be important.
- Some sociologists, notably **Parsons**, say that disengagement is probably a good thing because it means that the churches can focus more effectively on their **central role of providing moral goals for society to achieve**.

Religious pluralism

> Another aspect of secularisation identified by Wilson is **religious pluralism**. The established church no longer ministers to all members of society. Instead, as **Bruce** argues, industrialisation has fragmented society into a **market-place of religions**. Wilson argues that competition between religions undermines their credibility and they can no longer take loyalty for granted as they compete for **'spiritual shoppers'**. Religion thus no longer acts as an integrating force in society.

KEY POINT

Sects are seen here as caused by the social change brought about by secularisation.

In particular, the growth in the number of sects, cults and new religious movements has been seen by Wilson as evidence of secularisation. He argues that sects are the **last outpost of religion in a secular society** and are a symptom of religion's decline. Wilson suggests that members of sects are only temporarily committed to religious beliefs. They are more committed to following a charismatic leader or attracted by the lifestyle. He sees sects as **short-lived** with members drifting in and out of them.

However, studies by **Greely** and **Nelson** argue that the growth of new religious movements indicates that society is undergoing a **religious revival**. Nelson argues that this revival is a **product of the secularisation of the established churches** which have lost touch with people's spiritual needs. The rituals of organisations like the Church of England are interpreted as stale, boring and lacking in genuine commitment. Nelson suggests people have turned to evangelical Christian fundamentalism in the form of house churches and charismatic pastors who encourage a more informal and exciting form of worship, which is especially attractive to young people.

Conclusions about secularisation

Some sociologists suggest that it is too one-dimensional to associate secularisation with a decline in religious activity. **Hervieu-Leger (1993)** suggests that what Wilson sees as secularisation is merely **the reorganisation of religion so that it is more relevant to the needs of modern societies**. He suggests that the role of religion in rational and increasingly globalised societies has changed. Religion today, and especially NRMs, function to provide **supportive emotional communities in increasingly impersonal societies**. Religion provides **a counter to globalisation** by providing a focus for cultural identity, e.g. many Muslims see their religious identity as more important than their ethnic and national identity. Religion is more important today because it resists modernity – **fundamentalists**, whether Christian or Islamic, reject modernity and aim to return to the 'traditional'. Hervieu-Leger points out that religions that perform these functions are still strong.

KEY POINT

Grace Davie (1995) suggests that theories of secularisation need to **separate believing and belonging**. She argues that religion in the UK is characterised by **believing without belonging** and there may even be a case for arguing that church attendance for many people is **belonging without believing**.

Profound changes are clearly occurring in institutional religion in the UK. However, whether these changes can be described as secularisation is difficult to ascertain. A major problem is that **sociologists cannot agree on a universal definition of religious belief and therefore secularisation**. Consequently statistical tools may be fine for measuring attendance and membership but they are probably too crude for uncovering the real level of religious belief – which is difficult to measure because it is often private, contradictory in nature and not articulated. At best, then, the evidence for secularisation is mixed.

KEY POINT

Stark and Bainbridge argue that secularisation is probably a **cyclical process** and we are now passing out of a period of low religious belief into an upswing as we anxiously enter the 21st century. In conclusion, then, it may be that **religion is merely changing and adapting, rather than being in decline**.

Progress check

1 What has replaced religion in explaining the world, according to Bryan Wilson?

2 What is disengagement?

3 What is religious pluralism?

4 What statistical evidence contradicts the idea that active participation in religious practices is in decline?

5 Who argues that for true religion to flourish the established churches have to undergo secularisation?

6 In what ways might increased participation in fundamentalist religions, evangelical churches and sects be a reaction to globalisation?

7 Define what is meant by fundamentalist religion.

1 Scientific or rational thinking.
2 The withdrawal of the Church from important areas of social life such as politics.
3 The fragmentation of monolithic religion into hundreds of religions competing with each other.
4 The rising number of young people involved in the evangelical Christian movement and the increase in ethnic-minority religions such as Islam in the UK.
5 G.K. Nelson.
6 It provides a basis for cultural identity and emotional community in an increasingly impersonal society.
7 It refers to religions that oppose modernity and wish to return society to traditional values and institutions. Such religions usually insist on a literal interpretation of their holy writings.

Sample question and model answer

Item A
Gender and church attendance, Britain and Northern Ireland, 1991 (%)

Attendance	Britain		Northern Ireland	
	Men	Women	Men	Women
Frequent	37	63	39	61
Regular	35	65	57	43
Rare	48	52	49	51

(Source: British Social Attitudes Survey (1991) in Investigating Religion *(1999) by John Bird, p. 38, Collins Educational.)*

(a) Using material from Item A, describe and briefly explain gender variations in patterns of church attendance in Britain and Northern Ireland. **(12 marks)**

Use Item A first to set the context.

In Britain and Northern Ireland, women are almost twice as likely as men to attend church frequently. In Britain, women make up 65% of regular attenders but this is largely reversed in Northern Ireland where men make up the majority figure. This may partly be due to the political nature of religion in this area as much as religious belief. In terms of those who attend church only rarely, numbers are fairly evenly balanced between the sexes both in Britain and Northern Ireland.

Brief explanation.

Generally, then, women attend church more than men. It has been suggested that women are more religious than men. However this may merely be a demographic effect – there are more older women than men and it is a fact that religious belief is more common in middle and old age. Also, as Davie notes, many people belong to churches without believing. Women may be attracted to the social networks provided by churches rather than the belief system.

(b) Examine some of the problems that sociologists face in quantifying religious belief. **(8 marks)**

It's only worth 8 marks so don't over-do this response; 3–4 points will suffice.

Sociologists have attempted to quantify religious belief and its alleged decline, i.e. secularisation, by using official statistics collected by church organisations mainly relating to membership of the established churches and Sunday attendance. Some have seen the decline in the number of confirmations, Sunday school attendance, church weddings and marriage as a quantifiable symptom of the decline in religious belief. However, the official statistics have problems because different churches define membership and count attendance in different ways. Bellah argues that religion is a private experience and it does not need attendance at church for it to be valid. Davie notes that many people attend church for social reasons, e.g. the elderly.

Note that this response outlines *how* religious belief is quantified *before* outlining the problems.

Sample question and model answer (continued)

Essay question – aim for 2 sides at least.

(c) Assess the sociological arguments and evidence for the view that religion is a conservative force in society but may be associated with social change in certain circumstances. **(40 marks)**

Identify the view that religion is a conservative force, i.e. functionalism.

The functionalist, E. Durkheim, claimed that religion is fundamental to the maintenance of collective consciousness, i.e. shared beliefs, values, customs and norms that make social life possible. He claimed that the worship of religion is essentially the unconscious worship of society and results in the reinforcement of values that the group shares and the binding of the group together. Religion therefore functions to promote social solidarity. Religion is a conservative force because its role is to ensure commitment to the existing social order and minimisation of conflict and disruption. In this way, religion is a major contributor to the maintenance of social order.

Elaborate on the functionalist view.

Other functionalists support this view. Parsons noted that religion provides and legitimates key social values by investing them with a sacred quality, i.e. such values become moral codes. Members of society internalise such codes during socialisation and they become guidelines for behaviour ensuring that people interact with each other in an ordered and stable fashion.

Assess the functionalist view.

However, critics of functionalism point to two factors that seem to contradict and challenge this theory. First, we now live in a secular society rather than a religious society, and consequently religion has little everyday influence. How, therefore, can religion function to bind society together? Second, religion is seen as the cause of much conflict in the world rather than social order.

Identify another view that suggests religion is a conservative force, i.e. Marxism.

Marxists argue that religion functions to socially control the subordinated working class by transmitting the ideological messages that the social order of wealth and poverty may be the product of God's plan and therefore unchangeable. Some religious ideology – especially that associated with sects and some evangelical Protestant religions – socialises its followers into seeing lack of power, poverty and suffering as a sign of salvation or exclusivity. Therefore, people are discouraged from attempting to transform their material circumstances in case they threaten their spiritual place in heaven, etc. Marx refers to religion as the 'opium of the masses' because it dulls their senses in regard to their exploitation – it is the imaginary flowers of religion that cover our chains. In this sense, religion functions as a conservative force to promote false class-consciousness, and the capitalist system and ruling-class power continue undisturbed.

Elaborate the Marxist view.

Marxists point to a range of evidence that suggests that religion inhibits social change. Halevy, in particular, notes that the British working class were probably diverted from revolutionary zeal by religions such as Methodism which encouraged the much safer (for capitalists) path of non-conformity. However, there is also evidence that religion has not always acted as a conservative ideological force and may be a catalyst for change in certain circumstances.

Sample question and model answer (continued)

Identify a view that suggests religion can promote change.

Maduro argues that most religions tend to take a traditional and conservative line but some churches have undergone significant internal reorganisation which may fuel social change in wider society. For example, the hierarchy of most religions tends to be recruited from élite groups. However, when clergy are recruited from the subordinated class, conflict between bishops and clergy can lead to the emergence of a more radical religion. This seems to have been the case in relation to liberation theology in Latin America. The view held by many Roman Catholic priests in South America working with the poor is that Jesus Christ and Karl Marx had a great deal in common and that the clergy should work towards ending poverty and the political oppression of ordinary people by élites.

Maduro points out that such religions may become the focus for protest if the ruling élite block all normal and democratic avenues of social change and arrest opposition politicians. The Church may then become the opposition. Support for revolutionary change from religious leaders may motivate the mass to rise up against their oppressors. The Sandinista revolution in Nicaragua is seen as a good example of this, whilst the role of religion in South Africa, Iran and Eastern Europe is also seen as important in bringing about profound social change in those societies.

Conclusion briefly summarising main arguments.

In conclusion, then, religion can be an ideological tool of the ruling class but it can also be transformed by internal changes or a charismatic leader into a force which can assist major social change.

Practice examination question

Item A

Ceremony and ritual, in Durkheim's view, are essential in binding the members of society together. This is why they are found in the various life crises at which major social transitions are experienced – for example, birth, marriage and death. In virtually all societies, ritual and ceremonial procedures are observed on such occasions. Funeral rituals demonstrate that the values of the group outlive the passing of particular individuals, and so provide a means for bereaved people to adjust to their altered circumstances. Mourning is only a spontaneous expression of grief for those personally affected by the death, whilst for others it is a duty imposed by the social group. With the development of modern societies, Durkheim believed, the influence of religion has waned. Scientific thinking has increasingly replaced religious belief and explanation for the majority whilst ceremonial and ritual activities come to occupy only a small part of individual's lives.

(a) Using Item A, describe and briefly explain how religious rituals and ceremonies function to bind members of society together. (12 marks)

(b) Examine some of the problems sociologists face in measuring the view that scientific thinking has replaced religious belief and explanation for the majority. (8 marks)

(c) Assess the sociological arguments and evidence for and against the view that sects and cults are the product of the anxieties created by profound social change. (40 marks)

Chapter 4

World sociology

The following topics are covered in this chapter:

- Definitions of development and under-development
- Sociological explanations for development and under-development
- Recent developments in world sociology
- Population in the less-developed world
- Gender and development
- Health-care in the developing world

4.1 Definitions of development and under-development

After studying this section you should be able to:

- define the key concepts of development and under-development
- identify and illustrate the characteristics of development

Key concepts

AQA U4

World sociology is concerned with explaining the relationship and, specifically, the **economic inequalities**, between different regions and different countries of the world. Generally the term **'development'** is used by Western sociologists to mean **industrialisation, economic growth and the living standards associated with prosperity, such as increased life expectancy, health-care, free education, etc**. Those countries that have not yet achieved these objectives are said to be **'undeveloped'** and are often termed **'less-developed countries'** (LDCs).

The problematical nature of 'development'

However, some sociologists suggest that this definition of development is both **loaded** and **ethnocentric** – it reflects the view that **Westernisation** is the only worthwhile and desirable direction development should take. Not all sociologists agree with this definition of development. For example, some regard **liberation from oppression** as more important to progress than industrialisation. Others regard industrial development as a problem if it means increasing social and economic divisions within a country. Islamic societies regard development as constituting progress to becoming nearer to Allah whereas Westerners might regard this as a backward step.

> Marxists equate development with socialism or communism.

It is also important to distinguish between **'undeveloped'** and **'under-developed'** societies. The former have not yet developed but there is no reason why they should not do so in the future. The latter have not developed because they have been prevented from doing so by richer countries. Their poverty may have been directly caused by richer countries exploiting them.

Until the 1990s, world sociology mainly focused on the relationship between the rich countries of the **First World** (consisting of the USA, Japan, Western Europe, etc.) and the **Third World** (consisting of most of Africa, South and Central America, the Indian subcontinent and most of East Asia). The **Second World** was a political entity made up of the socialist/communist societies such as the USSR, Eastern Europe, China, etc.

Today, the distinction between these three worlds is problematical for three reasons.

- The **Second World** has largely collapsed – even China now has elements of free-market capitalism as part of its economic policy.
- Some Third World countries have **rapidly industrialised** in the last thirty years, e.g. the so-called '**Asian Tigers**' of South-East Asia (South Korea, Malaysia, Taiwan, Indonesia and Singapore) and South American countries such as Brazil, Mexico and Argentina. However, such development has tended only to benefit the political and economic élite. Nevertheless, **there is no longer one single Third World**.
- It can be argued that we can no longer split the world up into distinct sections because of **globalisation**. Global communications, the easy movement of international capital, and the activities of multi- and transnational companies may mean that we live in **one global system in which national and regional boundaries are less important**.

The economic and social differences between developed nations and undeveloped nations

Despite these observations, the **economic and social differences** between First World and Third World or less-developed countries (**LDCs**) remain striking. In contrast with First World nations, LDCs display the following characteristics.

- Their economies are based on production of **cash crops and raw materials** for export with **little or no manufacturing industry**.
- They have **low economic growth**, little capital to invest, and high levels of **unemployment** and underemployment.
- There is little, or no, formal education, with **low levels of literacy**.
- There is **famine and malnutrition**, the latter being found in both rural and urban (e.g. shanty towns) areas.
- There is a lack of basic health-care, with high levels of **disease, high infant-mortality and low life-expectancy**.
- There are poor or non-existent communications and transport networks.

Indicators of development: economic growth, levels of literacy, health care, infrastructure.

Progress check

1 What do most Western sociologists mean by 'development'?

2 What is meant by under-development?

3 What is meant by the Second World?

4 How do the Asian Tigers make the concept of the Third World problematic?

5 What aspects of health indicate lack of development in a country?

5 Low life-expectancy, high infant-mortality and people dying of diseases they would survive if they lived in the West, e.g. measles.

4 The Asian Tigers are a set of countries in South-East Asia that have rapidly industrialised and challenged Western countries as producers of manufactured goods. Their newly acquired wealth means they cannot be categorised with other poorer Third World nations.

3 The Communist world which has now largely collapsed.

2 The idea that some countries are undeveloped because they have been prevented from developing or have been exploited by Western nations.

1 The movement towards Western versions of industrialisation.

4.2 Sociological explanations for development and under-development

After studying this section you should be able to:

- compare and contrast modernisation and dependency theories of development and under-development
- outline the cultural, political and economic relationships between developed and undeveloped countries.
- describe the role of aid, trade and transnational companies in regard to development strategies.

LEARNING SUMMARY

Modernisation theory

AQA ▸ U4

> Modernisation theory is largely based on the view that to develop means to become 'modern' by adopting **Western cultural values and social institutions**. It is suggested that undeveloped societies subscribe to value systems and institutions that **hinder** the development process.
>
> *KEY POINT*

Development as an evolutionary process

The leading modernisation thinker, **Bill Rostow**, suggested that development should be seen as an **evolutionary** process in which countries progress up a development ladder of **five stages**.

1 Undeveloped societies are '**traditional societies**' dominated by institutions such as families, tribes and clans, within which roles are **ascribed** (i.e. people are born into them) rather than achieved. Production is agricultural.

2 **The 'pre-conditions for take-off'** stage involves the introduction of material factors such as capital and technology from the West in the form of **capital investment by Western companies and official aid**.

3 The '**take-off stage**' is the most important and involves traditional attitudes and social institutions being overcome and replaced with their Western equivalents. For example, **achievement** replaces ascription and **the nuclear family** replaces the extended family or clan/tribe as people become more **geographically mobile** in their search for work in the factories set up by Western companies.

4 The '**drive to maturity stage**' is marked by **export** of manufactured goods to the West as the country takes its place in the international trading system.

5 Development is achieved in the final stage which Rostow calls '**the age of high mass consumption**'. In this stage, the majority of citizens live in urban rather than rural areas and enjoy a comfortable lifestyle. Life expectancy is high and most citizens have access to health-care and free education.

Western societies are said by Rostow to be at the 5th stage. The 'Asian Tigers' are said to be at the 4th stage because not all the population share the same standard of living.

Modernisation and cultural change

Other modernisation writers such as **Parsons** have stressed the need for **cultural change** in the LDCs if development is to come about. In particular, **traditional religions** such as Islam and Hinduism are seen to be a problem because they are perceived to be:

Values.

- anti-science and anti-secular
- ascriptive and therefore an obstacle to both social and geographical mobility
- responsible for 'population explosions'.

Lerner suggests that cultural change could be encouraged by **educating the children of LDC élites** in Western schools and universities.

Criticisms of modernisation theory

Modernisation theory has been very influential, particularly on US foreign policy, but it has attracted four key criticisms.

It is an ethnocentric theory – meaning it judges other cultures relative to Western, especially American culture.

- It implies that traditional values and institutions have little or no value compared with their Western equivalents. However, there is evidence from Japan and the 'Asian Tigers' that the traditional (e.g. religion and extended family) can exist successfully alongside the modern.
- It assumes Western forms of capitalism to be the ideal and conveniently ignores the social and economic problems that are common in those societies, e.g. high divorce-rates, crime, poverty, suicide, etc.
- Western encouragement of LDC élites has created inequalities in wealth and power which have led to human-rights abuses. In particular, the USA has propped up abusive right-wing regimes because they are anti-communist.
- In its emphasis on internal obstacles, modernisation theory underestimates the **external** obstacles to development.

Dependency theory

AQA   U4

> **KEY POINT**
>
> The **neo-Marxist dependency theory** rejects the view that the people of LDCs are responsible for the failure of their societies to develop. Instead, **Andre Gunder Frank**, the leading dependency theorist, suggests that lack of development is because **Western nations have deliberately under-developed them.**

Global capitalism

Frank argues that there exists a **global system of capitalism** in which **core** nations such as the USA and UK exploit what Frank calls the **peripheral** nations or LDCs. The periphery is kept in a state of dependency and under-development because the developed world requires cheap raw materials and labour. Frank argued that this relationship of exploitation and dependency occurred **historically** through slavery and colonialism, and **continues today** through Western dominance of the international trading system, the practices of multinational companies and the LDC's reliance on Western aid.

Historical exploitation – slavery and colonialism

Frank argued that the trade in **slavery** resulted in tremendous profits for both slave-traders and plantation owners in the 18th century. This led to a **super-accumulation of capital** which was invested in Britain's industrial revolution and consequently helped kick-start industrial development in the UK.

According to **Paul Harrison**, in the 18th century Europe was able to use its advanced military technology to **conquer and colonise** many parts of the Third World. First World countries exploited the colonies for cheap food, raw materials and labour. For example, land traditionally used for growing food was turned over to the production of **cash crops** for export.

Contemporary exploitation

International trade

The way world trade is organised today is a **legacy of colonialism**. Most colonies have achieved political independence but their economies still tend to be based on exporting cash crops and raw materials to the West. Moreover, many LDCs find it difficult to achieve full economic independence because many are **over-dependent on either one or two primary products or Western demand for those products**. Therefore, any over-production or fall in Western demand can have a severe effect upon LDC economies. Western nations further limit the export earnings of LDCs by setting the prices for many LDC products and setting **tariffs and quotas** which tax or limit LDC products entering the First World, especially manufactured products.

Neo-colonialism

Frank and others such as Therese Hayter argue that traditional forms of colonialism are giving way to new forms: **neo-colonialism**. At the forefront of this type of exploitation are the **multinational companies (MNCs)**. In their search for profit, these companies allegedly exploit LDCs for cheap labour, cheap raw materials and new markets.

Multinationals

The search for new markets encouraged Western companies to expand in size and market their products globally. These **multinational companies (MNCs)** imported raw materials from the LDCs and exported manufactured goods back to them. After World War II, increasing numbers of companies started to produce manufactured goods in the LDCs, taking advantage of cheap labour, relaxed health and safety laws and low taxes.

Simpson and Sinclair point out that MNCs now dominate the capitalist world economy and many have greater economic and political power than LDCs. Moreover, the MNCs are not accountable for their actions in law. Many have been accused of **interfering in the internal politics of LDCs** to ensure that local élites supportive of their activities retain power. Others have been accused of **environmental destruction** and **pollution** and playing a major role in **the eviction of native peoples from their land**. Moreover, some have been accused of **marketing drugs and pesticides banned in the West**. **Illich** argues that MNCs are guilty of creating **'false needs'** in their marketing of products in LDCs which may have detrimental effects on health such as high-tar tobacco, soft drinks such as Coca-Cola, hamburgers and baby-milk powder.

According to Marxists, then, MNCs do not invest in LDCs because they want to kick-start their economies. Their motive is primarily **profit**.

Official aid

Another form of neo-colonialism according to dependency theory is official aid. **Bilateral aid** refers to the flow of resources from one country to another – most usually in the form of loans but also as weapons, medicines and human expertise. **Multi-lateral aid** involves financial institutions such as the World Bank and the International Monetary Fund lending money to LDCs.

Most loans to the Third World involve **interest**. However, economies grow too slowly and long-term development projects such as irrigation schemes, dams, etc. can be slow to generate the predicted income or may fail. In the meantime, the interest builds up and can eventually outstrip the initial loan.

Visit the Guardian or Telegraph website and update these statistics and Western government's response to debt.

By 1980 LDCs owed the West $600 billion. By 1998, this had increased to **$2.2 trillion**. Most of the countries in real trouble are extremely poor African states, e.g. in 1998 Sub-Saharan Africa owed $222 billion (which makes up 71% of its national earnings) whilst Mozambique and Ethiopia spent almost half their export earnings servicing their debts. Nearly a quarter of the aid African countries receive this year will be immediately repaid to the West to repay debts.

Hayter argues that debt has a number of consequences.

- It leads to **dependency**. LDC governments may find themselves pressurised into accepting MNC investment, into making internal political changes and ensuring LDC support for Western strategic interests, e.g. Kenya was rewarded with aid for providing US forces with port facilities during the Gulf War.

- Debt contributes to high infant-mortality rates and low life-expectancy because the money spent servicing debt could be spent on improving the **infrastructure** of LDCs, especially health and education.

- Aid benefits the donor country because they can insist that future aid is **tied**, i.e. spent in the donor country – which may not be the cheapest market. For example, it is estimated that for every British pound lent to LDCs, 70 pence is spent in the UK or spent on projects which primarily employ expertise from the donor country.

In 2000 many Western governments including the UK announced that they were looking at ways in which LDC debt could be **cancelled or reduced**. In 2001 the UK announced its intention to put a stop to tied aid.

In summary, Frank's theory of dependency suggests that the LDCs can never develop so long as they remain part of the world capitalist system. For Frank, development and under-development are two sides of a world process by which the **First World developed at the expense of the LDCs**. Such poor countries are locked into a system that is almost impossible for them to escape. One possible solution is 'isolation' as in the example of some Islamic states such as Iran and Afghanistan. Frank also suggests a **socialist revolution** may be necessary in some LDCs to overcome the ruling classes who collaborate with the West. However, Frank believes that sooner or later, the West would reassert its control.

Criticisms of dependency theory

John Goldthorpe and other **liberals** have argued that colonialism did have **positive benefits** because it provided LDCs with a basic infrastructure in terms of transport and communications. Never colonised LDCs such as Ethiopia and Afghanistan experience severe problems today because they lack the infrastructure provided by the colonial powers. Goldthorpe also points out that those countries without colonies such as the USA and Japan have performed economically better than those with empires.

The **Marxist, Frank Warren** argues that colonialism and neo-colonialism were, on balance, conducive to development rather than under-development. However, **Hancock** notes that a great deal of the aid that remains within LDCs ends up in the bank accounts of LDC élites. Despite extensive investment and aid, some LDCs have experienced little or no economic growth. Some countries such as Bangladesh have grown poorer despite increased aid from the West over two decades.

Criticisms of both modernisation and dependency theory

AQA ▶ U4

Despite being ideological opposites, these two theories have a great deal in common.

Both modernisation and dependency theory make the mistake of treating LDCs as **homogeneous** (i.e. as having the same characteristics). They fail to understand that value systems and institutions tend to be **culture-specific**. For example, Ethiopia and Somalia may be neighbouring LDCs but their cultures are quite different from one another and may each require different development programmes. Some sociologists therefore argue that **each LDC needs to be analysed and understood independently.**

Both theories also make the mistake of treating capitalist societies as homogeneous and consequently **fail to acknowledge that there are different types of capitalism and cultural reactions to it**. For example, American capitalism (based upon **Fordism**) tends to have a different character to Japanese capitalism (which tends to be more **paternalistic**).

Both theories can be accused of being **over-deterministic** in that they make little attempt to **explore the interpretations of people in the LDCs**. They fail to acknowledge that LDC people might **rationally choose** to take a capitalist path, might rationally choose to hang on to their own culture or might rationally choose to combine elements of capitalism and their own cultures – as in Japan.

Finally, **Foster-Carter** accuses both theories of presenting the relationship between LDCs and the West in terms of **conflict or 'them versus us'**. For example, modernisation theory sees LDCs as **'backward'** societies that **'need'** our help to develop, whilst dependency theory **sees 'us' as exploiting 'them'** for cheap labour and raw materials. Foster-Carter argues that this disguises the **similarities** that exist between LDCs and the West.

Progress check

1 What should initiate development according to Rostow?
2 What does modernisation theory blame for lack of development in the Third World?
3 Identify one Western value and one Western institution which modernisation theory claims should be introduced into the Third World.
4 Identify two types of historical exploitation of Third World countries according to dependency theory.
5 What do dependency theorists mean by neo-colonialism?
6 What causes under-development according to dependency theory?
7 What does Foster-Carter mean when he accuses both modernisation and dependency theories of being over-deterministic?

7 They both ignore or neglect the capacity of Third World people themselves to bring about development and/or resist Western exploitation.
6 The systematic and deliberate exploitation of Third World countries by the West.
5 Modern forms of exploitation such as Western domination of world trade, debt dependency and multinational/transnational use of cheap labour, etc.
4 Slavery and colonialism.
3 Any values from: achievement, competition, individualism. Any institutions from: the nuclear family, Western-type schools, democracy and Western forms of media especially radio and television.
2 The culture and institutions of Third World countries.
1 Western aid and multinational investment.

4.3 Recent developments in world sociology

After studying this section you should be able to:

- *identify and outline recent developments in theories of world sociology*
- *outline and assess the impact of globalisation*

LEARNING SUMMARY

World systems theory

AQA ▶ U4

Wallerstein was heavily influenced by Frank but goes much further. His approach insists that individual countries are not an adequate unit of sociological analysis. He argues that we must look at the totality, the overall social system that transcends (and has done for centuries) national boundaries. He calls this the '**Modern World System**' **(MWS)** and suggests that it is characterised by one world economy (i.e. **capitalism**) although it has no common political structure.

Wallerstein uses Frank's concepts of core and periphery states, but adds that in the MWS there is also a **semi-periphery**. A core country like Britain can become a semi-periphery just as a periphery can become a semi-periphery, e.g. the Asian Tigers. The periphery countries are those whose economy still revolves around the export of cash crops, e.g. much of Africa. Wallerstein argues that it is impossible for authentically socialist states to operate within the MWS, e.g. China is engaged in capitalist practices in its trade with the West.

Wallerstein's analysis is therefore more **flexible** than Frank's. It looks at the global system as a whole but is also able to explain the changes in fortune of individual nations as part of the MWS.

New international division of labour theory

AQA ▶ U4

Note that this theory supports dependency theory rather than modernisation theory.

This theory suggests that multinational companies have evolved into transnational companies (TNCs). TNCs have three important characteristics that distinguish them from multinationals.

- **They do not have a clearly identifiable home base** and consequently tend to have major holdings across both the developed and undeveloped worlds.
- **Their interests tend to be diversified across several economic areas.**
- These companies are not **over-reliant on one country in the production of their goods.** Since the 1970s they have set up international production systems in which different parts of the finished products are made in different countries, e.g. the more technical parts may be made in the West whilst the assembly of the product may be done in a low-wage LDC. A great deal of world trade between countries is actually between different parts of the same TNC scattered across the world.

There has been a massive movement of industrial capital from the core to the LDCs in the last thirty years as TNCs establish '**world market factories**' because high labour costs in the West were seen to be eating into profits. TNCs were attracted by the large supplies of **cheap labour** available in the LDCs. Developments in manufacturing (especially in electronics) were such that the work process could be divided up into hundreds of tiny unskilled or semi-skilled tasks that could be done with minimal training. **Hinchliffe** notes that this transfer of industrial capital has resulted in the decline of manufacturing in the West and high unemployment, 'as Kuala Lumpur rises, so Liverpool and Birmingham will continue to fall'. TNCs therefore **exploit Western capitalist economies**, too, because the only way countries like Britain can attract TNC investment is by keeping labour costs low.

Globalisation

AQA ▶ U4

There is no one single theory of globalisation but most contemporary theories of world sociology take into account globalising tendencies. **Foster-Carter** argues that technology and modern communications mean that we no longer live in societies that are self-contained or insular. Our standard of living is increasingly being affected by events across the world and by the increased **interdependence** of countries in terms of economics, culture and social problems. He suggests that **one world is not just a slogan but increasingly a social fact.**

> Think about your consumption of global products from films and music to clothing and food.

KEY POINT

Giddens notes that we now live in a **global world economy** in which TNC production and marketing exert considerable economic and cultural influence over our daily lives. According to **post-modernists**, a global system based on **consumption** rather than on production has evolved and the most important element behind this move is the **global mass media**. Continuing advances being made in communications technology such as satellite TV, the Internet and e-mail mean that the world has become a smaller place and consequently **symbols of consumption** such as Coca-Cola, Levi's, McDonalds and Disney have become globally very powerful.

Foster-Carter notes that social problems, too, increasingly have a global dimension. AIDS, drugs, refugees, migration, debt, environmental pollution and destruction, global warming, genetically modified crops and terrorism, etc. are common concerns and problems that have a bearing on all our futures.

Therefore, Foster-Carter notes that no country or region of the world can be looked at in isolation from the whole world system, although cultural and religious differences are not transformed so easily. Many sociologists are now interested in the **emergence of nationalist and fundamentalist movements** that may have developed as a means of **resisting** globalisation.

4.4 Population in the less-developed world

After studying this section you should be able to:

- *describe the pattern of demographic change in developing countries*
- *explain and evaluate sociological explanations of the 'population explosion' in the developing world*

LEARNING SUMMARY

The pattern of demographic change in the developing world

AQA ▶ U4

> The study of population is known as demography.

In 1994, the population of the world numbered 5.7 billion. By the year 2050, it is estimated that it will reach 10 billion. Three-quarters of humanity, including 94% of the newly born, live in the Third World.

The population of the Third World is increasing at approximately 2% annually. This implies a doubling every 35 years. For example, in 1800 Egypt had a population of just 2 million. By 1978 this had increased to 38 million.

High population-growth was first identified as a problem by **Malthus** in 1978. He argued that populations increase in size at a much faster rate than the capacity of those same populations to feed themselves. Malthus claimed that the increase in world population was posing a serious threat to the world's natural resources.

Modernisation theory and population

The modernisation theorist **Ehrlich** sees rapid population growth in the LDCs as an obstacle to development. He claims that much of the poverty found in the LDCs is caused by a '**population explosion**' which has put too much **strain** on the limited resources (i.e. food and energy) of these societies and resulted in famine and malnutrition and consequent high rates of infant mortality. High population allegedly puts a great strain on the infrastructure of the LDCs and services such as education and health are stretched to the limit. Economic growth is also difficult to achieve because any economic surplus in the form of capital must be spent on feeding the population and developing an infrastructure to cope with it. If population was not increasing, such economic surplus could be invested in industrial development. There is also concern that high population puts a strain on the environment in terms of pollution and the over-use of land, whilst the need for more land may lead to deforestation.

Population and religion

Some LDC religions see contraception as a Western attempt to control their population growth.

The **culture** of LDCs, and specifically **religions** such as Islam and Hinduism, are blamed for high birth-rates. The patriarchal nature of these religions means that the **status of women is very low** in many LDC societies. Women have few opportunities for paid work and are consequently likely to be dependent upon men. As a result they are likely to **lack reproductive rights**, i.e. they cannot choose not to have children or when to have children. Men may deny them access to contraception and abortion.

Modernisation solutions

According to modernisation theory, there are three solutions to high population.

As in, e.g. China.

- First, the governments of LDCs should be encouraged to adopt **family-planning policies** limiting the number of children in families.

- Second, **official aid** from the West should be used to finance **birth-control programmes**.

- Third, aid should also be used to promote **health education** and media programmes which encourage the use of contraception. In particular, education should be aimed at **women** because, given the choice, women will want to have fewer children. Moreover, educated women are generally better able and willing to use contraceptives.

Dependency theory and population

Dependency theory is critical of the idea that the LDCs' populations are out of control and the idea that high population is responsible for the problems faced by LDCs today.

- First, **Harrison** points out that birth rates in the LDCs have not dramatically changed in the last 200 years. High population growth is mainly due to a dramatic **decline in the death rate**, especially the infant-mortality rate, which, ironically, is due to Western intervention in the fields of public hygiene, the processing of food and medical advances in the eradication of diseases such as smallpox and malaria.

- Second, there is little evidence that the world's food resources are under strain. Food production has actually increased this century due to advances in technology. Moreover, European farmers are actually paid by the EC not to produce food because of surpluses in the West.

- A third argument suggests that the real cause of famine and its related problems is **inequalities in access to land** (and therefore food) rather than high population. Famine may occur where food production is high but land use is controlled by local élites and multinationals for cash-crop production.

Such **inequality causes high population** because children are seen as economic assets by parents. They bring in extra income and can be a source of welfare support when their parents can no longer work. Therefore the decision to have large families may be rational.

Poverty causes high population rather than high population causing poverty.

KEY POINT

Dependency theory argues that the real problem is not population but the **unequal global distribution of resources and power** between the developed nations and the LDCs. It is pointed out that the world has the space, the wealth, the resources and productive capacity to provide a decent standard of living for all, but that the West monopolises the consumption of food and energy resources. For example, the USA has 6% of the world's population but consumes 40% of its resources. In their lifetime, an average person in the West will consume 30 times the resources that an average person in the Third World consumes. This means that the 16 million babies born a year in the West put more strain on the world's resources than the 119 million babies born in the Third World.

Finally, dependency theory claims that high population in the LDCs suits Western interests because it keeps the LDCs in a constant state of dependency and distracts from the real causes of Third-World problems such as inequalities in the world trading system, multinational exploitation and the international debt crisis.

Progress check

1 What did Malthus argue about high population?

2 What evidence does dependency theory cite which contradicts Malthus?

3 Why is the so-called population explosion in developing countries a problem according to modernisation theory?

4 What does modernisation theory blame for the so-called population explosion?

5 What solutions does modernisation theory propose?

6 What does dependency theory blame for famine in the developing world?

7 What does dependency theory mean when it says poverty causes high population?

8 What is a more important problem than population according to dependency theory?

8 The West's overuse of the world's resources.
7 People have children because children can be put to work and earn a wage, as well as looking after their parents in the absence of a Welfare State.
6 Inequalities in access to fertile land for growing food – the best land is monopolised by Western multinationals to grow cash crops for export to the West.
5 Family planning and education for women.
4 Culture and especially religion, which denies women reproductive rights.
3 Because it uses up valuable capital that could be used to invest in industry and puts considerable strain on the infrastructure.
2 World food resources have actually increased.
1 That it would put the world food resources under strain.

4.5 Gender and development

After studying this section you should be able to:

- identity and describe gender inequalities apparent in the developing world
- outline and assess sociological explanations of the role of women in the Third World

LEARNING SUMMARY

Gender inequalities in the developing world

AQA ▶ U4

An increasingly popular area for exam questions.

Women make up 50% of the world's population yet they generally occupy **subordinate** positions compared with men. For example, women only own 1% of the world's property. In the LDCs women do 50–60% of all agricultural work and 50% of animal husbandry. They are the main providers of food as well as primarily responsible for children and housekeeping. In LDCs three out of five women are illiterate.

Moreover, women tend to **lack reproductive rights** in LDCs – they do not exercise power over decisions to have children, when to have them, how many to have, whether to use contraception or access to abortion. All these decisions are controlled by men. This has two major implications for women in LDCs. It ties them firmly to household responsibilities by **denying them economic independence**. It also has a **negative effect upon health**. In the LDCs women do not live as long as men. They are more likely than Western women to die in childbirth.

Modernisation theory and gender

Patriarchal = dominated by males.

Modernisation theory sees women's oppression in the LDCs as caused by **patriarchal cultural factors**. For example, the extended family and tribal system which are common in some LDCs stress the importance of **ascription** rather than achievement. Men are viewed as having natural authority and are therefore seen as the head of the household.

Modernisation theory argues that such pressures result in high population which hinders development. Their solution is the introduction of meritocratic education systems to replace ascription. It is argued that women should be given **educational opportunities** whilst Rostow argued that MNC investment in the LDCs should aim at providing employment primarily for women. Moreover modernisation theory encourages **health education** and specifically **family planning** to reduce population growth and to improve both womens' life expectancy and their independence from men.

Feminist explanations of gender inequality

However, **feminists** working from a dependency theory position are critical of these ideas.

- First, feminists point out that a great deal of gender inequality in the LDCs is the product of colonialism. When the colonial powers conquered these territories they brought with them and **imposed Western values about males and females**, especially the idea that males should be breadwinners and females should be primarily mothers and housewives.

- Second, **Deere and Van Allen** argue that **female labour has been exploited by MNCs** because women are seen to be cheap, willing to work long hours and suited to monotonous unskilled work. MNCs see women as '**pliable and docile**' and know that they will put up with lower wages because they are used to occupying a subordinate position in those societies.

- Third, **Leonard** criticises official aid because it is not **gender-neutral**. Western aid experts often arrive in LDCs with Western **patriarchal** prejudices. For example, science and technology is regarded as men's work and consequently men are the main recipients of aid programmes in this field.

However, dependency theory has also been criticised for implying that socialism is the answer to women's problems in the LDCs. **Ellwood** points out that in the old USSR 'women could fly into space but they still had to do the ironing when they got home again'. **Foster-Carter** suggests that we should acknowledge that **women's oppression is a global fact** because although Western women are better off than LDC women they still remain subordinate to men and Western societies are still predominately patriarchal.

Progress check

1 What percentage of the world's property is owned by women?

2 What are reproductive rights?

3 What does modernisation theory recommend to improve the rights of women in developing nations?

4 What is responsible for the subordinate position of women in developing nations according to modernisation theory?

5 What is responsible for patriarchy in developing nations according to feminist thought?

6 What does Foster-Carter conclude about the patriarchal subordination and exploitation of women?

6 It's a global fact and exists both in the developed and developing world.
5 Western value systems which have entered developing nations via colonialism, aid and MNC investment.
4 Patriarchal culture and religion.
3 Family planning, birth control, health education and education into skills for factory work.
2 The ability to choose to have children, when to have them, how many to have, whether to use contraception, etc.
1 1%.

4.6 Health-care in the developing world

After studying this section you should be able to:

- *identify and evaluate theories that explain health inequalities in developing nations*
- *outline how the causes of health inequalities in the developing world can be linked to the developed world*

LEARNING SUMMARY

Explanations for morbidity and mortality rates in the developing world

AQA   U4

Morbidity = illness.
Mortality = death.

LDCs experience low life-expectancy and high infant-mortality rates compared with the West. Many diseases such as measles are major killers of children.

Modernisation theory and health-care

Modernisation theory argues that the traditional practices and medical remedies found in many LDCs are actually dangerous for health. Modernisation theorists would argue that only modern medicines can provide the cure for many LDC health problems and that LDCs require European-style health-care systems. Moreover, health education is also required – especially in the field of family planning. It is suggested that this would improve female mortality and morbidity rates (which are worsened by constant childbearing) and reduce population. It is envisaged that these health improvements could be funded from official aid-packages, the income generated by world trade and, in the long term, improvements in the standard of living as the country progresses up the development ladder.

Dependency theory and health-care

Dependency theory does not question the need for universal health-care but points out that many of the LDC's health problems are linked to **global inequalities**, i.e. which stem from the First World's exploitation of LDC peoples and resources. A number of points can be made to support this idea.

- **Colonialism introduced European diseases** to LDC populations who were unable to resist them. The effects of such diseases were, and still are, devastating.

- Colonialism also entailed the **replacement of crops for food with cash crops**. In some cases, this resulted in famine and mass starvation. Cash crops have meant that people's diets in the LDCs have become less balanced over time, resulting in less resistance to disease.

They die of diseases of poverty whilst we die of diseases of affluence.

- **Poverty** is the major killer in the LDCs. This is partly a result of a world trading system that prevents the LDCs getting a fair price for their goods.

- **Aid and the debt** it generates also means that less money is available to spend on health-care. There is evidence that as countries pay more in interest repayments so infant mortality increases. Organisations such as the World Bank and IMF will only lend money if countries cut public spending – health-care is one of the main types of public spending in the LDCs.

- Existing health-care systems and medical aid from the West tends to **focus on cure rather than prevention**. It is argued that much disease could be prevented by focusing aid and health-care on **clean water (80% of all LDC disease is water-related) and sanitation**.

- There is evidence that multinationals have had a negative effect on LDC health. Their failure to provide workers with health and safety equipment, their poor record on pollution (e.g. the Bhopal disaster in India), the selling of products banned in the West for health reasons (e.g. high-tar cigarettes) and the promotion and advertising of false needs (e.g. Nestlé and baby-milk powder) have all contributed to poor health in the developing world.

Some socialist countries (e.g. Cuba) have adopted **socialist** development strategies which strongly emphasise **preventative medicine and a system of universal medical care**. They have also acknowledged the need to raise general living standards in order to raise resistance to disease. Such strategies have generally proved successful despite, in the case of Cuba, attempts by the USA to prevent medical supplies entering the country.

Progress check

1   What does modernisation theory recommend to bring about good health in the Third World?

2   What does dependency theory blame for poor health in the developing nations?

3   How does debt dependency contribute to poor health?

4   Why might Western-style health-care systems not be suitable for developing nations?

5   What type of aid programme could bring about dramatic changes in morbidity and mortality levels in the LDCs?

6   How do MNCs contribute to ill-health in the LDCs?

6   They expose workers to toxic substances, they pollute and they market products banned in the West on health grounds, etc.
5   Clean water and sanitation programmes.
4   Because they focus on cure rather than prevention.
3   Capital is spent repaying the interest on loans rather than on disease prevention or health-care systems.
2   Global inequalities brought about by Western intervention.
1   Western-style health systems and family planning programmes for women.

Sample question and model answer

Item A

Development is one of those areas where it's usually more helpful to quantify things. How many people can read? How many children live to adulthood? How many doctors and hospitals does the country have? How many people are unemployed or living in poverty? Ideally, all of these and other important indicators of development could be fed into a computer, and out would come a single number measurement of how developed a society is. Most sociologists see economic growth as the main indicator of development and spend their time examining the gross national product (GNP) of developing nations. However, although this may be useful, it does not tell us about how wealth and income are distributed or anything about people's physical and social environment. Finally the concept of 'development' is not objective. How it is defined is both loaded and contentious. Sociological debate about what counts as development is dominated by Western definitions. Modernisation theory, for example, sees development as moving towards the Western model of industrial capitalism. However not all sociologists agree that this is an ideal goal.

(Adapted from Think sociology, *(1998) P. Stephens et al., page 580, Stanley Thornes.)*

(a) Describe and briefly explain how sociologists measure development using social and economic indicators as in Item A. (12 marks)

> The information in Item A should be the main focus of your response.

The main indicator of development according to Western sociologists is economic growth measured by reference to the wealth produced by nations, i.e. the gross national product (GNP). However, this tells us little about how that wealth is divided up. Some sociologists prefer to examine child mortality, life expectancy, health and illness, levels of employment and unemployment, literacy levels, population levels and numbers in poverty as more powerful social indicators of development and lack of development.

(b) Examine what is meant by the view that the concept of development is not objective. (8 marks)

> Don't overdo your response – it's only worth 8 marks. This response outlines and criticises the dominant definition of development and suggests an alternative definition.

The dominant definition of development in the West for many years was invented and dominated by modernisation theory which sees it as movement towards a Western model of industrial capitalism. Rostow even claimed communism was a disease which acted as an obstacle to development. Islamic societies, which tend to be suspicious of and hostile to any forms of Americanisation, would reject the modernisation definition. They tend to see a return to traditional institutions and values as progress.

(c) Evaluate the view that the concept of under-development is more useful than the concept of development in explaining the relationship between developed and developing countries. (40 marks)

> Essay question – aim for two sides at least.

> Begins with a definition of key terms; development and under-development.

The concept of development is generally used to refer to industrialisation and economic growth. Those countries that have industrialised and enjoyed prosperity in terms of wealth and income, high standards of living, etc. are said to have developed. Those countries that have not yet experienced these processes are said to be undeveloped. Many countries obviously fall somewhere in between these two points. Under-development is a concept mainly used by the Marxist-influenced dependency theory. This

Sample question and model answer *(continued)*

theory argues that poor countries have not developed and may not do so because they have been prevented from doing so by the developed West. Moreover, LDC poverty may be caused by their relationship with Western countries which is characterised by exploitation.

Identifies the view associated with the concept of development, i.e. modernisation theory.

Modernisation theorists such as Rostow argue that LDCs themselves are responsible for their lack of development. It is argued that such societies are characterised by social institutions and values that hinder development. For example, LDC families tend to be extended and this encourages values such as collectivism, ascription, etc. which prevent the geographical mobility of the workforce needed for efficient industrial development. It is suggested that Western-style institutions and values be introduced via official aid and multinational investment. For example, LDC people should be encouraged to live in geographically mobile nuclear families.

Elaboration and illustration.

Meritocratic education systems should be introduced in order to encourage the values of individualism and achievement which are seen as essential to capitalist development. Essentially, then, modernisation theory equates progress with Westernisation.

Evaluation of modernisation theory.

Modernisation theory has been criticised for its ethnocentric view of development. It implies that LDC cultures have little to offer and ignores the fact that the developed West is plagued with social problems such as crime, poverty, etc.

Identifies the view associated with the concept of under-development, i.e. dependency theory.

Dependency theory suggests that the poverty of the LDCs is caused by deliberate under-development of LDC economies by Western countries. Frank argues that the West has systematically exploited the LDCs. In the past this was done through slavery and colonialism which resulted in a super-accumulation of capital, cheap raw materials and labour which financed the industrial revolution in the West. Colonialism also shaped contemporary world trade by ensuring that LDC economies were overly dependent on producing one or two cash crops or raw materials.

Elaboration and illustration.

Other dependency theorists such as Hayter suggest that multinationals (MNCs) and official aid are a form of neo-colonialism which ensure the contemporary exploitation and underdevelopment of the LDCs. She argues that MNCs are attracted to the LDCs because of low wages and taxes, the lack of health and safety legislation and the fact that trade union rights often don't exist. There is evidence that MNCs create problems for the LDCs by marketing goods banned in the West, e.g. drugs and pesticides, causing environmental pollution and disasters, e.g. Bhopal, Shell in Nigeria, etc. and interfering with internal politics, e.g. Chile.

Official aid is also criticised because it results in LDCs' dependency on the West. A great deal of aid is tied – it must be spent in the donor country. In this sense, aid is a form of repatriated profit. Aid also means debt because a great deal of it comes in the shape of loans with interest. Hayter argues that this creates debt dependency as countries have to spend large proportions of their export income servicing their debt. Aid also means political compliancy. Loans may only be made if the LDC agrees to open up its markets to Western MNCs (e.g. Russia) or agrees political co-operation, e.g. the use of military bases. Dependency theory has been criticised by the Marxist, Bill Warren, who claims that colonialism, MNCs and aid have brought benefits to the LDCs, although Hayter claims most of these benefits went to LDC élites rather than the

Sample question and model answer *(continued)*

Conclusion focuses on recent theoretical developments.

poor. She points out that the Tiger Economies of the Far East look very successful but they are economies distorted by debt.

Foster-Carter argues that sociology should move on from what he sees as the rather dated modernisation versus dependency theory debate. He argues that global interconnectedness now characterises the whole world and that we now have one global system. Modern systems of transport and communication mean that national boundaries are less important, especially in economic terms. For example, Japanese, Korean and American companies have built factories in the UK, British companies like Marks and Spencer have their products manufactured in the low-wage economies of the Far East and Coca-Cola, McDonald's, Sony, etc. advertise and sell globally. Of course, this also means we share global problems, too, such as environmental pollution and, recently, economic recession.

Practice examination question

Item A

Since 1969 Western countries have repeatedly promised to give the United Nations target of 0.7% of their GNP in aid to developing countries. But this target has never been hit. In 1994 the average aid given by Western nations was 0.3% of GNP. Japan is now by far the world's largest donor whilst the USA gives the smallest percentage of its GNP of all donors. Most estimates suggest that less than 20% of aid ever reaches poor people directly. Two-thirds of the world's poor live in 10 countries that together receive less than a third of official aid. The Arab States have more than six times the per-capita income of South Asia, yet in 1992 (shortly after the Gulf War) they received more aid, especially from the USA. Today a large number of developing countries are practically bankrupt. They owe foreign investors so much money that just paying the interest means that their governments cannot afford basic education and health systems.

(a) Using **Item A** only, describe and briefly explain the trends in aid and debt that developing countries have experienced since 1969.　　(12 marks)

(b) Examine some of the problems that developing nations face because of debt dependency.　　(8 marks)

(c) Assess the claim that sociological accounts of development have neglected gender issues.　　(40 marks)

Chapter 5

Education

The following topics are covered in this chapter:

- Education, socialisation and identity
- Patterns and trends in educational achievement
- Power, control and the relationship between education and the economy

5.1 Education, socialisation and identity

After studying this section you should be able to:

- compare and contrast functionalist and Marxist theories about education, socialisation, cultural transmission and reproduction
- define and illustrate the concept of 'the hidden curriculum' and its relationship to streaming and labelling

LEARNING SUMMARY

The functions of education

OCR | U2536

Cultural transmission and reproduction

The Functionalist view

> **Functionalists** such as **Durkheim and Parsons** saw education as a crucial **agency of secondary socialisation** functioning to transmit **shared cultural values** to the next generation. Both thinkers argued that this process of **social reproduction** is central to the construction and maintenance of social order because education produces ideal citizens committed to consensus and conformity.
>
> **KEY POINT**

Durkheim believed that societies are stable and ordered when their members feel a strong **sense of belonging** to the greater social group. He argued that the teaching of subjects like history and religious education promotes **social solidarity** because it enables children to see the links between themselves and society. They can feel a sense of pride and therefore a sense of belonging to their society.

Parsons argued that schools act as a **bridge** between the family and society. In families, we learn that our parents will love us regardless of our abilities or lack of them. However, children need to get used to the universalistic value system that operates outside the family in order that they are efficiently prepared for their future role both as citizens and workers. This value system judges all members of society according to the same standards, i.e. on the basis of achievement. School, therefore, is the halfway house in which we first encounter the rules, standards and values of wider society. The role of education is to socialise children into universal values such as **achievement, individualism, competition and equality of opportunity**. The internalisation of such values means that the products of Western schooling move effortlessly into the world of work – which is underpinned by the same value system.

The Marxist view

KEY POINT

In contrast with functionalism, the **Marxist**, **Louis Althusser** argues that education is an **ideological state apparatus** which functions to maintain, legitimate and reproduce, generation by generation, **class inequalities** in wealth and power. In other words, education functions to ensure that the minority capitalist class continues unchallenged to dominate disproportionately and unfairly élite positions and to make sure the working class continue to take on manual jobs in which the value of their labour far outstrips the wage they are paid.

Marxists argue that there is no such thing as a common culture because the capitalist class has the economic and political power to impose its culture on less powerful groups, i.e. **cultural reproduction**.

KEY POINT

The role of education is therefore **ideological** – it promotes capitalist values as shared or common values. Althusser argued that this is mainly done through the **hidden curriculum**. From a Marxist perspective, this refers to the informal ways in which conformity and acceptance of failure and inequality are encouraged in working-class young people.

The hidden curriculum

The concept of 'the hidden curriculum' is a popular one with examiners.

Althusser identified two ways in which the hidden curriculum convinces the working class that the capitalist system is fair and natural.

- The **knowledge** taught in schools is vetted and stripped of anything which might motivate students to criticise or challenge the existing capitalist order. Students rarely come into contact with facts or ways of thinking that focus on inequalities or injustices resulting from capitalism.

  Marxist thinkers have criticised the national curriculum as 'highly prescriptive' and suggest that critical subjects such as economics, politics and sociology have been deliberately excluded from mainstream schooling for ideological reasons. Moreover, few students leave school or college with knowledge about the distribution of wealth and poverty, theories such as socialism, communism and republicanism or the more dubious aspects of British history such as slavery, the imperial suppression of native peoples or Northern Ireland.

- **The way that schools are organised**, i.e. the everyday rules and routines, transmit very different messages to middle-class and working-class pupils about the purpose of school.

  Educational processes such as **labelling** by teachers, **streaming** and examinations serve to convince working-class pupils that their knowledge and experiences are irrelevant and to accept failure as their fault. For example, Marxists argue that teachers tend to see middle-class and conformist pupils as **ideal pupils**. Those pupils who challenge teacher authority or the purpose of schooling may be banished to the bottom streams where they are socialised into believing that their educational failure is caused by their own inadequacies and therefore deserved. In other words, education socialises pupils into **false class-consciousness** – working-class pupils are encouraged to see educational failure as self-inflicted rather than caused by capitalism's need for a conformist, factory labour force.

Role allocation

OCR ➤ U2536

The functionalists Davis and Moore argue that the role of education is to select and allocate people to occupations which best suit their abilities and talents. Educational mechanisms such as grades, examinations, references and qualifications are used to sift and sort individuals. Society is a **meritocracy** in which people are rewarded for intelligence, ability and effort.

Functionalists argue that both the most talented and the least talented end up in jobs in which they make efficient contributions to the smooth running of capitalist society. The most qualified are motivated by the high financial rewards attached to top jobs. In this sense, inequalities in income and wealth are seen as **functional** and necessary by functionalists because high rewards promote competition – which sifts the best from the rest.

However, Marxists and other critical thinkers reject the view that the UK educational system is meritocratic for three broad reasons.

Try and find statistics to support this argument.

- They argue that as long as **private education** continues to exist that the UK can never be meritocratic. Public schools symbolise class inequality and injustice because their products are vastly over-represented in top jobs. There is evidence that this is the result of '**old boy networks**' rather than any superior intelligence or ability. However, supporters of private education believe it to be an essential part of a free market and argue that parents should have the right to choose what type of education they want for their children and how to spend their money.

Exclusion can also be seen as a form of selection.

- Some have argued that the focus on choice and diversity has created a hierarchy of educational institutions based on forms of **selection** rather than equal opportunities. In the secondary sector, grammar schools practise overt selection whilst **selection by mortgage** is becoming a norm in the comprehensive sector as middle-class parents buy houses in areas with good comprehensives. The focus on parental choice and league tables has created an incentive for schools to be more selective in their intake and to exclude children likely to perform badly.

- The **disproportionate inequalities** in achievement experienced by groups such as the working class and particular ethnic minorities in the British education system also undermine the concept of meritocracy.

Similarities in the functionalist and Marxist approaches to education

Despite their differences, functionalist and Marxist accounts of education do share three broad similarities.

In any essay which asks you to examine functionalist and Marxist approaches, it is worth concluding by examining these similarities.

- They are both **structuralist** theories in that they see social institutions as being more important than individuals.

- They do not pay much attention to **classroom interaction** or the **interpretations** of teachers and pupils.

- Both theories are **over-deterministic**, meaning they both see pupils as passive products of the educational system. Functionalists see pupils being turned into model citizens whilst Marxists argue that the hidden curriculum turns working-class children into conformist workers. Both theories, argues Willis, fail to take into account the power of pupils to resist these processes.

1 Identify two ways in which schools act as agents of socialisation.

2 What do functionalists mean by the term 'social reproduction'?

3 What do Marxists mean by the term 'cultural reproduction'?

4 Define the concept 'hidden curriculum'.

5 Why are the working class generally doomed to fail by the education system?

6 What do functionalist sociologists mean when they describe education as meritocratic?

6 They believe that intelligence, effort and achievement are the main criteria for educational mobility and rewards.
5 Because of capitalism's need for a manual labour force.
4 This refers to the way in which certain cultural values and attitudes (e.g. obedience to authority, conformity, etc.) are transmitted through teaching and the organisation of schools.
3 The socialisation of each generation into the cultural values of the ruling class.
2 The socialisation of each generation into the cultural values of society.
1 Any two from: They socialise pupils into key social values such as achievement, competition and individualism. They encourage social integration through the teaching of English, History and RE. They encourage conformity through the hidden curriculum.

5.2 Patterns and trends in educational achievement

After studying this section you should be able to:

- describe the patterns of educational achievement according to social class, gender and ethnicity
- outline and assess explanations of differential educational achievement
- identify the implications for educational policy and provision of trends in achievement

LEARNING SUMMARY

Class and achievement

OCR ▶ U2536

At all levels of education, students from working-class backgrounds achieve less than their middle-class counterparts. They are less likely to be found in nursery schools, will have fallen behind significantly in reading, writing and arithmetic by the age of 9, are more likely to leave school at the age of 16 and are three times less likely to go on to university.

Explanations of differential educational achievement

OCR ▶ U2536

Intelligence

A victim-blaming theory. ▶

It is argued that the working class have lesser innate intelligence as shown by IQ tests. **Peter Saunders (1996)** claims that the middle class do better in education quite simply because they inherit their parents' talent. Saunders argues that the differences in educational achievement and, therefore, relative mobility between social classes may be the result of natural inequalities, i.e. genetic or **hereditary factors**. Saunders suggests that it may not be the case that talents and abilities are randomly distributed across all social classes. Saunders claims that there are genetic differences in aptitude between social classes as measured by IQ tests. Saunders furthermore claims that it is normal to expect successful middle-class parents to pass on genetic advantages to their offspring.

However, some sociologists point out that it is impossible to separate genetic influences from environmental influences such as poverty, education, racism, etc. which may exert greater influence. IQ test results may be **culturally biased** and can never be neutral because they measure what middle-class academics regard as intelligence.

Cultural-deprivation theory

Another victim-blaming theory.

KEY POINT

This blames working-class culture for lack of achievement. It suggests that the reason working-class children fail is because their **home culture is inadequate**, especially in terms of parental attitudes, child-rearing practices and language development. Key studies, mainly conducted in the 1960s, argued that **working-class parents are less interested in their children's education.** J.W.B. Douglas' classic study of achievement measured parental interest by counting the number of times parents visited schools for parents' evenings, etc. Other studies have suggested that middle-class parents are more child-centred than working-class parents.

The work of Basil **Bernstein** on linguistic deprivation was hijacked by **cultural-deprivation theory in the 1970s.** Briefly, Bernstein identified two speech patterns used in the UK, the **'restricted code'** and the **'elaborated code'** and argued that while members of the middle class are able to converse in both, members of the working class are limited to the use of the restricted code.

Restricted codes are a kind of **shorthand speech** characterised by short, grammatically simple, often unfinished sentences lacking in adverbs and adjectives. Meaning is not clearly spelled out because it is used amongst intimates such as family and friends. An outsider would find it difficult to understand. Elaborated codes, on the other hand, explicitly make clear the meanings that restricted codes take for granted because care is taken to give a complete explanation of details and relationships. Bernstein suggested that the educational system is conducted in the elaborated code and therefore the working-class child is at a disadvantage.

The **'underclass theory' of Charles Murray** is a 1990s version of cultural-deprivation theory because it argues that there exists a **culture of welfare dependency** in the inner cities which is socialising its children into an anti-education culture.

Cultural deprivation: educational policy and provision

Cultural-deprivation theory influenced educational policy in the 1960s and led to the founding of six **Educational Priority Areas** made up of deprived inner-city areas. Extra money was spent on their primary schools. This type of scheme was known as **positive discrimination or compensatory education** because it aimed to discriminate positively in favour of the working class and compensate for 'deficiencies' in working-class culture. However, the scheme failed and supporters argued that this was because not enough money was poured into it – whilst Marxists argued it failed because educational inequality is only a small part of a wider pattern of class inequality which needs to be treated as a whole. However, in 1999 the Labour government announced its **Excellence in Cities** programme, the creation of **'education action zones'** in six major cities in which £350 million worth of extra help will be given to under-achievers in schools.

Material-deprivation theory

Blames social factors rather than the victim.

Cultural-deprivation theory has been attacked for seeing cultural factors as more important than material disadvantages. Writers such as **Wedge and Prosser (1973)** have documented the effects of **poverty** on educational achievement. They point out that a **poor material environment** means that children are more likely to suffer from illness and accidents and to be handicapped by speech and learning difficulties. Consequently they are more likely to take time off school and fall behind with their studies.

Halsey *et al.* in *Origins and Destinations* **(1980)** also argue that material factors such as **low income** become more significant as the child gets older. In particular, they note that the cost of maintaining a child at school after the minimum school leaving age is sufficient to deter many working-class families from keeping their children at school.

Marxism

Blames capitalism.

> **KEY POINT**
>
> The Marxist, **Bourdieu**, points out that schools are middle-class institutions, run by the middle class which primarily benefit middle-class children. Working-class children may lack the **cultural capital** required (i.e. middle-class values and ways of looking at the world) for academic success in these institutions.

Bourdieu blames the organisation of schools for working-class failure because **the hidden curriculum defines the knowledge, skills and behaviour of middle-class pupils (i.e. their cultural capital) as appropriate to success, whilst working-class knowledge and experience are devalued.** Schools fail to compensate working-class pupils for their lack of cultural capital because the function of education, according to Bourdieu, is to ensure that the working class fail in order that they continue to enter manual work.

Labelling theory

Blames school and teachers.

> **KEY POINT**
>
> This theory focuses exclusively on school factors and specifically **classroom interaction** between teachers and pupils. It argues that teachers judge or label pupils on the basis of factors such as social class, gender, race, behaviour, attitude and appearance rather than just ability and intelligence. Middle-class pupils are seen as **'ideal pupils'**.

Studies such as those carried out by **Becker** and **Rist** confirm that ideal pupils tend to be pupils who have conformed to the demands of the hidden curriculum – they are generally middle-class children who have learnt to passively accept the authority of teachers

According to **Rosenthal and Jacobsen**, teachers transmit their judgements about pupils to them through everyday classroom interaction. Pupils internalise these positive and negative labels and the result is a **self-fulfilling prophecy** as pupils come to see themselves in terms of the label attached to them by teachers. The status of 'good' student, 'academic', 'skiver', 'troublesome', etc. becomes the dominant or **'master status'** used by the teacher to judge the student and consequently encourages or inhibits their progress in the subject.

Positive labelling may lead to middle-class pupils being streamed more highly than working-class pupils. **Streaming is a form of institutional labelling.** **Keddie** discovered that top streams are treated more favourably than bottom streams in terms of teacher control and access to high-status knowledge. On the other hand, bottom-stream pupils pick up the hidden curriculum message that failure is their fault.

Those pupils that develop a negative self-image may turn to **deviant subcultures** to compensate for their lack of status from teachers. **Hargreaves** notes that pupils award each other the status denied to them by the school by carrying out anti-school behaviour. This confirms their failure in the school's eyes.

The criticism of this theory focuses on:

- its neglect of social influences **external** to the classroom. For example, Marxists point out that schools are shaped by social-class inequalities rooted in the organisation of wider capitalist society

- its neglect of **working-class culture**. Willis argues that working-class boys don't fail because they are labelled by teachers. Many of them reject qualifications because they don't see them as relevant to the type of factory jobs they want to do. Their behaviour is a result of a conscious choice to reject schooling rather than a reaction to teacher labelling

- its neglect of **pupil resistance** to teacher labelling. Pupils can resist teacher labels. A negative label may result in hard work to disprove the label

- the lack of **empirical evidence** for the existence of the self-fulfilling prophecy.

Progress check

1 How does Peter Saunders explain working-class educational underachievement?

2 Identify the three home factors focused on by cultural deprivation theory.

3 What is ignored by cultural deprivation theory, according to Halsey?

4 What is the main influence on success and failure, according to Becker?

5 What theory of achievement is described by the phrase 'what teachers believe, their students will achieve'?

6 Identify two ways in which the concept of the self-fulfilling prophecy has been criticised.

6 There is little empirical evidence for it. Pupils may resist such processes.
5 Labelling theory.
4 Teacher expectations and the consequent labelling of pupils.
3 Material influences such as poverty.
2 Parental interest in education, child-rearing practices and language use.
1 Lack of inherited intelligence.

Ethnicity and achievement

OCR ▶ U2536

It is important to acknowledge differential educational achievement across different ethnic minorities – don't lump them all in together!

Children from Pakistani/Bangladeshi homes and males from Afro-Caribbean homes tend to get fewer and poorer GCSE results than white or Indian children. They are less likely to get A Levels and go on to university. Afro-Caribbean males are six times more likely than any other group to be excluded from schools. Afro-Caribbean boys are disproportionately found in bottom-stream sets in comprehensive schools and are under-represented in the top sets.

However, recent research by Modood (1997) suggests that both male and female members of ethnic-minority groups are more likely to stay on at school post-16 – although the higher level qualifications achieved by Afro-Caribbeans are more likely to be vocational than academic. Evidence also suggests that Indians, particularly females, are enjoying improved success at degree level.

Cultural-deprivation theory

Victim-blaming.

This theory blames black people themselves for their educational underachievement. It argues that Afro-Caribbean, Pakistani and Bangladeshi failure at school can be blamed on the **home and family background, i.e. the culture**, of the child. Some sociologists have argued that Afro-Caribbean parents lack understanding of the importance of play, toys, communication and parent–child one-to-one interaction in the early years. These alleged shortcomings in primary socialisation supposedly lead to low motivation and disruptive behaviour. Other sociologists have focused on Pakistani and Bangladeshi culture and argue that children are handicapped by a poor grasp of English, and the Muslim religion which allegedly stresses education in Islamic values and teachings at the expense of academic education. Females are seen to be held back by an alleged Islamic focus on traditional roles for women. However, in criticism of this theory, there is empirical evidence that Asian culture and Afro-Caribbean parents value education very highly.

Underclass theory

Victim-blaming.

Afro-Caribbean underachievement in boys has been linked to the large number of **female-headed, one-parent families** in this community. It is argued that boys are disruptive in the classroom because of the lack of authoritative fathers to control their behaviour. This allegedly accounts for the over-proportionate number of Afro-Caribbean children excluded from schools. **Murray** argues that black one-parent families are part of an '**underclass**' that is not committed to mainstream values and consequently fails to value education.

The influence of black youth-culture

Blames popular culture.

Sewell (2000) argues **that black youth-culture's concern with money and consumer goods** is almost as damaging to black pupils' chances in school as racism. He acknowledges that black children have gained much needed self-esteem from their youth culture. However, this culture is superficial in character and encourages black youth to see trainers, rap music and street credibility as more important than intellectual activity.

Material deprivation and racism

Blames social factors.

Sociologists who are critical of cultural-deprivation theory and the concept of an underclass point out that the economic environment in which ethnic-minority groups live may be more influential than culture in explaining educational under-achievement. Afro-Caribbeans, Pakistanis and Bangladeshis are more likely than the white population to be **economically disadvantaged** or to be living in **poverty**. They are likely to earn low incomes, to be unemployed or be in insecure employment. In addition, they may be subjected to **racist name-calling and racist attacks**. All of these factors may act as obstacles to educational success.

The school, teacher expectations and labelling

Blames school and teachers.

In the mid-1980s, **the Swann Report** argued that the knowledge, teaching methods and means of assessment found in most British schools were probably partly responsible for the underachievement of Afro-Caribbean children. In particular, Swann was critical of the **stereotyping** of such pupils as good at music, dance and sport and the channelling of children into these areas at the expense of academic lessons.

Interactionist sociologists have found that **teacher expectations** about Afro-Caribbean pupils have written them off as 'lazy', 'less able' and 'disruptive'. Other studies have suggested that these stereotypes lead to black children being given less teacher attention and being treated in harsher ways than white children. The result of such treatment is often **conflict and confrontation** because teachers interpret black pupils as challenging their authority. Consequently black children are assessed according to their *attitude* rather than their ability and placed in bottom bands in order to control them rather than for good academic reasons. Suspensions and exclusions are also used more extensively by white teachers in their dealings with black pupils. A recent OFSTED report by **Gillborn and Mirza (2000)** suggests **institutional racism** may be an integral part of the hidden curriculum and organisation of some British schools.

Negative treatment of Afro-Caribbean children may result in a **self-fulfilling prophecy** as these children internalise low self-esteem. One means of compensating for the lack of status, at school is to join a **deviant subculture** that stresses a common Afro-Caribbean identity, perhaps in terms of music, dress, Rastafarianism and use of slang or patois. The subculture will probably reward anti-school activities with status thus confirming teacher expectations that such children are not interested in education.

Ken Pryce

Blames racist nature of society.

Pryce's **ethnographic study** of Afro-Caribbean youth in Bristol suggests that all previous accounts have neglected how such youth **interprets** their situation. Pryce concludes that many young Afro-Caribbeans interpret school as an agency that benefits whites only. In addition, they are aware that in a predominantly white society, the odds are against them in the form of **racism**, etc. They therefore choose to reject what school has to offer and deliberately take up 'deviant' careers because they see this as the only way to achieve success in a racist society.

Gender and achievement

OCR ▷ U2536

As you can see, this is no longer a straightforward topic. Don't oversimplify the issue by suggesting all boys or all girls underachieve or achieve.

Until the late 1980s, most sociological literature focused on the underachievement of girls. They were less likely than boys to pursue A Levels and consequently to enter higher education. However, in the early 1990s, it was argued that girls had begun to outperform boys at most levels of the education system. The main sociological focus today therefore is on the underachievement of boys. However, it is now clear that female underachievement was exaggerated. Females have always outperformed males across a range of levels and subjects. The idea that females perform poorly in school was, and is, a myth.

> Epstein et al. (1999) point out that boys' underachievement is not something new. They suggest that in the past boys' underachievement was not a worrying trend for two reasons:
> - working-class boys used to move easily into jobs without good qualifications in the days when sons followed fathers into mines, factories, etc.
> - the structural and cultural barriers preventing females access to high-status jobs and the pressure on women to become wives and mothers, etc. meant that males always achieved better jobs in the long run.

KEY POINT

However, today Epstein notes that governments are anxious about large numbers of unemployed young men because they are a potential threat to social order. However, feminists still lobby on behalf of females. They still have concerns about the subject choices made by girls. **Burgess and Parker** point out that where students have the choice of options at GCSE there is still a tendency for chemistry and computer studies to be taken up by boys. This division is even more pronounced at A Level. Females are still less likely than boys to apply for degree courses in the hard sciences and information technology. Feminists point out that the message 'the future Is female' distracts from the inequalities in employment, training and pay that characterise women's work. However, on a positive note, in 2000, the number of women gaining first-class honours degrees outnumbered males for the very first time.

Why are girls now succeeding?

There is some evidence that the women's movement has raised the expectations of females. Many women are looking beyond the mother–housewife role as illustrated by Sue Sharpe who in a 1976 survey discovered that girls' priorities were 'love, marriage, husbands, children, jobs and careers, more or less in that order'. When the research was repeated in 1994, she found that the priorities had changed to 'job, career and being able to support themselves'.

There are **increasing job opportunities** for women in the service sector of the economy. Many girls have mothers in paid employment who provide positive **role models** for them. As a result females recognise that the future offers girls more **choices** – economic independence and careers are a real possibility.

The **work of feminist sociologists** in the 1980s especially Dale Spender, Michelle Stanworth and Alison Kelly highlighted the educational underperformance of girls and led to a greater emphasis on **equal opportunities** in schools. Policies included monitoring teaching and teaching materials for sex bias to ensure **more girl-friendly schooling**, especially in the sciences. Consequently teachers are now more sensitive about avoiding gender stereotyping in the classroom.

Why are boys underachieving?

A very popular area with examiners.

In some schools, the extent of boys' underachievement has become so serious that twice as many girls are getting five GCSEs grades A–C. In inner-city schools that serve economically and socially deprived communities, the achievement of girls compared with boys is even greater. It has been estimated that by the age of 16, nearly 40% of boys are 'lost' to education.

Sociological explanations for these male underachievements fall into three broad areas.

- Some sociologists have suggested that the **fault lies with teachers**. Studies of classroom interaction and the relationship between pupils and teachers suggest that teachers are not as strict with boys as with girls. It is claimed that teachers tend to have lower expectations of boys, e.g. they expect work to be late, to be untidy and boys to be disruptive. Emphasis in the past has been on excluding such boys rather than looking for ways to motivate them. Consequently a **culture of low achievement** evolved among boys and was not acted upon because the emphasis in schools for many years was to make education more relevant and interesting for girls.

- Other sociologists have pointed to the **feminine culture which surrounds younger children** as a possible influence on male underachievement. At school, primary teachers are mainly women and evidence suggests that it is mothers rather than fathers who spend most time with their children helping them to read. Children, both male and female, may therefore equate learning and therefore schooling with **femininity**. As boys grow up, they identify with more masculine role-models and may reject academic learning and skills such as presentation and reading as feminine.

Examine proposed solutions to these aspects of boys' failure by visiting tes.co.uk and using its archive to search for articles on this topic.

- **Mac An Ghaill (1996)** argues that working-class boys are experiencing a **'crisis of masculinity'**. Their socialisation into traditional masculine identity has been undermined by **the decline of traditional men's jobs** in manufacturing and primary industries such as mining. **Mass unemployment** found in working-class areas means that boys are no longer sure about their future role as men. This confusion about their future role may lead working-class boys to conclude that qualifications are a waste of time because there are only limited opportunities in the job market. The future looks bleak and without purpose so they don't see the point in working hard. They may temporarily resolve this crisis by constructing delinquent or anti-school subcultures which tend to be anti-learning. Research evidence indicates that boys appear to gain street credibility and status in such cultures for not working.

> However, there is evidence that the problem is not solely a gender problem. Sociologists point out the focus on gender can distract us from other important educational problems. **Not all boys are doing worse than all girls**. For example, although working-class and middle-class girls do better than working-class and middle-class boys respectively, middle-class boys outperform working-class girls. The picture is far from simple. If we ask 'which boys, in which areas, are doing badly?' we find that **the impact of class and ethnicity on achievement is greater than that of gender**.

KEY POINT

Progress check

1 Which ethnic-minority group does very well in education?

2 Which ethnic-minority group experiences the highest rate of exclusion from school?

3 What does Sewell blame for Afro-Caribbean underachievement?

4 What did the Ofsted report conclude about British education in regard to black children in 2000?

5 Why was it not a problem in the past that boys failed in education?

6 Why do feminists argue that despite female success in education we should still be concerned about them?

7 What is the crisis in masculinity?

8 What might be more important than gender in explaining male and female achievement?

8 Social class and ethnicity.
7 Confusion about the male role and status caused by a decline in men's jobs.
6 The subject choices they make are stereotypically female and consequently do not impact on male-dominated occupations.
5 There were plenty of jobs available for the semi-skilled and unskilled.
4 That the educational system is institutionally racist.
3 Black youth-culture and commercial culture.
2 Afro-Caribbean.
1 Indians.

5.3 Power, control and the relationship between education and the economy

After studying this section you should be able to:

- *describe and evaluate theories of the transition from school to work*
- *outline the relationship between education, vocational training and education*

LEARNING SUMMARY

Theories of the transition from school to work

OCR   U2536

The relationship between education and the economy.

Functionalists argue that a major function of education is to transmit the skills required by a developing economy. The implication is that if educational systems are performing effectively the transition from school to work will be smooth, as employers use educational qualifications to sift and sort people into jobs that suit their abilities. However, some sociologists have raised doubts about the effectiveness of this transition. **Braverman** argues that in modern societies not many jobs actually require skills, because of technology. Therefore we may be over-educating people.

New Right thinkers suggested in the 1980s that Britain's industrial decline was due to the educational system's failure to produce young people with the appropriate attitudes and technical skills. This skills shortage was a result of schooling being divorced from the needs of work.

I.e. the hidden curriculum.

Marxists claim that the transition from school to work is shaped by the demands of the capitalist system for a passive and docile workforce prepared to accept low skills, pay and job satisfaction. Education therefore is not really about transmitting skills but about transmitting **'good worker' attitudes**.

Bowles and Gintis note that what goes on in schools **'corresponds'** with what goes on in factories. Most work is boring and routine (e.g. assembly-line production in factories) and school functions to prepare working-class pupils for their future role as factory workers, e.g. they note that students are socialised into accepting authority, powerlessness, different rewards for different abilities and lack of satisfaction. These experiences prepare them for their future experience of the factory floor.

A key study – know it well.

> **Willis'** research **'Learning to Labour'** indicates that early in their school careers, many working-class boys come to realise that they are not going to succeed educationally. Their experience of their community and the fact that their fathers are factory workers leads them to understand and accept that they will end up in manual factory-jobs. The lads' reaction to this is to reject the official school culture and its definitions of success and failure. They construct an alternative or counter school culture. This involves them going to school but resisting teacher authority and school rules.

KEY POINT

Willis is critical of Bowles and Gintis in seeing school as preparing working-class people for the boredom and monotony of factory work. Willis suggests that **the counter-culture of the lads prepares them for a shop-floor culture** which resists management by fostering community spirit and creating a work environment based on having a laugh.

Vocational training and education

OCR ▶ U2536

Educational thinking in the UK has long been characterised by **a cultural divide** between the view that children require an **academic** education in order to encourage critical and creative thinking and the view that children need to be **trained** in order that they acquire **vocational skills** relevant to the workplace. Generally until the 1970s the former view dominated educational social policy. For example, the attempt to introduce technical schools in 1944 was a failure whilst the vocational higher education establishments set up in the 1960s – the polytechnics – have become universities and increasingly stress their academic credentials.

In the late 1970s, a **'great debate'** about the relationship between education and the economy was initiated by the Labour Government and developed by the Conservative administration of Mrs Thatcher. This debate focused on Britain's poor economic performance in the 1960s and concluded that it was the result of British schools being out of touch with the changing industrial world and consequently producing a poorly trained workforce. Britain was seen to experiencing a **'skills crisis'**.

Educational social policy 1979–97

Economic recession and rising unemployment, especially amongst youth, led to a fundamental change in educational social policy in the 1970s and 1980s. Consequently the period 1979–97 saw Conservative Governments make radical changes to the organisation of schooling. This was in order to make schooling more **relevant to work** and thereby produce the skills required by industry to make Britain more competitive in the global market-place. In particular, a package of vocational measures were introduced throughout the 1980s which collectively became known as the **'new vocationalism'**.

KEY POINT

Dealing with youth unemployment

In the 1980s the Thatcher Government concluded that youth unemployment in the late 1970s was rising partly because many school leavers were unemployable. It was claimed that schools were focusing on the wrong issues and not doing enough to prepare youngsters for the world of work. It was also believed that young people expected too much in terms of job satisfaction and that they had priced themselves out of the job market. In other words, youth needed to be provided with 'appropriate' skills and attitudes for the workplace. They were to be made more **'employable'**.

One strategy that aimed to reduce youth unemployment was the expansion of **youth training schemes**, which underwent several developments in the 1980s. For example, in 1983 a one-year training scheme (**Youth Training Scheme or YTS**) combining work experience and training courses was introduced for school-leavers and extended to two years in 1986. After 1987 it was decided to deny benefit to those young people who refused to take part in this scheme. In May 1990 the government replaced YTS with YT. Later in the 1990s management of YT was devolved to local quangos called **Training and Enterprise Councils (TECs)**. These bodies fund training both for youth and adults on the basis of local employer's needs. Training is delivered by a combination of local further-education colleges, private training organisations and work experience with employers.

School initiatives

Other vocational qualifications include the TVEI and CPVE. Look them up!

The 1980s also saw the introduction of two qualifications in schools aimed at bringing an end to the culture divide of the academic and vocational. The **National Vocational Qualifications (NVQ)** are specific to certain industries and aim to test the competence of candidates in terms of both knowledge and skills. The **General National Vocational Qualifications (GNVQ)** are aimed at occupational fields, e.g. health and social care rather than specific types of jobs. These have been specifically designed to reduce the culture gap between school and work and have equivalence with GCSEs and A Levels.

The critique of new vocationalism

The new vocationalism has been strongly attacked by critics who suggest that the reality of vocational programmes for young people is very different from the philosophy that underpins it.

The Marxist critique

Vocationalism as cheap labour.

The **Marxist** critique has tended to question either the aims of youth training schemes or their outcomes. **Phil Cohen** argued that the real function of YTS was to cultivate in young people conformist attitudes, work discipline and the acceptance of a likely future of low paid and unskilled work with frequent bouts of unemployment and job changes.

Andy Green's empirical research indicated that most schemes resulted in jobs that were relatively unskilled, insecure, low paid and offered little chance of promotion.

> Green also argues that **vocational schemes legitimate traditional class divisions** because they are based on the idea that the middle class should be educated and the working class should be trained. In other words, the cultural divide still exists as another form of selection.
>
> **KEY POINT**

Recent developments are important. Keep your eyes and ears open.

In regard to GNVQs, there has been criticism that the academic bias within schools means that they have not been marketed properly or have been accorded low status by teachers. Some employers and universities have been reluctant to recognise them and they still suffer the stigma of being thought less demanding than GCSEs and A Levels. However, in January 2001 the Labour government announced plans to give 14-year-olds the option of a vocational path with the introduction of vocational GCSEs in 2002 which may lead to foundation apprenticeships for 16–18 year olds. The Government is also intending a complete reshaping of training programmes for young people in 2002.

Changing the curriculum

OCR ▸ U2536

In 1988 the Conservative government introduced the **Education Reform Act** to take more centralised control of the curriculum and teaching methods. Their aim was to raise standards in education in order that pupils leave school with knowledge and skills relevant to the workplace.

The national curriculum

A centralised standardised curriculum was introduced. The content of this national curriculum was determined by national government. It was based around three core subjects (English, science and maths) and seven foundation subjects for pupils aged 5 to 16. National **standardised assessment tests (SATs)** at 7, 11 and 14 were also introduced, although the number of these tests was substantially cut back after 1994. However, the results of these tests (along with other criteria such as GCSE, A Level and truancy statistics) are published annually as part of **league tables** that aim to compare the performance of schools.

It is argued that the national curriculum was underpinned by vocationalist ideas in that the stress on science, maths and technology aims to produce pupils with more work-friendly skills.

City technology colleges

The 1988 Act led to the setting up of **city technology colleges (CTCs)** (specialising in the arts, maths, science and technology) in some inner-city areas. These were independent of local authorities and supposed to be financed by private industry. Their aim was to prepare young people to work in the high-technology industries. However, the goal of creating 20 of these colleges has not been achieved. There are also signs that the vocational element has been diluted in favour of academic qualifications. However, they have achieved excellent exam results because the money spent on them by government means they have low staff–pupil ratios.

Labour educational policy 1997 onwards

Keep an eye on Labour's educational policy – it is constantly changing!

In 1997 New Labour were elected and this brought the introduction of a '**third way**' into educational policy. This aims to continue to modernise the educational system whilst providing more opportunities for groups who are '**socially excluded**' to enter the labour market as skilled workers. The **New Deal**, for example, is aimed at improving educational opportunities for the long-term unemployed and single mothers by providing them with financial assistance to attend further education.

Progress check

1 What do Bowles and Gintis argue about the relationship between school and work?

2 Why is Willis critical of Bowles and Gintis?

3 What was the skills crisis identified in the 1970s?

4 What is the new vocationalism?

5 What hidden-curriculum function of YTS was identified by Green?

6 What type of vocational educational establishment was introduced by the 1988 Education Reform Act?

6 City technology colleges.
5 That the middle class receive an academic education whilst the working class are trained.
4 A package of vocational initiatives aimed at producing people with work-oriented attitudes and skills.
3 The view that the UK was not producing people with the right sort of skills and that there was a shortage of technical skills.
2 Because working-class boys are realistic about what to expect from factory work. They choose to do it.
1 What goes on in school prepares the working class for the boredom they can expect in factory work.

Sample question and model answer

An essay question – you should aim for at least two sides.

Outline and assess sociological contributions to an understanding of the hidden curriculum. (60 marks)

Begins with a definition of hidden curriculum.

The hidden curriculum refers to the way in which the organisation of teaching, knowledge and school regulations shape pupil's attitudes and behaviour. Many sociologists argue that its main function is to encourage conformity to the values and definitions of success and failure held by dominant social groups. It consequently promotes feelings of superiority and inferiority among some groups. It can be contrasted with the formal curriculum which is usually concerned with the transmission of subject-based and assessment-centred knowledge. Much work on the hidden curriculum has been focused on the allegedly negative consequences of the hidden curriculum in promoting inequalities relating to class, gender and race. Marxists, feminists and those sociologists who focus on classroom interaction between teachers and pupils have all contributed to our understanding of the concept of the hidden curriculum.

Outlines Marxist contribution.

Marxists argue that education is an ideological agency which functions to maintain, legitimate and reproduce, generation by generation, class inequalities in wealth and power. Louis Althusser argued that the educational system conditions young people to accept social inequalities through the use of the 'hidden curriculum'. He argues that hidden messages stressing conformity to the capitalist system are transmitted to pupils through the knowledge that is taught in schools and through the everyday routines and rules of school organisation.

Elaboration and illustration.

Althusser insists that many academic subjects reflect ruling class and capitalist values. Ways of thinking that offer a critique of capitalist inequality or that offer an alternative to it are simply not covered by the formal curriculum. Althusser believed that history teaches pupils to believe that hierarchy, inequality, nationalism, racism, conflict, etc. are 'normal' facts of life that cannot be changed. Althusser also argued that the everyday rules and routines of schools transmit very different messages to middle-class and working-class pupils about the purpose of school. Devices such as streaming and examinations serve to convince working-class pupils that their knowledge and experiences are irrelevant and to accept failure as their fault.

Bowles and Gintis argue that capitalism requires a passive and docile workforce which is prepared to accept low skills and pay. They, too, focus on the hidden curriculum of schools. They note that what goes on in schools 'corresponds' with what goes on in factories. Most work is boring and routine (e.g. assembly-line production in factories). Therefore school functions to prepare working-class pupils for their future role as factory workers. For example, they note that students are socialised into accepting authority, powerlessness, different rewards for different abilities and lack of satisfaction. These experiences correspond with experience on the factory floor.

Outlines interactionist contribution.

Interactionist approaches have also touched upon the idea of the hidden curriculum in their studies of teacher expectations. Becker found that teachers classify and evaluate pupils using an 'ideal pupil' standard or yardstick. Teachers have a very clear idea about what constitutes ideal work, conduct, attitude and appearance. Middle-class, white and male students are seen as closest to this ideal whilst those students from working-class, ethnic-minority and female backgrounds are seen as furthest

Sample question and model answer (continued)

from it. In other words, ideal pupils meet all the requirements of conformity which the hidden curriculum demands. They are the hidden curriculum personified.

Outlines contribution of hidden curriculum in explaining ethnic minority under achievement.

Studies into ethnic-minority underachievement have also highlighted the role of the hidden curriculum. The Swann Report (1986) argued that the school curriculum is ethnocentric – knowledge, teaching methods and forms of assessment are biased in favour of white, middle-class children.

Outlines feminist contribution.

Feminists have also focused on the role of the 'hidden curriculum' in female underachievement, subject stereotyping and conformity to traditional gender roles. Marion Scott analysed the content of school textbooks and found that in physics and chemistry textbooks the main discoverers 'all seem to be men' whilst history textbooks tended to contain 'a view of the past which left women invisible'.

Assessment of sociological contributions.

The idea of the hidden curriculum has been criticised as over-deterministic. Willis argues that pupils are not merely passive recipients of educational processes but are actively involved in shaping their educational experience. In other words, not all pupils and students accept what goes on at school. Some pupils resist the hidden curriculum. Willis found that the working-class lads in his study rejected the official school culture and its definitions of success and failure. They constructed an alternative or counter school culture based around 'having a laff'. This involved them going to school but resisting teacher labels, authority and school rules, i.e. the hidden curriculum.

Practice examination question

Outline and assess the view that males are now the disadvantaged sex in education.

(60 marks)

Chapter 6

Health

The following topics are covered in this chapter:

- *The social nature of health and illness*
- *Trends and patterns in health and illness*
- *Medicine, power and control*

6.1 The social nature of health and illness

After studying this section you should be able to:

- *outline how health and illness are socially constructed*
- *describe and assess sociological explanations of mental illness and disability*
- *critically examine the relationship between deviance, social control and the sick role*

LEARNING SUMMARY

The social construction of illness

OCR ▷ U2536

Gomm (1980) argues that **sickness and health are the product of culture** rather than nature. He does not deny that bacteria or viruses exist and that these cause pain and discomfort but he points out that in modern societies, physical symptoms are only defined as sickness and disease when officially recognised by a **biomedical élite**, i.e. doctors, using objective scientific diagnosis. Gomm notes that there is a three-stage social process involved in becoming ill.

The social process of becoming ill

An increasingly popular area with examiners.

First, he argues that people often feel 'unwell' or 'under the weather' but they have a considerable choice of action at this stage. They may choose to put up with the symptoms, treat themselves, use alternative medicines such as homeopathy or obtain an official agreement from a doctor that they are ill. Visiting the doctor and being officially defined as sick is not a straightforward decision. Our family may strongly encourage us to visit the doctor and there are official rules about taking time off work with pay which may force a visit.

Our culture, social class, gender and ethnicity also affect our choice of action. For example, many people in the developing world experience pain or discomfort as a taken-for-granted part of their lives and therefore do not see themselves as suffering from illness. Even in our own culture, men may be less likely to recognise symptoms as illness because they are socialised not to show weakness.

Second, our symptoms need to be defined as sickness by doctors. However, this is not as straightforward as it seems – misdiagnosis is fairly common. The interaction between the doctor and the patient is crucial here. Research by **Cartwright and O'Brien** suggests that working-class patients feel intimidated by the middle-class nature of health-care and consequently may be less willing to visit their doctor. Middle-class patients feel more comfortable with their doctors, are more articulate about their symptoms and consequently are more likely to be officially diagnosed as ill and treated.

Third, diagnosis leads to action being proposed by doctors. Recently, sociologists have suggested medical treatment can help *create* illness as medical professionals make mistakes and prescribe drugs that lead to dependency.

Definitions of health and illness are therefore not fixed or universal. They are subjected to constant change. Gomm notes how medical definitions of what counts as illness have expanded over the course of the last century. For example, pregnancy has gradually become defined as a dangerous medical condition and obesity, impotence, frigidity, fear of strangers and misbehaviour at school have become medical matters. Homosexuality, on the other hand, was once defined as a disease but is no longer regarded as such by doctors in the Western world.

Finally, **the social distribution of morbidity (illness) and mortality (death)** also supports the view that health and illness are socially constructed. If health and illness were a product of the natural order of things then we could expect to see both sickness rates and death rates distributed fairly equally across all social groups. However, death rates and sickness rates are disproportionately affecting groups such as the working class and ethnic minorities.

Mental health and illness

OCR   U2536

Mental health and deviance

Some types of mental disorder are clearly biological or physiological in origin, e.g. Alzheimer's disease. However, some types of mental illness are less clearly linked with biological malfunctions or disease. Mental health and illness is not fully understood by the medical profession. Sociologists have long argued that this has resulted in mental illness being treated in a stigmatised fashion as deviance rather than in the sympathetic fashion that society tends to treat most physical disease. Consequently, the social treatment of mental health has tended to be prejudiced and discriminatory as society fears the behavioural consequences of mental-health problems. Contact with psychiatric services is therefore seen as shameful by some families who may seek to conceal members who have been defined as suffering from mental-health problems.

Health professionals have not always dominated definitions of mental health and illness. For example, mental illness in the 16th century was often defined as possession by evil spirits, therefore clerics rather than health professionals were responsible for its treatment, whilst in the 18th century it was seen as being caused by moral weakness.

Henshaw and Howells (1999) define mental illness as behaviour preventing individuals functioning adequately in their society. However, 'functioning adequately' can be dependent upon interpretation by powerful groups. For example, dissidents in the former USSR were interpreted as 'mentally ill' and treated in psychiatric units. In the USA homosexuality was officially classed as a mental illness until the 1980s. Definitions of mental health can therefore be manipulated to control 'problem' groups.

Labelling theory and mental health

Both Scheff (1966) and Szasz have claimed that mental illness is merely a label applied to the behaviour of certain people at certain times and in certain situations. In other words, what is 'normal' or 'mad' behaviour is a matter of interpretation. For example, Szasz points out that there is often little difference between being defined as 'mad', 'eccentric' or just plain 'odd'. Moreover definitions of such behaviour are relative – they vary over historical period and across societies. For example, Foucault argued that in medieval times, madness was often associated with genius and in pre-industrial societies, it was equated with holiness and great wisdom. However, Porter claims this is an over-romanticised view and the rest of society rarely regarded such individuals as part of society.

Scheff argued that there is no such thing as mental illness. Instead there exist a range of behaviours, some of which are defined by those with power supported by the medical profession as objectionable behaviour that needs to be controlled. For example, women who did not conform to social expectations about feminine behaviour in terms of their sexual behaviour or because they refused to conform to the good wife or mother stereotype were often treated as mentally ill.

Szasz argues that mental-health labels often confuse people's problems and result in misdiagnosis. For example, the label of clinical depression disguises the fact that someone may be very miserable for good reason.

Goffman (1968) claims that there is great **stigma** attached to mental illness in Western society. Therefore societal reaction to the label is likely to be negative and such labelling (and the consequent treatment by mental-health professionals) can result in a **'deviant career'**. In other words, those labelled as mentally ill will come to accept the definition of themselves as 'ill'. This is especially likely to be the case if they are institutionalised.

Community care

Research newspaper websites for articles on this topic.

Today, however, institutionalisation is less likely in the UK because in the 1980s many large mental hospitals were closed down and replaced by 'community care'. People were either treated at home or they were placed in accommodation and treated in day-care centres. The aims of community care were threefold:

- to avoid the problems of institutionalisation
- to avoid marginalising the mentally ill – it was hoped that they would be treated as normal members of the community
- to save money – institutional care is expensive.

However, over the past ten years two major problems have been perceived in relation to community care.

- There is public concern that the release of psychiatric patients into the community puts 'ordinary' people at risk. This is partly the product of stereotypical and distorted fears about the 'mentally ill' – the label is extremely powerful in the social reaction it gets from the general public. However, it may also be a realistic response to the well-documented cases of violence by schizophrenics who had failed to take their medication.
- The policy has not been properly organised or funded. For example, in some areas ex-patients receive insufficient support in terms of hostels and trained staff. This, too, may reflect the low status and negative labelling mental health has in the overall health and welfare system.

The sociology of disability

OCR ▸ U2536

Defining disability

Three concepts – impairment, disability and handicap – are important in understanding the medical treatment of the disabled. For example, someone who has a hearing impairment might have difficulty in listening to a conversation (they are regarded as disabled) and consequently have problems interacting face-to-face with others (they are handicapped). This may seem a logical process but it is challenged by sociologists subscribing to the social model of disability.

The social model of disability

Shearer (1991) argues that 'handicap' is not something that naturally results from impairment. The idea that impairment should mean 'handicapped' is something imposed on the disabled by a society which is largely organised for the non-disabled and which ends up defining disability as a type of deviance. **Barnes (1991)** also suggests that 'disability' is not the result of impairment. Rather it refers to the loss of opportunities to take part in the normal life of a community because of social barriers put up by the non-disabled. In other words, the social model of disability argues that people with impairments are **disabled by society**. This is known as 'disableism'.

Disableism

A good topic for a Personal Study.

Thompson suggests there is a combination of social forces, cultural values and personal prejudices which marginalises disabled people and portrays them in a negative and deviant light. This includes the following.

- Failing to build physical environments in which the disabled can move about freely, e.g. wheelchair-friendly access to buildings. Changes are taking place slowly in this field.

- Institutional discrimination – for example, Barnes (1991) found that disabled applicants were six times more likely to be turned down for a job than non-disabled applicants.

- Stigmatisation – **Davies (1994)** points out that disabled people are seen by the non-disabled as possessing a deviant identity in that they are stereotyped as being ugly, asexual, intellectually impaired, unable to speak for themselves and dependent.

- Media representations – research by **Barnes (1992)** indicates that disabled people are largely absent from our screens and newspapers. However, when they *are* portrayed it is usually as pitiable and pathetic or coverage focuses on how the non-disabled view the activities of the disabled as 'extraordinary' or as the product of 'remarkable courage'.

The consequences of disableism for the disabled

Stereotypes about the disabled are extremely powerful because the label 'disabled' acts as a master status – disabled people come to be seen by the non-disabled exclusively in terms of their impairment, e.g. it is assumed by many people that those in wheelchairs are mentally handicapped as well as physically handicapped (i.e. 'does he take sugar?'). Social segregation rather than the social integration of the disabled into society becomes the norm. This may result in a 'self-fulfilling prophecy' as the disabled come to accept their dependence on the non-disabled. Moreover, it can mean that the disabled person's sense of identity is mainly based on what is wrong or abnormal about them rather than what they have in common with the non-disabled. There have been recent signs that some sections of the disabled are politically mobilising against disableism or what Davies calls 'the last civil-rights battle'.

Deviance, social control and the sick role

OCR   U2536

Functionalists see medicine as important as an **agency of social control**. They argue that social order depends upon value consensus and the inter-dependence of skills. Illness disrupts the industrial system because it involves people dropping out to recuperate. People may use illness as an excuse to withdraw from their social obligations. In this sense, illness is deviant and must be socially controlled.

Parsons argues that the power of doctors is used in the interests of society. Doctors officially confirm **the 'sick role'** and thus sanction the withdrawal of people from the economy. The doctor's social control role then is to maintain social responsibility amongst the ill and to encourage their swift return to their social roles. However, this theory implies that ill people are passive social actors who obey the demands of doctors without questions but evidence from **Cartwright** suggests that conflict between doctors and patients is the norm.

Progress check

1 How was mental illness explained before the 20th century?
2 What are the three stages of the social process of becoming ill?
3 What are morbidity and mortality?
4 What according to Scheff and Szasz is mental illness?
5 What is a deviant career?
6 What is meant by the phrase 'disabled by society'?
7 What is the relationship between community care and institutionalisation?
8 What is the 'sick role'?

8 The obligation of sick members of society to attempt to return to their social obligations as quickly as possible by consulting doctors.
7 One of the main objectives of care in the community was to avoid the negative consequences of incarceration in homes and hospitals.
6 It is the way that society treats the disabled that causes handicaps for them.
5 People labelled as mentally ill may come to see themselves as such.
4 A label applied by society to people whose behaviour is regarded as different or threatening.
3 Morbidity is illness and mortality is death.
2 Recognition, definition and action.
1 As either demonic possession or moral weakness.

6.2 Trends and patterns in health and illness

After studying this section you should be able to:

- *identify trends in the unequal social distribution of health and illness in regard to social class, gender and ethnicity*
- *outline and assess different explanations of inequalities in the provision of, and access to, health-care*

LEARNING SUMMARY

The social distribution of health and illness

OCR   U2536

If health and illness were chance occurrences we could expect to see them randomly distributed across the population. However, some groups can expect an over-proportionate amount of illness.

- The working-class experience worse mortality and morbidity rates than the middle classes. For example, more than 3500 extra working-class babies would survive per year if the working-class infant mortality rate was reduced to middle-class levels.
- Life expectancy is seven years longer for someone born into social class I compared with someone born into social class V.
- The working class are also more likely to die pre-retirement of cancer, stroke and heart disease than the middle class. Between 1972 and 1993 rates of death from all causes fell by nearly 50% for social class I but only 10% for social class V.

Explanations for social-class inequalities in health and illness

OCR U2536

Artefact theory

Blames the statistics.

This theory is sceptical about the connection between social class and health and argues that the official statistics are loaded with unintentional bias which distort the true picture of health. This theory suggests that the collection of statistics is unreliable because of variation in the interpretation and recording of death. It also suggests that we cannot trust the social-class categories used by sociologists because some occupational groups have dramatically expanded in size whilst some have shrunk. For example, social class V has diminished so much in recent years that comparisons over time with social class I are allegedly pointless.

Cultural-deprivation theory: blaming the individual

Blames the victim.

> **KEY POINT**
>
> This theory argues that inequalities in health between the working class and middle class are the product of culture. Working-class culture is seen to be composed of values that are harmful to health.

Cultural deprivationists suggest that working-class people are less likely to eat a healthy diet and more likely to excessively smoke and drink. **Roberts** argues that the working class indulge in less exercise and are more passive in terms of their leisure pursuits. Cultural deprivationists have also suggested that the working class are less likely to take advantage of preventative health-care, vaccination or ante-natal care. They are supposedly less likely to breastfeed – which can lower children's resistance to disease. For example, **Ann Howlett and John Ashley** suggest that the middle class have more knowledge of what constitutes good health than the working class. Consequently the middle class attempt to prevent health problems through exercise and diet. In conclusion, working-class ill health is seen to be the product of irresponsible individual behaviour and the failure to make rational choices about their lifestyle.

Material-deprivation theory

Blames social factors.

> **KEY POINT**
>
> Critics suggest that working-class cultural values may be a realistic response to the poverty and material deprivation caused by unemployment and/or low wages.

Cost may be the major reason why working-class people do not subscribe to healthy diets, take exercise and or take up NHS facilities. They may be well aware of the benefits of these but unable to afford them. Smoking and drinking may be an attempt to relieve stress. Graham's research suggests smoking among working-class women may be a rational choice because it protects women's emotional health by relieving the stress of a heavily demanding routine.

Social-cohesion theory

Blames social factors.

Wilkinson (1998) acknowledges that poverty is a significant factor in bringing about poor health but argues that lack of social cohesion in a society is the most important contributor. He notes that societies with large income differences between social groups are less healthy than societies with narrower income differences. Inequalities in income lead to conflict and competition between people which raises stress levels and results in greater levels of ill-health. Societies in which there are few differences in income are more cohesive and experience better health. Wilkinson argues that these appear to be less stressful because people are more supportive of each other.

The social-administration theory

This view argues that there are regional inequalities that are largely caused by inequalities in the distribution of NHS resources.

Blames the NHS.

> **KEY POINT**
>
> **Tudor Hart (1971)** suggests that the allocation of NHS resources is so unequal that it conforms to an **'inverse care law'**. This law states that those whose need is less get more health resources whilst those in greatest need get less. Working-class areas tend to be provided with the fewest and worse health facilities in terms of numbers of GPs and hospitals.

However, in criticism of Tudor Hart, the healthiest part of the UK (I.e. East Anglia) has never received a fair share of funding whilst Scotland which has the highest levels of ill-health has always received more funding than England and Wales.

There have been attempts by governments to deal with regional health inequalities by preventing GPs from starting new practices or taking over practices in areas where there are too many doctors. However, it is still the case that the NHS system of funding health facilities benefits those areas with more hospitals, doctors, etc. These tend to be the more affluent areas located in the south-east.

Marxism

Blames capitalism.

Marxist sociologists suggest that in capitalist societies it is inevitable that health will become a **market commodity** like any other. Marxists suggest that government cutbacks in health spending in the 1980s were aimed at encouraging people to turn to private health-care. The ability to pay for health clearly benefits some groups at the expense of others.

The Marxists, **Doyal and Pennell**, note that the fundamental purpose of capitalism is the pursuit of profit. They suggest that this has two negative consequences for the health of the working classes.

- Less attention is paid to the welfare of workers. For example, approximately 700 workers are killed in industrial accidents every year in the UK whilst death from industrial disease is also common.
- Employers have a vested interest in keeping wages at a low level in order to maximise profits. This may result in **poverty**. Two Government-sponsored reports, **The Black Report (1980) and The Health Divide (1987)** identify the chief causes of ill health amongst the working class as poverty.

> **KEY POINT**
>
> **Townsend and Phillimore (1986)** in a study of health in the north-east note the relationship between bad housing, poor diet, lack of play areas, overcrowding, poor education and exposure to infection. They conclude 'the health gap is a consequence of the wealth gap'.

However, **Nicky Hart** accuses Doyal and Pennell of being **selective** in their use of evidence. She notes that they fail to acknowledge that many of the commodities and medical technologies of advanced capitalist society are very beneficial to health. Moreover, the former socialist countries of Eastern Europe probably experience worse health levels than the West. Hart concludes that poor health is linked to **industrialisation** rather than its organisation along capitalist or socialist lines.

Gender and health

OCR   U2536

Patterns of health and illness

A number of differences in mortality and morbidity can be perceived between men and women.

- Women tend to live longer than men in all social classes. Life expectancy at birth in the UK is 77 years for females but 71 for males.
- Women experience more chronic sickness (i.e. long-standing illness, disability or infirmity) than men. Two-thirds of the four million disabled people in the UK are women.
- Women are more likely to suffer from emotional disturbance, depression and acute stress than men. Women are much more likely to be receiving drug treatment for such problems.
- Women see their doctor more frequently than men.

Explanations for gender inequalities

OCR   U2536

Artefact theory

Blames the statistics.

Alison McFarlane suggests that the statistics are misleading. She notes that once admissions for childbirth are taken into account, differences in admission rates to hospitals between men and women virtually disappear. Moreover, she notes that once visits to the GP in connection with contraception, menstruation, gynaecology and post-natal care are taken into consideration the differences between males and females disappear.

However, it is still a fact that more women are treated for mental-health problems and degenerative diseases. The latter is probably due to the fact that women are more likely than men to survive beyond retirement age.

Gender-role socialisation

This is seen by some liberal feminists as being the reason for differences in mortality and morbidity rates for the following reasons.

Blames social factors, i.e. patriarchal culture.

> - Men are socialised into being more aggressive and to take more risks. This could account for the death rate for males aged between 15 and 35. Many of these deaths result from acts of violence and motor accidents.
> - It is more acceptable for men to smoke and drink alcohol – which may account for the higher rate of death from cancer and heart disease in the 45–55 age group.
> - Men are expected to be breadwinners in our culture. Therefore they are more likely to be victims of industrial accidents, disease and stress. They are more likely to suffer the stress of unemployment.

KEY POINT

The mother–housewife role

Blames patriarchal culture.

Some **feminists** have also contributed to this gender-role socialisation argument by focusing on the **mother–housewife role. Ann Oakley's (1976)** interviews with working-class and middle-class housewives discovered that they experienced housework as both monotonous and isolating. **Jesse Bernard** argues that **marriage makes women sick**. She found that married men have better mental and physical health than single men but this position is reversed with married and single women. **Hilary Graham** suggests women's responsibility for family health makes them more conscious of health and results in their greater take-up of health facilities.

Labelling theory

Busfield (1983) notes that the diagnosis of mental illness in women may reflect negative stereotypes held by doctors about female behaviour. Certain types of behaviour, e.g. being angry, shouting etc. may be labelled deviant because they do not fit conventional perceptions of femininity.

Marxist–feminism

The mother-housewife role benefits capitalism.

Marxist feminists argue that the labelling of some women as mentally ill has an **ideological function** because it neglects women's domestic environment – which is the real cause of the problem.

Ethnicity and health

OCR   U2536

A number of trends can be seen in regard to ethnicity and health in the UK.

• Asians and Afro-Caribbeans suffer higher than average levels of liver cancer, diabetes, tuberculosis and high blood-pressure.
• Stillbirths and infant mortality are higher than average amongst immigrant Asians.
• Admission rates to psychiatric hospitals for Afro-Caribbeans, especially Rastafarians, are higher than average.

Explanations for ethnic inequalities

OCR   U2536

Cultural-deprivation theory

This theory focuses on health-damaging behaviour which allegedly is caused by the cultural or religious beliefs of ethnic minorities. It is suggested that:

Blames the victim.

• Asian mothers fail to attend ante-natal classes
• the Asian diet (especially the use of ghee fat and the alleged carbohydrate content of food) is unhealthy
• immigrant groups experience 'language difficulties' and this is responsible for their failure to use NHS facilities.

However, Marmot (1984) suggests that such lifestyle factors play only a minor role. He argues that:

• Asian diets are arguably closer to health education advice on low fat diets than the traditional British diet
• language should not be a problem as the numbers of British-born ethnic minorities increase.

Social-administration theory

Blame the NHS.

This view of health is critical of the NHS's treatment of ethnic minorities. It is suggested that ethnic minorities are likely to experience unequal access to health services because:

KEY POINT

- ethnic-minority needs are often unrecognised or ignored, and consequently ethnic-minority groups may find medical treatment or advice irrelevant, offensive, unhelpful or threatening (Mares, 1987)
- NHS facilities may fail to provide health information in the appropriate language
- NHS facilities may fail to make knowledge of religious, dietary and cultural norms basic to health-professional training
- NHS facilities may fail to provide amenities which support cultural beliefs such as the importance of, for example, prayer in hospital, death rites, etc.

Marxism

Marxists argue that it is important to consider the location of the black population in the **class structure**. Ethnic minorities are more likely to be:

Blames capitalism.

- concentrated in low-paid manual occupations and particularly in industries that are most hazardous to health
- subjected to the stresses of unemployment and lack of job security
- subjected to the stresses of shift work
- located in poor-quality, overcrowded housing and sharing bathroom/toilets.

Such problems will be compounded by **racism**. **Brown** suggests that racist practices by employers and landlords mean that ethnic minorities are more likely to face these problems than whites in poverty. Racism may also have a more direct impact in the form of racial attacks.

KEY POINT

It is important to note that race interacts with other important social factors especially social class and gender. For example, some Asian groups (notably East-African Asians) tend to occupy higher social class positions than other Asian groups and consequently enjoy health levels similar to the white middle-class. Ethnic-minority women may experience worse health than ethnic-minority men according to Blackburn (1991).

Solutions to the problem of health inequality

OCR ▶ U2536

The National Health Service

The National Health Service was set up in 1948 by the Labour Government. The intention was to create a system of universal and free health-care. Both Labour and Conservative governments subscribed to a consensus about how the NHS should be run until 1979 when Mrs Thatcher took power.

Conservative reform of the NHS focused on four key areas.

- The principles of the free market such as competition were introduced to health-care. An internal market was created. GPs became responsible for their own budgets (fundholders). They could purchase services on behalf of patients registered to them from hospital trusts. The idea was that competition would promote efficiency and reduce costs as trusts competed with each other to provide services. Managers were recruited from business to oversee this system.
- Care in the community was designed to take the old, sick, disabled and mentally ill out of institutional care and put them back into the care of family and the wider community.
- Private health schemes and hospitals were encouraged. This period also saw an expansion of private homes for the elderly.

- A Patient's Charter was introduced in 1992 in order to make clear what performance standards the health service was supposed to achieve.

Criticism of Conservative reforms

It has been suggested that the health service has been transformed into a three-tier service which merely reproduces the inverse care law, i.e. those in greatest need receive less resources. The wealthy have access to a private health-care system. The middle class are registered with GPs in rural or suburban practices in which demand on funds is not so great. This gives GPs more choice of services. Working-class patients tend to be registered to GPs in inner-cities who face intensive demands on their funds. They therefore have less flexibility in how they spend their funds.

The Labour Government and the NHS post-1998

The Labour Government experienced a crisis in its handling of the NHS in January 2000. It was noted that the UK has fewer doctors and hospital beds than almost any other country in Europe per head of population. However, Labour intends to:

- abolish the internal market
- raise health expenditure to the European average by 2002
- set up Primary care trusts – autonomous, statutory bodies run by GPs, nurses and other health professionals, handling annual budgets of at least £60m. They will offer services such as high-street health centres and more convenient day surgery, providing more flexible health-care that also reduces the strain on hospitals
- put more emphasis on preventative health-care
- focus on the relationship between health, poverty, housing, environment and lifestyle
- reduce waiting lists.

Note any changes to the NHS you see referred to in the news.

Progress check

1 What does cultural deprivation theory blame for inequalities in health?

2 What do material deprivationists blame for inequalities in health?

3 What is the 'inverse care law'?

4 What do Marxists claim is the major cause of ill health?

5 What female social role is blamed by Oakley, Bernard and Graham for the poor health of women?

6 What is the 'internal market' in the NHS?

7 Give examples of the way the NHS may institutionally discriminate against Asians.

8 Ethnic minority needs such as diets and the importance of religion may not be recognised or ignored and NHS facilities may fail to provide health information in the appropriate language.
6 Competition between providers of health-care (e.g. hospital trusts) to provide services to purchasers such as fundholding GPs.
5 The mother/housewife role.
4 Capitalism.
3 Those whose need is less get more health resources whilst those in greatest need get less.
2 Poverty.
1 The cultural habits of the poor.

6.3 Medicine, power and control

After studying this section you should be able to:

LEARNING SUMMARY

- *describe the biomedical model of health and social models of health and assess their roles in regard to levels of health and illness*
- *outline and assess different explanations of the role of medical professions*
- *evaluate the role of medicine in the control and regulation of the body, mind and sexuality*

The role of the biomedical élite in creating good health

OCR   U2536

It is often assumed that medicine is primarily responsible for levels of good health in UK society today. The medical profession has convinced society through its dominance of the NHS that the way that it has organised the treatment of illness is the main reason why infant mortality has fallen and life expectancy has increased during the course of the 20th century.

> The dominant model of health.

KEY POINT

Nicky Hart notes that the biomedical model has five characteristics.
- It concentrates on the organic or physical symptoms of disease. Doctors are portrayed as being the only people who have the necessary skills to identify symptoms of illness.
- It is cure-oriented and stresses treatments such as surgery, drugs, etc.
- Illness is seen as a temporary affair. Germs, etc. are identified and driven off by medical expertise.
- The individual is the site of the disease. The causes of disease are rarely located in the environment that the individual occupies.
- Treatment is best located in a medical environment, i.e. hospital rather than in the environment where the symptoms may have risen.

However, this model has attracted criticism because it tends to react to illness rather than be preventative. Only a small amount of the NHS budget is spent on health education. Alternative or holistic medicine is critical of the biomedical neglect of the relationship between the body and the mind or the person and his/her immediate environment.

The social model of health

> McKeown is worth knowing in detail.

KEY POINT

McKeown points out that health levels as measured by increases in life expectancy and improvements in child mortality had dramatically improved before the development of modern biomedical techniques such as vaccination. McKeown argues that 19th-century public-health measures, e.g. sewage systems, clean water supplies, etc., improvements in nutrition and diet and birth limitation are mainly responsible for good health today.

Health, professionals and social control

OCR U2536

Functionalism, medical professionals and altruism

Doctors as public servants.

Functionalists see the medical profession as primarily **altruistic**. Doctors serve the public interest rather than pursue private gain. The Hippocratic Oath is indicative of this social commitment. Doctors swear to do all they can to help the sick, regardless of material interest. However, functionalists tend to neglect **private medicine**. Its existence questions the idea that the medical profession is primarily altruistic. **Hart also** notes that if altruism were the primary motivation of doctors, the NHS would devote more resources to disease **prevention** than it currently does. There is some evidence that the general public's confidence in doctors as altruistic individuals working for the public good has been severely shaken by a number of recent public scandals. The Harold Shipman serial killing, the controversy surrounding the removal of children's organs at Liverpool Alder Hey Children's Hospital and the finding of a number of consultants and surgeons as grossly negligent undermine the functionalist argument.

Marxism, medical professionals and ideological control

Doctors as agents of capitalism.

Marxists generally see medicine as a social institution that supports capitalist interests. They suggests that the power of doctors is not geared to altruism. Rather, Marxists argue it functions to reproduce class inequality.

Doyal see doctors as performing a conservative social function. Marxists argue that doctors and the NHS are part of an ideological state apparatus working on behalf of the capitalist class to reproduce and legitimate class inequality. The role of doctors therefore is to:

* maintain the health and productivity of the workforce
* validate or otherwise the claims of workers to have time off work – doctors therefore prevent workers from dropping out of the system and thus minimise disruption to the capitalist system
* obscure the real causes of disease such as class inequality and exploitation caused by capitalism, e.g. poverty, low wages, etc. by blaming the sick for their illness or by suggesting that illness is a random phenomenon.

Marxists such as Doyal argue that in return for performing this ideological function doctors are rewarded with status, high financial rewards and monopoly over medical knowledge. The power of doctors is therefore granted to them by the capitalist class in return for acting as agents of social control.

Medical professionals and occupational strategies

Doctors as self-serving professionals.

The Weberian sociologist, Friedson points out that the medical profession has achieved a legal monopoly over health in the UK. The British Medical Association controls recruitment, training and practice and regulates professional conduct. Only doctors have a legal right to diagnose and treat illness. They also have a major say in the running of the NHS. In return, the medical profession is supposed to guarantee high ethical standards. Doctors appear to the public as a standard product, equally skilful and equally trustworthy – in other words, as altruistic.

Friedson argues that the basis of professional power is rational–legal rather than economic. Doctors are socially autonomous of the capitalist class. Friedson, too, is sceptical of the altruistic role of doctors. He notes that medical power is mainly aimed at serving the interests of doctors. It is an occupational strategy that has ensured high financial rewards.

Medicine and the control and regulation of the body, mind and sexuality

OCR ▷ U2536

The social control of women's health

Western scientific medicine claims to be objective and value-free. However, **feminists** see medical knowledge as a means of maintaining patriarchal control over women. It is argued by **Abbott and Wallace** that medicine seeks to control women who deviate from a feminine stereotype as seen in the following areas.

- Both the pill and IUDs carry significant health risks which men would not be expected to tolerate. Radical feminists argue that the worldwide business in contraceptive pills is huge and consequently the profits for the multinational pharmaceutical companies are massive. It is therefore in the interests of such companies to restrict women's ability to choose how they control their own fertility by encouraging doctors to prescribe the pill.

- Control over **childbirth** has been taken away from women. Pregnancy is seen as an **'illness'** and pregnant women are viewed as patients. As Abbott and Wallace note, pregnant women are treated as potential problems, they are required to make regular ante-natal visits and are almost forced to have a hospital birth where mainly male doctors control the management of labour and childbirth.

- Doctors make the decision as to whether a woman can have an abortion. They may refuse abortion to young married women whilst single women and women from ethnic-minority groups may be positively encouraged to have abortions.

- Doctors control the new reproductive technologies which came about to help women to conceive and have children. Doctors decide which women should have access to technologies such as IVF and decisions are often motivated by doctor's definitions of morality, e.g. certain types of women, i.e. single or lesbian, may be refused such treatment.

- Post-natal depression, problematic menstruation and the menopause have been neglected by biomedicine. There has been very little medical research into these conditions. Feminists suggest that very few male doctors take these conditions and their effects on women seriously.

- The giving of tranquillisers to housewives with depression does nothing to address the real causes of the problem, e.g. the fact that the mother–housewife role is not valued by society. Similarly, feminists feel that doctors don't do enough to protect women from domestic violence, i.e. they merely treat the physical injuries but are reluctant to intervene by offering women support.

Post-modernist theory

OCR ▷ U2536

Post-modernists note that the biomedical model of health has dominance over all other theories of health such as complementary medicine. However, post-modernists argue that in a rapidly changing and fragmented world **no single approach to health and illness can be regarded as the 'truth'**. As Senior argues, all theories are simply ideas that compete to become recognised as the illusory truth.

Post-modernists claim that power can be acquired through language. **Foucault** argued that words and phrases can affect the way people think. This is the **power of discourse**. Medical discourse is dominated by doctors who are able to **medicalise** (apply medical language) to **human behaviour**. The power that arises from such discourse allows doctors to impose their views on others as unquestioningly correct. Foucault suggests that medical discourse is involved in the **social control of the body and sexuality**.

There is some evidence that medical discourses are underpinned by a language of morality. **Sontag (1991)** shows how AIDS was viewed as a social problem as well as an illness. People attached **social meaning** to AIDS so that it became more than an unfortunate disease. As a result, certain types of behaviour, e.g. homosexuality and prostitution, were morally condemned. For many years in the UK, AIDS was interpreted as a **'gay plague'** and the result of immoral practices which had allowed 'unclean' illness to invade the body. People with AIDS were perceived as **'guilty'** victims and consequently discourse about the illness was used to control and even punish homosexual behaviour. Sontag points out that the stigmatisation attached to AIDS may well have changed the ways in which people with AIDS viewed their bodies and self-identity.

Ideology of the body

Some sociologists have examined the **cultural meanings** placed upon the body especially in terms of desirable body size, weight and shape. **Kirk and Tinning (1994)** note that consumer societies treat the body as a **commodity**. **Senior (1999)** notes that this commercial idea of the body as a **'thing'** that can be thought about, presented and gazed at has implications for health and illness. For example, media definitions of what constitutes the **'desirable'** body may result in people believing they are healthy or ill. In Western societies, a **thin body shape offers high status** and is sought after. The pursuit of the perfect body through dieting may contribute to eating disorders such as **anorexia and bulimia** or result in the desire for cosmetic surgery. Increasingly medical science is reflecting dominant ideas about what counts as beauty by defining certain characteristics such as ageing, obesity and teenage acne as medical problems or illnesses that can be treated. **Nettleton (1995)** claims that this has led to a **body fascism** that is intolerant of those who fail to live up the body norm, e.g. those who are overweight or disabled.

Progress check

1 What does altruism mean?
2 Which sociological theory claims that doctors are altruistic?
3 How do Marxists view doctors?
4 Why does Friedson reject the view that doctors are altruistic?
5 How is pregnancy viewed by the biomedical model of health?
6 How might cultural ideas about the 'perfect body' negatively affect health?
7 How do post-modernists see the biomedical model of health?
8 How did the medicalisation of AIDS lead to the social control of homosexuality?

8 The disease was not treated solely as an unfortunate medical condition. Instead pronouncements were made that it was caused by immoral, i.e. promiscuous and 'unhealthy', types of behaviour.
7 As a powerful discourse that dominates thinking about health and socially controls behaviour by medicalising it.
6 Intensive dieting and anxiety may lead to problems such as anorexia and bulimia.
5 As an illness.
4 Because control over medicine is an occupational strategy aimed at ensuring high status and rewards.
3 As ideological agents of capitalism.
2 Functionalism.
1 Working primarily for the public good.

Sample question and model answer

An essay question – you should aim for at least two sides.

Outline and assess the view that health and illness are socially constructed and distributed. (60 marks)

Outlining what is meant by health and illness are socially constructed.

Many sociologists argue that definitions of health and illness are socially constructed because there is no universal agreement about what constitutes these conditions. Instead, what we can see is that different cultures and even different social groups within our own culture have different ideas about what constitutes 'good health' and sickness. In this sense, health and illness are relative concepts and consequently definitions are dependent upon what set of ideas dominate a particular historical period or culture. For example, mental illness has not always been seen as a medical condition. It has at various stages been seen as caused by possession by evil spirits and as lack of moral fibre. Today, definitions of health and illness are socially constructed by a biomedical élite, i.e. the medical profession. Gomm notes

Elaboration.

that this dominance has led to the increasing medicalisation of behaviour. He points out that alcoholism, obesity, learning difficulties, sexual problems and pregnancy have all come to be defined as medical problems in recent years. Moreover there is evidence that definitions of health and illness have been used in certain cultures to control both homosexuality and political dissent.

Outlining what is meant by health and illness are socially distributed.

If health and illness were chance occurrences we could expect to see them randomly distributed across the population. However, this is not the case – rather we see that some groups can expect an over-proportionate amount of illness. The working-class experience poorer mortality and morbidity rates than the middle classes. For example, more than 3500 extra working-class babies would survive per year if the working-class infant mortality rate was reduced to middle-class levels. The working class are also more likely to die pre-retirement of cancer, stroke and heart disease than the middle class. Statistics indicate that women suffer greater morbidity than men. For

Elaboration.

example, statistics for hospital admissions indicate that women experience more nervous breakdowns than men. Therefore we can see that illness is not the product of chance – it is socially produced in that your chances of being ill seem to depend upon your social class, gender, ethnic group and the region in which you live.

Explanations of why health and illness are unequally distributed.

Sociologists have attempted to explain these social variations in morbidity and mortality. Cultural deprivationists argue that working class people lead unhealthy lifestyles in terms of smoking and diet. They also suggest that lack of education may mean the working class are less likely to take advantage of NHS facilities – especially visiting the doctor and preventative medicine. However, this theory has been criticised for neglecting the economic circumstances of this group. For example, poverty may be the cause of poor diet rather than lack of education. Feminists suggest that the high levels of morbidity that women suffer may be the product of the mother-housewife role. Bernard's study concluded that married housebound women suffer more depression, etc. than married women or single women. However, the statistics may merely reflect women's biological condition, i.e. they visit the doctor more

Evaluation.

because of menstruation, contraception, pregnancy, menopause, etc. Gender-role socialisation may also be responsible for males consulting doctors less because it is culturally expected that men be more tolerant of pain than women. Finally, Busfield questions the statistics because she argues that men and women are labelled differently by doctors. For example, what passes as overwork in a man may be labelled as depression in a woman.

Sample question and model answer (continued)

Marxists such as Doyal and Pennell link ill health specifically to capitalism's pursuit of profit which they claim means that less attention is paid to the welfare of workers. For example, approximately 700 people are killed at work annually. Kinnersley estimates 10 million are injured. Industrial disease is also a major problem. Marxists also argue that ill health is brought about by the poverty created by low wages. Certainly the government-sponsored papers, The Black Report (1980) and The Health Divide (1992) noted a strong link between low wages, unemployment, poor housing, etc. and poor health. Critics note that communist societies actually experience worse health than the West and that capitalism has dramatically improved the life expectancy of all sections of society. In conclusion, this view helps illustrate the idea that health is socially defined and produced because we no longer die from the diseases of poverty that characterised the 19th century. Today we are more likely to die of diseases of affluence although some of us are more likely to die earlier than others.

Evaluation.

Practice examination question

Outline and assess the view that class inequalities in health and illness are the product of the social circumstances in which individuals live.   (60 marks)

Chapter 7

Social policy and welfare

The following topics are covered in this chapter:

- *Theories and ideologies of welfare*
- *Patterns of welfare provision*
- *Welfare, power and social control*

7.1 Theories and ideologies of welfare

After studying this section you should be able to:

LEARNING SUMMARY

- *clearly define key concepts in welfare*
- *outline and evaluate ideologies and theories of welfare*

Defining key concepts in welfare

OCR ▷ U2536

Marshall (1965) defines **social policy** as the action of governments that has a direct impact on the welfare of its citizens in the form of services or income. It generally includes national insurance, income support, health and welfare services, housing, education, and policing and punishing crime. Social policy tends to aim to reduce potential or actual social problems.

In social democracies such as the UK, the state is the guardian of the welfare of the community and is committed to the concept of **social citizenship**, i.e. the idea that equal welfare rights allow citizens to be healthy, secure and educated, and so enjoy equal opportunities with other citizens. This involves a certain amount of **collectivism** – that is, people contribute to the **public good of all** through mechanisms such as national insurance.

Individualism, which is the ideological opposite of collectivism, refers to the concept of individuals and families taking responsibility for their own lives and reducing their reliance on the state.

State welfare refers to policies specifically aimed at welfare. Most countries have developed some form of state welfare system, e.g. all Western states tend to provide support for the very poor although not all Western states have developed a Welfare State.

All industrialised societies have some sort of welfare system, either provided by the state or regulated by it. Sociologists tend to focus on two types of **welfare regime** in the UK, according to **Esping-Anderson**.

- **Liberal welfare regimes** are based on the idea that individuals should work hard and only use state welfare as a last resort. **Welfare is seen as the responsibility of the individual rather than the state**. As a result of this philosophy, benefits are deliberately kept low to discourage dependency on the state (**welfare dependency**). Those benefits that are available are **means-tested**, i.e. they are given only to those whose income falls below an officially defined level. The rest of the population is encouraged to buy into private welfare schemes such as pensions and health-care.

- **Social-democratic regimes** emphasise people's **right to welfare**. They are based on the idea that all citizens, regardless of income, should have access to state welfare provision and that a comprehensive range of services and benefits should be available to all. **Services and benefits are therefore universal – they are paid as of right** rather than means-tested. The social-democratic approach also aims to reduce inequalities caused by market forces and **regressive taxation** or indirect taxes (e.g. people, whether rich or poor, pay the same rate of VAT, therefore, this type of tax hits the poor harder). State welfare is funded by **'progressive taxation'** – which means that those with higher incomes pay more income tax.

Ideologies and theories of welfare

OCR ▸ U2536

There are essentially three political ideologies associated with the provision of welfare.

The New Right

The tabloid media subscribe to this perspective too.

This group of thinkers subscribe to the **market model** of welfare provision which basically argues that minimal state resources should be spent on welfare. What is spent should be targeted at the most needy who will be identified via means tests. Three related ideas underpin this ideology.

- It is believed that welfare encourages **dependency**. Minimal welfare will encourage people to stand on their own two feet and take responsibility for their situation.

> - There exists a culture of dependency in the UK because welfare benefits are too generous. It is suggested that these act as a **disincentive** to work and consequently a social grouping called an **'underclass'** has developed which socialises its children into anti-social values and behaviour. **Murray**, for example, is keen to stress that welfare payments have encouraged teenage pregnancy and the consequent crime and deviance that develops as single mothers fail to control their children. **Marsland** argues that a culture of dependency has eroded the capacity of the unemployed and single mothers to be self-reliant and independent.

KEY POINT

- **Marsland** believes that **universal benefits are too costly** and that consequently there is less capital to invest in the economy. Marsland claims the cost of the Welfare State is partly responsible for Britain's economic decline during the 1970s and 1980s. He subscribes to the view that **selective benefits** should replace universal benefits and the private sector should be encouraged to provide welfare services.

- The New Right stress the need to restore individual **freedom of choice** and to **minimise state intervention** both in the economy and in the lives of individuals. Free-market forces are seen to be more efficient for the economy than interventionist state policies. Such ideas were very popular with Mrs Thatcher's government in the 1980s and many of her social policies aimed to **privatise** state services or to introduce an element of free-market choice to areas such as education, health and social services.

The social-democratic view

Social democrats believe that government intervention in the economy is all important to make sure that inequalities between people do not become too great. They believe that the free market benefits the rich and harms the poor so there is a need for government regulation of the economy at the very least. Social democrats therefore believe that all citizens should have the right to vote, the right to justice under the law and the right to universal and comprehensive welfare benefits. This ideology, unlike the market model, does not make judgements about the 'deserving' and 'undeserving' poor. The Welfare State, then, should be the central defining institution of the modern state. One drawback of this model is the cost of a Welfare State – which is extremely high.

Social democrats like Jordan (1989) are Marsland's main critics. Jordan points out that universal benefits help maintain a reasonable standard of living for disadvantaged groups who under a more selective system may be forced to turn to crime or be trapped in a cycle of disadvantage. Other sociologists point out that if an underclass exists it is the product of structural constraints such as global recession over which they have no control. Therefore their unemployment may not be the result of choice as the New Right claim.

The 'third way'

Watch the media for new developments in welfare provision.

Traditionally Labour governments have tended to support a social-democratic ideology in regard to the Welfare State. However, the Labour party under Tony Blair has moved steadily away from collectivism towards individualism. In particular, Labour's **'welfare to work'** programme contains some elements of the market model of welfare. It requires people receiving benefit to accept a subsidised job, do voluntary work or take up full-time education or training. Labour claimed that the Welfare to Work policy would challenge 'the poverty of ambition and poverty of expectation' which suggests some adherence to ideas about an underclass or culture of dependence. However, Labour has made social-democratic noises about reducing the degree of child poverty in the UK. According to government figures, 750 000 children have so far been lifted out of poverty as a result of its reforms, although there is still a good way to go before it is eradicated. Labour has focused on using work as the lever to lift families with children out of poverty, rather than raise benefits. A range of measures, notably the working families tax credit, has been used to help parents into work and to make work pay for those already in low-income jobs. The setting up of the **social exclusion unit** suggests Labour is still committed to reducing inequality.

Progress check

1 Define social citizenship.

2 What is a liberal welfare regime?

3 What is a social-democratic system?

4 What is the market model of welfare?

5 What British Prime Minister was very influenced by the New Right market model?

6 What is Labour's welfare policy, known as 'the third way'?

6 Because it contains elements of both the social-democratic and market models.
5 Mrs Thatcher.
4 The belief that minimal state resources should be too much state spending can lead to welfare dependency.
3 States in which all citizens are entitled to welfare.
2 A state in which welfare is seen as the responsibility of the individual rather than the government.
1 The idea that equal welfare rights allow citizens to be healthy, etc. and to enjoy equal opportunities with other citizens.

7.2 Patterns of welfare provision

After studying this section you should be able to:

- *outline the development of state welfare in Britain*
- *identify and explain contemporary shifts in the pattern of welfare provision*
- *outline and assess patterns of welfare provision in housing, social security and personal services and their impact on social stratification*

The development of the Welfare State

OCR ➤ U2536

The Welfare State refers to the state taking responsibility for welfare provision. **G. Marshall (1999)** notes that the state offers services and benefits to meet people's basic needs for housing, health, education and income. The Welfare State has its origins in the Poor Law which provided relief for the poor, sick and elderly in the 17th century. During the 19th century, the state gradually more involved with the welfare of society through public health provision, e.g. sewers and clean water supplies and the 1870 Education Act. The Liberal Government of 1906–14 introduced free school meals, old age pensions for those aged 70, national insurance and limited unemployment benefits. However, the organisation of the present Welfare State and the principles underpinning it have their origin in the Labour Government of 1945 to 1951.

In 1942 the **Beveridge Report** was published with the aim of creating a modern Welfare State and defeating the **'five giant evils'** of:

- **want or poverty** through the introduction of a universal social security system embracing pensions, unemployment benefit, child benefit and sickness and disability benefits financed by national insurance – this would be supplemented with a selective means-tested benefit acting as a safety net for those who could not look after themselves, i.e. what is today known as income support
- **idleness** – the State intended to maintain full employment through intervention in the economy
- **ignorance** or lack of education was to be addressed mainly through the 1944 Education Act which introduced free secondary education for all
- **squalor** or poor housing was to be addressed through a programme of council house building
- **disease** or poor health would be addressed through the setting up of the National Health Service funded by the state.

The Welfare State, however, is not the sole provider of such services. It has always operated in the context of **welfare pluralism**. Private services exist in the fields of education, health and pensions. The voluntary sector, too, plays a major role in health and welfare, e.g. agencies such as Age Concern. Finally, the **informal sector**, i.e. family care, plays a central role especially in the care of the sick, disabled and elderly.

Welfare consensus

Between 1950 and 1979 there was a good deal of **consensus** in regard to how Labour and Conservative governments saw the Welfare State. Until the late 1960s both parties intervened in the economy to maintain full employment. There was some movement towards selective benefits in the 1970s as concerns grew about the costs of the Welfare State especially as unemployment rose. However, both parties were committed to the **social-democratic** view that Welfare State policies were the best way of meeting social needs.

The Conservative Government 1979–97

> Mrs Thatcher's government was influenced by a group of thinkers known collectively as the **'New Right'**. Generally the New Right stressed **free-market principles, self reliance and individual responsibility**. They argued that the rising costs of the Welfare State were interfering with economic growth. Moreover, the Welfare State had discouraged incentive and personal initiative by creating the conditions for welfare dependency. Mrs Thatcher consequently set about radically overhauling sections of the Welfare State in a number of ways.
>
> **KEY POINT**

- **Selectivity and means testing were increased**. This was aimed at ensuring that those receiving benefits really needed them. For example, discretionary grants for household items were replaced with loans from a social fund that had to be repaid.

- **Cuts were made in some benefits**. Housing benefit was significantly reduced after 1986. Income support for 16- and 17-year olds was abolished. The value of benefits did not generally keep up with inflation or average wage levels.

- **Privatisation of services was actively encouraged**. Private companies were encouraged to run old people's homes and local government services such as refuse collection. Council housing was sold off. Private schools and hospitals were encouraged to compete with the public sector. Incentives to opt into private welfare and health schemes were introduced.

- **Charges** were introduced especially within the NHS for services traditionally subsidised by the state.

- **The introduction of community care** led to the closing of institutions such as psychiatric and geriatric hospitals and day-care facilities for the severely disabled. Local authorities, families and voluntary organisations are now expected to take a greater responsibility in caring for these groups. Generally, then, welfare pluralism became more important as the state retreated from the provision of welfare services.

New Labour and welfare

New Labour came to office in 1997 and announced that in terms of spending and taxation, little would change. However, a number of policy changes relating to the Welfare State were announced as follows.

- **The Social Exclusion Unit** was set up. This is based on the idea that a number of social groups such as single mothers, the unemployed, the homeless and those living on deprived housing estates are **socially excluded from participating in society**. Its remit is to come up with solutions to integrate these groups back into society.

- **The 'New Deal'** is one such policy. This aims to reduce poverty and the cost of welfare by assisting the unemployed and single mothers to find employment. These **'welfare to work'** policies have included job advice interviews, help with child-care costs, encouragement to re-enter education or to embark upon re-training programmes and the introduction of a **national minimum wage**.

- **The Working Families Tax Credit** was introduced in 1998. This encourages return to work and employment because it supplements earned incomes.

- **Private stake-holder pensions** have been encouraged as a way of topping up the state pension. Pension credits will be given to family carers who have been unable to accrue pension rights through work.

Patterns of welfare provision

OCR   U2536

In the post-war period there was consensus between the two major political parties on welfare policies and provision relating to housing, social security and personal social services.

Housing

The 1950s saw a general agreement in society that everyone had a right to a home. Both Conservative and Labour governments therefore financed large council-house building programmes whilst encouraging private home-ownership through tax relief on mortgages. However, by the end of the 1960s, this traditional mix of public and private housing was failing to meet the demand for housing. The Conservative government abandoned the consensus because of its ideological belief in the free market and its view that the state interfered too much in the lives of its citizens. It consequently embarked upon a housing policy that strongly encouraged private builders and housing associations to build homes, whilst the Housing Act (1980) allowed council tenants to buy their council houses. This increased home ownership to over 70% of the population.

There has been a major decline in the number of council properties built and the overall stock of council houses available for rent since 1979. The better quality houses have largely been sold leaving a building stock still in local authority hands of poorer quality. In addition, local authorities have had less money to spend on upkeep and repairs because of cutbacks in central government grants. Little capital has been invested in building new properties by local authorities in recent years. The responsibility for most new public housing lies with the 2600 housing associations. These are voluntary agencies whose role is to provide low-rent accommodation. However, the government only funds 75% of the building programme. Housing associations have consequently had to charge high rents to make up the difference.

Think about sociological explanations of homelessness.

In terms of ethnic differences, Afro-Caribbeans and Asians experience very different housing patterns to each other and to whites. Blacks are much more likely to be living in council accommodation whilst Asians are more likely to own their home than any other group. However, Asians tend to buy older properties in inner-city areas which may lack basic amenities. For example, 7% of Asians are likely to be lacking or sharing basic amenities compared with 4% of whites. There is some evidence that Asians may be concentrated in inner-city areas because of discrimination by estate agents and building societies and the cultural importance of owning property in the same district as extended kin.

Social security

National insurance is the system that underpins social security in the UK. It involves people paying a contribution into a common fund along with their employer and the government. In the event of becoming unemployed, ill or retired, everyone has the right to claim for the appropriate benefits. Some of these benefits were universal (e.g. pensions) whilst some were means-tested (i.e. people were assessed on the basis of need). Between World War II and 1979 there were no major changes in the provision of social security, although the nature of society was beginning to change in profound ways. There was massive unemployment and an enormous growth in the number of one-parent families. It soon became apparent that the system was under great strain.

The Conservative Government of 1979 quickly concluded that the system was failing. In their view, it was excessively bureaucratic, wasteful and allegedly encouraging people not to work. There were also concerns that there would be an increase in pensioners in the future but a reduction in the number of tax-payers because the birth rate had fallen. This would make pensions impossible to finance. Child benefit was frozen in the 1980s in order to save money.

In 1988 the Conservatives simplified the system and introduced the notion of targeting particular groups. Income support was introduced for those with no work, with extra payments for lone parents, children and the disabled. However, the young and the voluntary unemployed were denied payments. The Social Fund loaned money for help with bills or necessities. Family Credit was paid to supplement low incomes for those workers with families. Despite these changes, a considerable number of people fail to take up their benefits due to lack of knowledge, the complexity of claiming, stigma and embarrassment.

In 1996, income support was replaced by Jobseekers Allowance which aims to make sure that the unemployed person is actively looking for work. The rigorous conditions involved in claiming are intended to discourage those who have no intention of working and those who are engaged in fraud. In 1996–97, 25,000 people lost their right to a state benefit because they failed to convince the authorities that they were looking for work.

Personal social services

These are services that are normally provided by local authorities or voluntary organisations which aim to take care of the needs of vulnerable groups such as children, the elderly, the physically disabled, people with mental-health problems and people with learning difficulties. Local-authority social services departments employing social workers have legal authority in the areas of disability, adoption, mental health, the rights of children, juvenile justice and carers. This means that social workers deal with a range of problems including sexual abuse of children, mental illness, parenting problems, family violence, physical handicap, etc.

The nature of social services has been particularly affected by the National Health and Community Care Act 1990 which changed the way that social services dealt with adults. The Act emphasises care in the community and distinguishes between purchasers of care and providers of care. Social services thus buy in services from nursing homes, etc.

See the section on community care in Chapter 6.

Community care ideally involves the person living at home, or in a hostel or sheltered accommodation rather than in a long-term institution. The individual is encouraged to take responsibility for themselves and there are, therefore, no staff living in – although the individual receives support from outside in the form of social work visits, day-care centres, etc.

There were three main reasons for the introduction of community care.

- First, the cost of residential accommodation was prohibitively expensive for the government.
- Second, the numbers of elderly and severely disabled have risen.
- Third, the ideological beliefs of the Conservative government stressed self-reliance and family support. It was believed that the family rather than the state should take responsibility for them.

Community care has experienced problems, especially in terms of its complexity and expense. There has been a gap between the ideology and the reality. It has turned out to be more expensive than running residential institutions. Provision has also been unequal in standard across the country and co-ordination of services even within specific districts has proved very difficult. It is also evident that 'community' does not exist in some areas – which has intensified pressures on families, and particularly women, who make up the bulk of carers. Lack of community has been particularly illustrated by the degree of resistance in some areas to community-care initiatives to do with the mentally ill. People have not been keen to have such groups live amongst them. Such fears have not been helped by a few cases of crime committed by people in community care and the resulting hysterical media coverage.

Progress check

1 Identify Beveridge's five giant evils.

2 What is the difference between universal and selective systems of benefits?

3 What is welfare pluralism?

4 What is the social exclusion unit?

5 What happened to public housing stock in the 1980s?

6 In which part of the welfare system are people most likely to come into contact with means tests?

7 What was the main motive behind community care?

7 To cut costs because institutionalisation was very expensive.
6 The social security system.
5 The Conservative government encouraged local authorities to sell council houses.
4 A Labour think-tank that aims to come up with social policy solutions which will integrate the socially excluded, i.e. encouraging the long-term unemployed and single mothers back into work.
3 The state sector, the voluntary sector, the informal sector and private sector combine to provide welfare services.
2 Universal are paid to all, e.g. child benefit is paid to all with children. Selective benefits are means-tested and paid to the most needy.
1 Want, squalor, ignorance, idleness and disease.

7.3 Welfare, power and social control

After studying this section you should be able to:

- outline the role of welfare as an agent of social control
- describe the relationship between total institutions and personal identity

LEARNING SUMMARY

Marxism, the Welfare State and social control

OCR   U2536

Marxists argue that the **Welfare State has functioned to benefit the capitalist class** in four main ways.

> You can link this to stratisfication. See Chapter 9.

KEY POINT

- The Welfare State is an **ideological state apparatus** which aims to convince the working class that they have an 'equal' stake in society. **Ginsberg (1979)** calls the improved standard of living that the working class have enjoyed during the last 30 years and their free access to health and education the **'welfare bribe'**, because there is no evidence that equality between the social classes is occurring. In fact, the evidence suggests that the gap is widening between the rich and poor.

Le Grand (1982) notes that the Welfare State has failed to tackle basic problems such as homelessness and poverty. He argues that the most wealthy have benefited from a **'hidden' welfare state** in terms of educational success, state subsidies on mortgages and housing and improved health and longer life expectancy.

KEY POINT

The Welfare State functions therefore to ensure that the working class do not challenge the fundamental inequalities in wealth and power that characterise capitalism. It plays a crucial role both in ensuring 'false class-consciousness' among the working class and reproducing class inequalities.

- Welfare rules have been designed to **reinforce labour discipline**, e.g. the unemployed have to prove that they are actively seeking work. They face the risk of losing benefits if they turn down training opportunities.
- The Welfare State creates an educated, healthy workforce and creates the conditions through the NHS and child benefit for the next generation of workers to be reproduced.
- Welfare professionals such as doctors, social security officers and social workers 'manage' the resentment of the exploited proletariat. Those alienated by capitalism benefit from welfare policy and this prevents them from becoming a discontented, revolutionary working-class.

Feminism, the Welfare State and social control

OCR   U2536

Feminists argue that the Welfare State functions to **maintain and reproduce patriarchy and especially the patriarchal family**. Welfare tends to be aimed at families but it is mainly within families that women are exploited and oppressed. Therefore welfare tends to **institutionalise gender inequalities** by assuming that women are economically dependent upon men and that women's main role is in the home as a mother and housewife. Welfare policy, by focusing on family needs, renders the needs of women invisible.

Feminists argue that the patriarchal nature of the Welfare State is dated in the current context of most women being in paid employment. Moreover, the number of women living alone has increased, as has the number of women choosing childlessness. The number of lone mothers who go out to work and rely on informal extended family networks to look after children has increased, too. Feminists argue that the Welfare State needs to be modernised in order to keep up with these developments.

Ethnicity, the Welfare State and social control

OCR ▶ U2536

Ethnic-minority groups who claim benefit are subject to a social control not experienced by the white majority. When ethnic-minority members claim benefits, checks are often made on their length of residence and their passports to ensure that they are legitimate claimants. It can be argued that this is a form of institutional racism.

Ahmad and Atkin (1996) are very critical of community-care policies because they do not recognise nor respond to the needs of people from ethnic minorities. They claim that **the dietary, linguistic and caring needs** of minority ethnic communities are often neglected because services are organised according to white norms. Second, ethnic-minority communities are often **stereotyped** as being to blame for their own problems because of their allegedly deviant lifestyles. Third, health and social service professionals often list black people as 'high risk' clients, 'unco-operative', 'difficult to work with' and as time-wasters. These attitudes suggest that **institutional racism** may be embedded in the procedures of community-care organisations. This obviously contributes to the low socio-economic position of ethnic minorities in British society.

Age, the Welfare State and social control

OCR ▶ U2536

Outram notes that the Welfare State creates dependency for young people and this is often experienced by them as regulation and control of their lives. For example, unemployed young adults are expected to enter training schemes. Changes to the rules regarding income support mean that young people are dependent upon their parents for a greater length of time.

A number of trends can be perceived which indicate that politicians are increasingly redefining the role of the Welfare State as far as the elderly are concerned.

- There has been **a move towards encouraging the private sector** to take over some of the functions of the Welfare State. For example, there has been an expansion in the number of private 'rest' homes for the elderly whilst both Conservative and Labour politicians have encouraged younger people to take out private pension and health plans. There has been concern expressed by some pressure groups for the old that the state is intending to withdraw entirely from the provision of pensions.

- Some old people have been 'forced' to give up their savings or sell their homes by local authorities in order to pay for their long-term residential care.

- There have been **cuts in services for old people especially in social services and the NHS**. In extreme cases, this has involved NHS trusts publicly stating that operations for the elderly are low on their list of priorities or refusing to admit the elderly to long-term care because they 'block' beds.

- In recent years, the state has emphasised the need for an expansion in **'community care'** for the elderly. This implies that the state intends to withdraw as much as possible from the care of the elderly and to encourage the family, especially children, to play a greater role in the care of their aged parents.

Institutionalisation

OCR ▶ U2536

In the 1960s **Goffman** was critical of the role of welfare agencies that commit people into care because his research identified a number of problems associated with **institutionalisation**. For example, social workers can commit people into psychiatric care and take children into protective care. Goffman referred to these hospitals and homes as **total institutions** – places where people exist cut off from wider society and in which people's lives and behaviour are controlled and regulated.

Goffman's observation of patients in a mental hospital suggested that such institutions attempt to make patients conform to institutional labels by stripping them of their old identities. Goffman calls this process **'mortification of self'**. Institutional life involves learning to conform to a new role as defined by the care workers.

The film *'One Flew Over the Cuckoo's Nest'* contains some excellent examples of these responses.

Goffman's observations noted that the patients responded in a variety of ways to institutional regulation. Some withdrew, i.e. they became introverted. Some rebelled but were subjected to harsher treatment for their trouble. Some patients co-operated with staff. Others became dependent upon their labels. These are institutionalised. Others 'played it cool' and attempted to avoid trouble.

Goffman's case-study was a useful insight into the relationship between identity and institutionalisation despite being too small to generalise from. His work was influential in the policy decision to close down many mental-health institutions in the USA and UK from the 1970s on. However, his research has been criticised by both Marxists and feminists for not examining the reasons why people had been committed in the first place. Marxists point out that poverty means that higher numbers of working-class people are treated for poor mental health, while feminists suggest that women rather than men are likely to be diagnosed as mentally ill because patriarchal ideology sees women as more unstable than men.

Progress check

1 What is the hidden Welfare State?
2 What is the welfare bribe?
3 What does the Welfare State maintain, according to feminists?
4 How does the informal caring role of women benefit the Welfare State?
5 Why are Ahmad and Atkin critical of the Welfare State?
6 How are the young treated by the Welfare State, according to Outram?

6 Changes to the Welfare State, e.g. in income support, have increased their dependency upon their families.
5 Because it does not meet the needs of ethnic minorities.
4 Women have taken on most of the burden of community care and consequently the Welfare State costs less than it should.
3 Patriarchy.
2 The ideology that the Welfare State primarily benefits working-class people. In reality, it does not.
1 The benefits the middle classes have taken from free education and the NHS.

Sample question and model answer

An essay question – you should aim for at least two sides.

Introduction sets the context and identifies who the Welfare State is allegedly failing.

Historical context of Welfare State outlined.

Identifies who subscribes to view contained in title, i.e. Marxists.

Elaboration and illustration of view.

Outline and assess the view that the Welfare State has only benefited the well-off and has failed to meet the needs of those that need it most.　　(60 marks)

There is no doubt that the central principles and goals on which the Welfare State was founded after the Second World War have undergone profound change. This is especially true since 1979 marked the end of a consensus between the two main political parties about how the Welfare State should be managed. However, the view that the Welfare State mainly benefits the middle class at the expense of the working class and consequently fails to meet the needs of the most vulnerable, (i.e. children, the elderly, the disabled, single-parent families, etc.) had emerged before the end of that post-war consensus.

The modern Welfare State aimed to defeat 'five giant evils', poverty, idleness, squalor, disease and ignorance. Consequently, a universal social-security system was established supplemented by a safety net of means-tested benefits aiming to tackle poverty. Management of the economy was intended to maintain full employment and prevent idleness. State housing would tackle squalor. The National Health Service and the tripartite system (lately the comprehensive system) would tackle disease and ignorance respectively.

Despite the focus within the Welfare State on assisting the poorest groups, Marxists have argued that it has done very little to challenge the gap between rich and poor. In fact, there is evidence that the gap is increasing in terms of income and wealthy, and especially health. Le Grande, for example, suggests that the most wealthy have actually benefited from a hidden Welfare State in terms of their children's educational success in comprehensive schools and higher education, state subsidies on mortgages and improved health and life expectancy due to their greater take-up of NHS services especially in preventative health-care. Moreover, those most in need have found that changes in the organisation of the Welfare State have actually resulted in a less efficient and effective set of services. This can be illustrated in a number of ways.

First, in regard to social security, the Thatcher reorganisation meant that selectivity and means testing were increased and cuts were made in some benefits. Income support for 16- and 17-year-olds was abolished. People were encouraged to take out private pensions. These changes were made partly because the Conservatives believed that a welfare culture had developed and people did not want to work. Benefits were therefore stopped for those who did not attend interviews or who refused training programmes. In 1996–97 25 000 people lost their right to state benefits because they failed to convince the authorities that they were looking for work.

Second, the NHS community-care policy in relation to the mentally ill, disabled and the elderly resulted in private residential homes, hostels and families and especially women taking over many of the responsibilities of the state in terms of long-term care. There is evidence that this was a response to the escalating costs of state care rather than motivated by a medical rationale. Community-care programmes have experienced great problems. Provision has been unequal across the country and co-ordination of services has proved very difficult. Generally, then, it can be argued that community care has failed to benefit its clients, i.e. those that need the support of the Welfare State most.

Sample question and model answer *(continued)*

Third, in the 1980s the Conservative government gave council tenants the right to buy their council houses and increased the power of private landlords over tenants. It is argued that the present problem of homelessness is a direct result of the shortage of public-sector housing caused by these sales.

Fourth, the Welfare State also underwent a partial privatisation at the hands of the Conservatives. Private companies were encouraged to run residential homes for the elderly. People were encouraged by tax schemes to buy into private pensions and health schemes. Charges were introduced into the NHS, whilst fees for prescriptions, dental work and eye tests went up.

It is argued that all these changes to welfare systems had the most negative effect on those that need the Welfare State the most, i.e. the elderly, disabled and single-parent families. Moreover, these groups lack the resources to opt into private care.

Contemporary trends.

There are signs that the Labour Government, whilst not reversing Conservative reforms, are attempting to ensure that the Welfare State provides for the most vulnerable or 'socially excluded'. In 1997 it set up the social exclusion unit whose function is to look at how poorer sections of the community can be reintegrated back into the community. This is a fairly urgent task considering that even government figures are suggesting that there has been a major rise in child poverty. However, it is interesting to see that Labour policy towards some of the more vulnerable groups is double-edged. For example, welfare-to-work policies are aimed at assisting the long-term unemployed and single parents to raise their living standards by helping them back into work. However, such programmes are also aimed at undermining the culture of welfare dependency which it is argued afflicts some sections of the poor.

This essay would benefit from more assessment – it is a little unbalanced..

Practice examination question

Outline and assess the view that the break-up of the post-war consensus about the running of the Welfare State has brought to an end the universal provision of welfare services and benefits.

(60 marks)

Chapter 8

Crime and deviance (AQA synoptic)

The following topics are covered in this chapter:

- *The social nature of crime and deviance*
- *Patterns of crime and victimisation*
- *Theories of crime and deviance*
- *Deviance, power and social control*
- *Suicide*

8.1 The social nature of crime and deviance

After studying this section you should be able to:

LEARNING SUMMARY

- *distinguish between crime and deviance*
- *illustrate how definitions of crime and deviance are socially constructed*

Defining crime and deviance

| AQA | U6 |
| OCR | U2536 |

Remember this is an AQA **SYNOPTIC** unit.

Deviance is **norm-breaking behaviour**. It is generally non-conformist and usually attracts moral disapproval from members of society. However, deviant activity is not necessarily illegal, e.g. breaking wind in public is regarded by many as deviant but it is not against the law! Such behaviour is controlled by the use of informal sanctions through social groups such as family, friends and peers. These can be positive, i.e. we may be rewarded for conformist behaviour, and negative, i.e. we may be punished in a variety of ways for actions which are defined as deviant. For example, in the family positive sanctions may take the form of praise, love and material rewards whilst negative sanctions may include smacking, scolding, threats to withdraw love and when older, grounding and disowning.

Crime is **deviant behaviour which is against the criminal law**. Such behaviour is controlled through the use of public sanctions which are enforced by agencies of social control such as the police, magistrates and the judiciary.

The social construction of crime

> Despite the legal definition of crime, defining crime is not a straightforward task because there is no universal agreement in society as to what is criminal. Sociologists argue that crime is socially constructed – definitions of crime often depend on how society interprets particular actions.
>
> **KEY POINT**

Croall (1998) points out that there is often a very narrow borderline between what is regarded as 'criminal' and 'normal, legal or illegal', e.g. many people 'borrow' items from work and frequently break the speed limit but would not define themselves as criminal. 'Real' crimes are seen by the general public as those that are morally wrong such as murder or serious assault. Defining crime is complicated by the fact that **there is rarely universal agreement about what is criminal**, e.g. one person's terrorist may be another person's freedom fighter. In this sense, definitions of crime are **relative** and may reflect:

- the **historical period**, e.g. abortion, homosexuality and blasphemy have all been defined as crimes in the past in the UK

127

- the **culture**, e.g. selling marijuana in Holland is legal but illegal in the UK
- particular **social situations** or a place, e.g. nudity in your bathroom is acceptable but not in the street or on football pitches
- the **interpretations of those who enforce the law**, e.g. the police have the right to use 'reasonable force' and in some cases, this has been known to mean 'justifiable homicide'
- the **interests of powerful groups**, e.g. the failure to see business crime as 'real' crime may reflect the ability of business groups to influence the law and its interpretation
- the **powerlessness of groups** such as the working class, young people, women and ethnic-minority groups – e.g. the existence of a number of laws controlling young people, the neglect of domestic violence and racially motivated crimes may reflect the lack of influence these groups have.

Progress check

1 Define crime.
2 Define deviance.
3 What is a 'sanction'?
4 Give an example of a formal sanction.
5 Give an example of an agency of social control.

5 The police, judicial system, prisons, etc.
4 A prison sentence, fine, etc.
3 A means of reward or punishment for acceptable/unacceptable behaviour.
2 Behaviour that challenges widely accepted norms and values.
1 Deviance that breaks the law.

8.2 Patterns of crime and victimisation

After studying this section you should be able to:

- *outline the social distribution of crime by age, social class, ethnicity, gender and locality*
- *assess the reliability and validity of the secondary data used to socially construct the official picture of crime and criminals*
- *compare and contrast official criminal statistics with the findings of victim studies*

LEARNING SUMMARY

Measuring crime

AQA   U6
OCR   U2536

> A popular area with examiners.

Official Criminal Statistics (OCS)

The OCS are collected by the police and the courts and collated and published by the Home Office. They are used to establish trends and patterns in criminal activity, especially in regard to the volume of crime and the social characteristics of criminality.

The volume of crime

Between 1971 and 1993 there was a dramatic rise in the volume of recorded crime in the UK. All major categories of crime experienced substantial increases, e.g. violent crime increased fourfold in this period, although the proportion of crimes that were recorded as violent never exceeded 12% of all crime. Most crime was, and indeed still remains, property crime.

Since 1993, the crime rate has significantly fallen, despite the fact that the general public, encouraged by the media, believe it to be rising. Recorded crime in England and Wales continued to fall in the 12 months to September 2000 although there was an 8% rise in violent crime – which now makes up 13% of all crime. In particular, street muggings (robbery) rose by 21% and violence against the person rose by 7%.

The social distribution of crime by age

> Who commits crime?

The peak age for known offenders for both males and females was 14 in 1958 and 18 in 1997. The official statistics show that juvenile crime has declined in recent years after having reached a peak in 1984–85. In 1958, 56% of all offenders found guilty were aged 20 years or under compared with 38% in 1997. However, the OCS do indicate that burglary, robbery, violence and criminal damage are likely to be juvenile rather than adult offences.

The social distribution of crime by social class

Examination of the employment status of convicted offenders suggests that over 80% are from the manual classes. Hagell and Newburn's study of persistent young offenders found that only 8% came from middle-class backgrounds. Offences are also distinguishable by social class. Middle-class offenders tend to be associated with white-collar crime, fraud and tax evasion, whilst working-class offenders are mainly found guilty of burglary and street crime.

The social distribution of crime by ethnicity

The statistics show an over-representation of ethnic-minority men and women, and particularly Afro-Caribbeans, in prison. One-tenth of male prisoners and one-fifth of female prisoners are Afro-Caribbean yet this ethnic-minority group only makes up 2.3% of the population. Smith (1997) notes that black youth are more likely to be cautioned than any other ethnic-minority group.

The social distribution of crime by gender

The number of female offenders has risen faster than the number of male offenders since 1958 but approximately 85%–90% of offenders found guilty or cautioned are male. Male crime generally outnumbers female crime by a ratio of 5 to 1. Men and women are generally convicted for different types of offences, e.g. men dominate all offences and when females are convicted it is likely to be for theft (shoplifting).

The social distribution of crime by region

Urban areas, especially inner-city council estates, have higher rates of crime than the suburbs or rural areas. Official surveys on crime risks indicate that members of young households living in inner cities, e.g. students, are ten times more likely to be burgled than older people living in rural areas.

The official criminal statistics, reliability and validity

Sociologists point out that the official statistics do not comprise the total volume of crime. There is **a 'dark figure' of unrecorded crime**, a phenomenon which is now more widely acknowledged. **Andy Pilkington (1995)** notes the following.

- The official statistics do not comprise a complete record of criminal offences known to the authorities, for example, they don't cover 'summary offences' (i.e. those tried in Magistrates as opposed to Crown Courts) and offences dealt with by the Inland Revenue and Customs and Excise.

- The number of recorded offences depends on **official counting procedures** – which frequently changes.

> Always illustrate with an example if possible.

KEY POINT

- Over 80% of all recorded crimes result from reports by the public but **crime may not be reported** to the police because:
  - people may not be aware a crime has taken place (e.g. fraud)
  - the victim may be relatively powerless (e.g. child abuse)
  - the offence may seem too trivial (e.g. vandalism)
  - the victim may feel that the offence won't be taken seriously or may fear embarrassment or humiliation at the hands of the police and/or courts (e.g. rape)
  - the victim or community may distrust the police (e.g. ethnic-minority-communities may feel the police do not take racial attacks seriously as shown by the Stephen Lawrence case).

- Around 40% of crimes reported to the police are not recorded by them and therefore do not end up in the official statistics.

KEY POINT

Barclay (1995) argues that the net sum of all these processes is that only 2% of offences committed lead to a conviction in the criminal courts.

The Home Office interpretation of the OCS

Home Office research suggests that the rise in crime is an **artificial** phenomenon – a rise in reporting rather than a real increase because of the following.

- Living standards have risen rapidly since the 1950s and modern society is more materialistic. This has resulted in more consumer items (e.g. cars, videos, etc.) to steal and a greater public intolerance of property crime. People are therefore more likely to report it. The popularity of insurance has given people more incentive to report theft whilst increased ownership of mobile phones may have made it easier to report crime.

- Public attitudes towards violence have changed, e.g. the greater stress on women's rights has produced a less tolerant attitude towards domestic violence.

- Changes in legislation and police practice may result in more crimes being reported.

- The OCS on soft drug use, prostitution and homosexual importuning cannot be regarded as reliable because some forces elect to crackdown on these offences regularly whilst others may ignore or neglect them.

- The increase in the number of police officers (15 000 extra since 1979) and the use of modern technology (especially computers and surveillance cameras in city centres and football stadiums) has led to more efficient monitoring and recording of crime.

Progress check

1   What agency is responsible for the collection of official statistics on crime?
2   What percentage of all crime was violent crime in 2000?
3   What is the peak age for committing a criminal act?
4   What is the 'dark figure of crime'?
5   What is the ratio of male crime to female crime?
6   Why is Home Office research sceptical that there has been a rise in crime?

6   They suggest it is a rise in reporting rather than actual crime.
5   5 to 1.
4   Unreported and unrecorded crime.
3   18 years.
2   13%.
1   The Home Office.

The interpretivist critique of the OCS

AQA   U6
OCR   U2536

Holdaway (1988) notes that official statistics of crime are not facts about crime. They are socially constructed, i.e. the end product of a complex series of decisions and interactions.

Policing

Interpretivist sociologists argue that the OCS are the result of **selective policing** – criminal statistics originate in interaction between police officers and suspects. However, social groups may receive differential treatment from the police. A police officer has the power to choose to ignore an incident, to give a warning or to arrest. The police response may depend upon the social characteristics of the suspect.

Policing and class

Interpretivists argue that the high proportion of working-class offenders in the OCS is the result of the police using indicators such as dress, speech and deference when deciding to stop people or make an arrest. Young working-class people are consequently stereotyped negatively by the police and are stopped more frequently.

Policing and gender

Other studies of policing indicate that police stereotyping may partly account for the low representation of females in the OCS. Smith and Gray's study of the London Metropolitan police suggests that male officers tend to adopt paternalistic attitudes towards female offenders who are less likely to be stopped, arrested and charged. In other words, females are less likely to be stereotyped as 'suspicious' or criminal.

Policing and race

Humphrey argues that the police stop and search black people indiscriminately for drug offences, carrying offensive weapons, etc. in a way that they will never in normal policing run the risk of doing in the white community. **Smith and Gray** confirm this picture and report that, on average, six out of ten young blacks are stopped five times a year.

> Studies therefore of race and policing indicate that the OCS may tell us more about police attitudes towards black people, i.e. institutional racism, than they do about black criminality. As Phillips argues, the OCS prove little 'except a tendency to arrest blacks'.

KEY POINT

The role of the courts in the social construction of the OCS

Research into the social background of magistrates and judges has raised the question of whether there is class, gender and racial bias in the system. **Hood** has shown that almost 80% of magistrates are from the professional classes I and II. There is an almost complete absence of unskilled working-class people on the magistrate's bench and marked under-representation of black and Asian magistrates. **Griffiths'** research indicates that the vast majority of judges are from social classes I and II and up to 70% of them attended the top public schools and Oxbridge. Furthermore, judges are, with only a few exceptions, male and white and rather old.

Hood's study of 3300 cases heard in the West Midlands Crown Courts in 1989 suggests that **black males have a 17% greater chance of receiving a custodial sentence than whites for the same offence.**

Judicial attitudes may be gender-biased too. Worrall notes that women who conform to a feminine stereotype are more likely to be treated leniently by the courts whereas women who confidently argue their case or who are interpreted as 'unfeminine' by judges may receive more severe sentences.

The Radical critique of the OCS

According to traditional **Marxists**, working-class crime may dominate the official statistics but it is a minor problem when compared with crimes committed by the powerful such as white-collar crime, corporate crime and state crime. These do not generally appear in the official statistics because:

- they are not defined as 'serious crimes'
- if they are defined as crimes, they tend to be unreported, undetected and are not pursued as relentlessly as working-class crime by the police
- if they are detected, they are 'under-punished'.

Stephen Box argued that the law and the OCS are used to criminalise the activities of the powerless and give society the impression that the 'problem population' is the working-class and ethnic-minority groups. However, the OCS render the crimes of the powerful invisible. From Box's perspective, the OCS are **ideological** – they support the interests of the powerful and justify the continuation of class inequality. They tell us very little about the real level of crime in society and do little to help us understand criminality.

The Left Realist view

The Left Realists Young and Lea agree that the OCS may be unreliable because of the over-policing of certain social groups and the neglect of white-collar crime. However, using data from victim surveys of inner-city areas they conclude that interpretivists are wrong to suggest that the OCS are mainly a product of police and judicial processes. They suggest that crime is mainly committed by working-class and black people and it causes real fear and pain for working-class and black people living in inner-city areas who are its main victims. They therefore conclude that the OCS are a useful tool used alongside victim surveys and self reports for uncovering the reality of crime.

Progress check

1 Define what is meant by the idea that crime statistics are socially constructed.
2 What do sociological studies conclude about the large number of Afro-Caribbeans in the OCS?
3 What did Hood's study of West Midlands Crown Courts conclude?
4 Why are Marxists critical of the OCS?
5 What do Left Realists conclude about the OCS?

5 They probably are valid in that most street crime is committed by the working class and ethnic minorities in inner-city areas.
4 Because the statistics give the misleading impression that groups like the working class and ethnic minorities are the crime problem and they ignore middle-class crime.
3 Afro-Caribbeans were more likely to be imprisoned for offences than whites for the same offence.
2 They may be there because of institutional racism rather than because they are more prone to crime.
1 They are the end result of a complex set of interactions between police officers and suspects, and decisions taken by officers based on stereotypes.

Victim studies

AQA   U6
OCR   U2537

A common mistake in exams is to mix up the BCS with the OCS.

Victim surveys are an attempt to give a better understanding of the reality of crime than is provided by the official criminal statistics. The **British Crime Survey (BCS)** started in 1983 and is now conducted annually by a team of researchers in the Home Office.

The 1998 BCS was based on approximately 15 000 households, selected from all over the country and designed to be as representative a sample as possible. The survey discovered that:

- only one in four crimes are reported to the police, although the survey excludes a large number of crimes such as victimless crimes (e.g. drug use and prostitution), white-collar crime, tax evasion, benefit fraud, etc.

- theft of motor vehicles is most likely to be reported (98%), but the vast majority of other crimes have a reporting rate of less than 50%. Vandalism is the most under-reported crime

- the evidence does not back up anxiety about violence. It is clear that men and women are more likely to be the victims of different sorts of violent crime and that those who fear violent crime the most (the elderly, women) are least likely to be victims of it – conversely those who have least fear of crime (young men) are most likely to be victims

- the most common reason for not reporting crime is that it is 'too trivial', followed by the feeling that the police could do nothing about it anyway

- the survey estimates that only 54% of reported crime is actually recorded by the police, so its estimates of crimes committed – some 16.5 million – are much higher than police figures suggest

- however, the survey agrees with the OCS in that most crimes are property crimes.

The BCS tend to suggest that **fear of serious crime is out of proportion to its reality** and is exaggerated by the media. Past surveys have estimated that the average person is likely to be burgled once every 40 years, assaulted once every 100 years, robbed once every 500 years, and have their car stolen once every 60 years.

Criticising the BCS

The findings of the BCS have been challenged by Jock Young's **Islington Crime Surveys** (ICS). Young argues that the BCS neglects the way that crime is finely concentrated in the inner city. According to Young, the inner-city dweller is not an average person and subscribes to realistic fears about crime. Young criticises the methodology of the BCS and suggests that the questionnaire survey is not the most reliable tool for uncovering victims of crime. The ICS surveyed 2000 people in the London borough of Islington using sympathetic interviewers. In particular, they took great care to use female interviewers to uncover details of sexual assault and domestic violence.

The ICS found that a third of all households had been affected by serious crime in the previous year. A quarter of all people always avoided going out after dark and 28% felt unsafe in their own homes. Over 50% of women never or seldom went out after dark because of fear of crime. Young concludes that **the BCS underestimates people's fears of crime.**

Progress check

1 What are victim studies?

2 In what way does the British Crime Survey support the idea that there is a dark figure of crime?

3 Who are the main victims of crime according to the BCS?

4 Why is Young critical of the BCS methodology?

5 In what way does the Islington survey contradict the BCS in regard to likely victims of crime?

1 Questionnaire surveys which aim to uncover from victims themselves the extent and nature of crime in the UK.
2 Only one in four crimes is reported to the police.
3 Young men.
4 Its method, i.e. surveys, are not reliable in getting victims to report sensitive violent crimes.
5 It concludes that in the inner city, females and the elderly are more likely than young men to be the victims of crime.

8.3 Theories of crime and deviance

After studying this section you should be able to:

- *compare and contrast theories of crime that blame the culture of the deviant with theories that blame society*
- *outline and evaluate explanations of white-collar and corporate crime*
- *explain why crime is mainly a male phenomenon*
- *describe and assess explanations for crime committed by ethnic minorities*

LEARNING SUMMARY

Theories that blame the culture of the individual

| AQA | U6 |
| OCR | U2536 |

Until the late 1960s theories of deviance tended to blame the deviant or deviant's home background and culture. Such theories saw definitions of deviance as fixed and universal. Usually these theories accepted the picture of crime portrayed by the official statistics, i.e. as a working-class problem.

Inadequate socialisation

D.J. West was typical of this approach. He argued that working-class criminality was due to **inadequate socialisation or poor parenting**. In his study of 411 working-class boys monitored from age 8–19, one-fifth became delinquent – these mainly came from broken homes (one-parent families) or from families in which fathers were unemployed or on low incomes.

Underclass theory

Individualistic approaches re-appeared in the 1990s. The New Right commentator **Charles Murray (1990)** suggests that both in the USA and UK there exists an '**underclass**' a distinct lower-class grouping that subscribes to 'deviant' rather than mainstream values which it transmits to its children.

Critics of Murray argue that he is scapegoating the poor for the effects of structural constraints such as economic recession which are well beyond their control. Murray's theory is accused of negatively labelling a section of the poor for their poverty, which results in their over-policing. There is no **empirical evidence** for the existence of a underclass that subscribes to fundamentally different values.

Theories that blame society

| AQA | U6 |
| OCR | U2536 |

The **functionalist**, Robert Merton, argued that society encourages its members to subscribe to the **goal of material success** through education and the mass media. However, **society is unable to provide the legitimate means for everyone to achieve** that success because not everyone can gain qualifications and not everyone can get access to jobs. Working-class people are more likely than any other group to be denied these means. Their **opportunities are blocked**. Most people cope by conforming; others may turn to illegitimate means such as crime (innovation), rebellion or retreat from society, e.g. commit suicide, turn to drugs, drop out, etc.

However, in criticism of Merton, it is not clear that all members of society share the goal of material success. He fails to account for **white-collar crime** which is usually committed by those who have achieved material success, nor does he account for violent crime or crime committed in groups such as juvenile delinquency.

American subcultural theory

Albert Cohen adapts Merton's theory to explain the **collectivist** or gang crime committed by juvenile delinquents. He argues that working-class boys commit juvenile delinquency for two reasons.

- Their parents fail to equip them with the right skills required for success in education.
- Society encourages its members to acquire status through educational success, jobs and materialism. However, due to working-class boys' lack of skills, schools and teachers deny **status**.

In frustration, working-class boys form **anti-school subcultures (counter-cultures)** which turn the value system of the school upside down and award status for deviant activities. Cohen therefore blames a combination of inadequate socialisation and society's stress on acquiring status. However, some sociologists have questioned the view that working-class boys are interested in acquiring status from teachers. **Willis**, for example, argues that the lads in his study who rejected school wanted factory jobs and therefore did not see the point of qualifications.

Traditional Marxism

David Gordon argues that crime is an **inevitable product of capitalism** and the **inequality** that it generates. He argues that inequalities in wealth and income create poverty and homelessness for the working class and crime is a **rational** response to these problems. This idea is supported by research which shows property crime rising during recession. Gordon suggests capitalism encourages values such as greed and materialism which are conducive to all classes committing crime. Such values promote non-economic crimes such as violence, rape, child abuse, vandalism and hooliganism because **inequalities in wealth and power** lead to frustration, hostility, envy and alienation for some members of the working class who may commit crime in an attempt **to retrieve power and status**. This theory argues that it is surprising that there is not *more* working-class crime.

White-collar crime

Be able to describe and explain this type of crime in detail.

Marxists argue that **white-collar crime and corporate crime** are neglected by society because they are both likely to be carried out by the capitalist class or its agents.

Croall argues that a number of factors combine to reduce the extent and seriousness of white-collar and corporate crime (e.g. fraud, tax evasion, breaking of health and safety rules, insider dealing, etc.) in the eyes of the general public.

- Such crimes are often **invisible** (there is no 'blood on the streets).
- They are **complex** (usually they involve the abuse of technical, financial and scientific knowledge).
- Victimisation tends to be **indirect** (offenders and victims rarely come face to face). Consequently we fear white-collar crime less than conventional crime.
- Such crimes also tend to be **morally ambiguous**, e.g. many people do not see crimes such as tax evasion as wrong in the same way that mugging, for example, is seen as wrong.
- Both the police (who only deal with a small amount of white-collar crime) and civil agencies may **lack the resources to detect and prosecute such crime**. They may prefer to deal with the offence 'off the record'.
- Most white-collar crime and corporate crime, if detected, is **rarely prosecuted**.

White-collar crime therefore **is not socially constructed as crime** and not seen by the general public as a problem despite the fact that its costs far exceed that of conventional working-class crime.

The New Criminology – Neo-Marxism

Taylor, Walton and Young argue that capitalist society is characterised by **class inequality**. This theory suggests that **working-class people choose to commit crime because of their experience of the injustices of capitalism**. Therefore working-class crime is **political** – it is a deliberate and conscious reaction to working-class people interpreting their position at the bottom of the socio-economic hierarchy as unfair and exploitative. Working-class crime therefore is an attempt to alter capitalism. For example, crimes against property such as theft and burglary are aimed at the redistribution of wealth, whilst vandalism is a symbolic attack on capitalism's obsession with property. However, these ideas have been accused of being overly romantic. They fail to explain why most victims of crime are working class or in what way violent crimes are political.

Left Realism

Probably the most influential and therefore most important theory of crime.

KEY POINT

Jock Young and John Lea agree that working-class crime committed by young people is a very real problem in the inner cities which is 'wearing down' whole working-class communities, as indicated by victim surveys. This theory argues that working-class and black youth turn to street crime because of **relative deprivation**. In comparison with their peers (i.e. middle-class and white youth) they feel deprived in terms of education, jobs, income, standard of living, etc. Moreover, they feel they have little power to change their situation. They may feel that nobody listens to them or that they are picked on, e.g. police harassment. In reaction to these interpretations of relative deprivation and feelings of being **marginalised**, some young people may turn to **subcultures** – these may be positive and offer status through legitimate and conventional means (e.g. a church group) or negative in that status is awarded for deviant behaviour which may involve crime.

Progress check

1 What explanation does Murray have for crime?
2 What three types of deviance are identified by Robert Merton?
3 What causes working-class juvenile delinquency according to Cohen?
4 What do Taylor, Walton and Young mean when they say crime is political?
5 What types of crime are neglected by the agents of social control in a capitalist system?
6 What two factors do Left Realists blame for crime?

6 Relative deprivation and lack of power (marginalisation).
5 Those carried out by members of the economically dominant classes such as white-collar and corporate crimes.
4 It is a conscious reaction to the inequalities, exploitation and oppression of capitalism.
3 Status frustration.
2 Innovation (crime), retreatism and rebellion.
1 He blames the emergence of a welfare-dependent underclass which subscribes to a deviant value system or culture.

Gender and crime

AQA ▶ U6
OCR ▶ U2536

> **KEY POINT**
>
> Studies of the police suggest that the police generally do not see women as criminal types. They are therefore less likely to be stopped, arrested and charged compared with males. Studies of the courts note that magistrates and judges are less willing to punish women with custodial sentences especially if they conform to a feminine stereotype.

Heidensohn argues that exploring why women commit fewer crimes than men could provide clues about why men commit most crime. Feminists suggest that the differences between the sexes in terms of criminality can be attributed to two broad explanations.

- **Different socialisation** – 'masculine' values are potentially criminal values because they revolve around risk-taking behaviour, toughness, aggression, proving oneself, etc. The 'crisis in masculinity' has recently been linked by **Mac En Ghaill** to rising male violence. Femininity, on the other hand, involves values that may be passive and potentially less criminal.

- **Women experience less opportunities to commit crime**. They are more likely to be constrained by the mother–housewife role or by caring for the sick and elderly. The crimes they do commit may reflect this, e.g. shoplifting. They are less likely to engage in crime at work compared with men, although recent movement into the workforce may change this.

Explanations for female crime

- **Poverty** may be an explanation for welfare fraud and prostitution (especially among young single mothers who experience limited job opportunities and low pay).

- There is some concern that the rising number of violent crimes committed by young working-class women in **gangs** is primarily for peer-group status in order to compensate for low-skilled, tedious, low-paid jobs.

Ethnicity and crime

AQA ▶ U6
OCR ▶ U2536

Afro-Caribbeans are over-represented in the OCS despite the fact that they only make up approximately 3% of the general population. Asians, on the other hand, are under-represented in the OCS.

Increasingly a popular area for exam questions.

> **KEY POINT**
>
> The OCS may not reflect black criminality but rather racist stereotyping by police officers. The enquiry into the death of Stephen Lawrence (1999) concluded that **institutionalised racism** was a feature of police forces in the UK.

A number of theories have attempted to explain why Afro-Caribbeans commit crime.

- **Cashmore**, using a Mertonian approach, argues that young blacks in the UK are trapped in a situation where their **material goals are blocked** by their economic situation, i.e. because of **racism** they are much more likely to be unemployed. Innovation or crime is their response. However, in criticism, this account fails to account for the fact that only a small percentage of young blacks are involved in crime.

- **Gilroy**, a neo-Marxist, argues that the crimes committed by young blacks are political. They are part of a continuing **colonial struggle** between imperialism and racism symbolised by the police, and black communities. Crime is a form of **organised resistance to white oppression**. This theory makes some sense in the context of **riots** but still fails to account for the fact that only a small percentage of black people take part in this so-called 'political struggle'. Gilroy has been accused of being naïve about crime, especially considering **most victims of black crime are themselves black**.

- **New Right** commentators such as **Murray** see young blacks in the inner cities as part of an **underclass** that subscribes to antisocial attitudes and values. However, Murray fails to consider the impact of poverty and racism on young blacks nor does he offer any convincing empirical evidence that such a unified culture exists among black people.

- The **Left Realists, Young and Lea**, note that young blacks are more likely than young whites or Asians to experience **relative deprivation** – their opportunities for jobs, housing, education, resources, etc. are more likely to be blocked because of **institutional racism**. Consequently they feel **marginalised**, i.e. lacking in power and frustrated. Young and Lea suggest that some young blacks may interpret their position as impossible and react by coming together in **subcultures**. One such subcultural response may be crime.

Finally, the **Asian** crime rate is low. This may be because they are less likely to be economically deprived or marginalised because they are more likely to be in family or professional employment. Asian families also exercise **stricter controls** over their children which may limit opportunities for crime. Asian culture may provide a safety net for failure. The low rate of **Chinese** crime may be explained by the **closed** nature of Chinese society in the UK.

Progress check

1 How might policing lead to the low representation of females in the OCS?

2 How might gender-role socialisation be responsible for male violence?

3 What might be the main causes of female crimes such as theft, welfare fraud and prostitution?

4 What did the Stephen Lawrence Inquiry conclude about policing in London?

5 What does Gilroy blame for Afro-Caribbean crime?

6 What do Lea and Young blame for black crime?

1 The police may not stereotype females as potential criminals and stop and arrest them less than males.
2 Socialisation into a masculine role might mean learning to be tough and aggressive for some social groups.
3 Poverty.
4 That it was characterised by institutional racism.
5 He suggests that it is a political response to racism and a sense of grievance caused by the historical exploitation of black people.
6 They point out that racism may lead to a keen sense of relative deprivation and feelings that they lack power or are discriminated against.

139

8.4 Deviance, power and social control

After studying this section you should be able to:

LEARNING SUMMARY

- *outline and assess theories of crime that focus on social order and social control*
- *identify agents of social control and the role of the law*
- *assess the role of the mass media in the social control of deviance*
- *describe the relationship between deviance, power and control*

Crime, deviance and social order

AQA U6
OCR U2536

Functionalists argue that social order depends upon shared norms and values, i.e. **value consensus**, that are acquired through **socialisation**. Deviance is behaviour that **challenges the consensus**.

Durkheim believed that **deviance is present in all societies** and consequently it has a **positive** function to play. He concluded that a certain amount of deviance was **functional or beneficial to society because**:

- acts of deviance can bring about necessary **social change**
- deviance can act as an **early-warning system** that part of society is malfunctioning and is in need of social engineering
- deviance provokes **collective outrage** and therefore **social integration** and solidarity against outsiders such as criminals
- **punishment** of criminals is applied on behalf of the collective and **reinforces value consensus**
- deviance and its punishments are part of the **secondary socialisation process** in that they **reinforce what counts as acceptable and unacceptable behaviour**.

Other functionalists such as **Davis and Polsky** argue that deviance can be a **safety valve** for problems within important institutions such as the family. They argue that prostitution and pornography respectively may be lesser evils than the breakdown of the family or sexual crime.

This functionalist theory of deviance has some fundamental weaknesses. First, it does not explain why some groups are more prone to deviance than others. Second, some types of deviance are never functional nor beneficial (e.g. child abuse). Third, they probably underestimate the degree of conflict in society and **exaggerate the importance of consensus** in society.

The social construction of crime

AQA U6
OCR U2536

Labelling theory argues that definitions of deviance and normality are not fixed or universal – rather they are **relative** to specific cultures, times and places. **Deviance is a matter of interpretation**. Definitions of deviance require two activities: a group or individual must act in a particular fashion and another group with more power must label the initial activity as deviant. **There is therefore no such thing as a deviant act – an act only becomes deviant when there is societal reaction to it.**

KEY POINT

Powerful groups such as the middle class shape **societal reaction** by making rules or laws. Those who break laws are labelled via policing or media moral-panics. Labelling theory suggests that the deviant label becomes a **master status** which may have negative consequences in terms of **prejudice and discrimination and self-fulfilling prophecies** (once labelled, people may then see themselves as deviant). Labelling theory notes that **subcultures** may be the consequence of negative labelling. These are viewed positively by labelling theory because **they confer normality and status on those negatively labelled by society** – which may compensate for the societal reaction, e.g. gay culture.

In criticism of labelling theory, it is argued that the act of deviance is always more important than the reaction. People who commit deviant acts know full well what they are doing – self-awareness of their deviant activity does not suddenly result from having a label slapped on them. Labelling theory also fails to explain why people commit deviance in the first place. Finally, its view that the consequences of being labelled is further deviance underestimates **the degree of choice** that deviants have.

Deviancy amplification theory

A type of labelling theory.

Stanley Cohen argues that **the mass media** plays a key role in the construction of criminal statistics through the creation of **moral panics and folk devils**. It is suggested that the media label or stereotype powerless groups such as the young by **sensationalising** stories about them. This creates a moral panic – that is, a **public fear of crime that is exaggerated and out of proportion to the real threat offered**. The result of this is 'demonisation', i.e. folk devils are created – the group under scrutiny is seen as a problem and pressure is put on the government, police and courts to **stamp down hard** on them, thus increasing the official statistics. This may result in **confrontation** and **resistance** which further increases the statistics. Deviance is therefore **amplified** – selective reporting actually creates the crime problem.

Crime, deviance and ideology

AQA	U6
OCR	U2536

Law as an ideological state apparatus.

Traditional Marxism argues that the law and agents of social control such as the police and courts exist to **reproduce, maintain and legitimate class inequality** on behalf of the ruling class. In other words, the OCS and law are **ideological**. Their function is to **protect the interests of the ruling class**, i.e. wealth, private property and profit, and to divert attention away from white-collar and corporate crime committed by the ruling capitalist class. The capitalist class have the power to prevent laws being passed that are not in their interest or to make sure that such laws are weak, e.g. breaking health and safety laws and endangering the lives of workers is not punishable by prison. Many infractions are dealt with by the Health and Safety Executive informally. **Enforcement of the law is also selective and partial** in that working-class crimes are more severely punished than middle-class crimes which are either poorly policed and/or weakly punished.

In criticism of Marxism, it is argued that they overemphasise social class and neglect how the law and criminal justice system may reflect **patriarchal** inequalities and **institutional racism**. They have been accused of being over-simplistic in their view that power is concentrated in the hands of a ruling capitalist class. There may be a **plurality** of interest groups who benefit from the law.

Crime, costs and benefits

AQA   U6
OCR   U2536

Hirschi's control theory has strongly influenced **New Right** theories of crime. He argues that much criminality is **opportunistic** – people choose to commit crime by **rationally weighing up the benefits against the risks and costs** (getting caught and being punished).

An influential theory especially in the USA.

> Most people do not commit crime because they have **controls** in their lives which mean that **the costs of crime far outweigh the benefits of crime.** Such controls include attachment to family (e.g. marriage and children), commitment to a career, active involvement in a community and reputation, and belief in rules and discipline. Certain groups, i.e. the young, the working class, the underclass, etc. are less likely to have such controls in their lives and the benefits of crime clearly outweigh the risks of being caught and punished.

KEY POINT

This theory advocates the use of **deterrent** – i.e. making punishments harsher, therefore increasing the costs of crime. **Target hardening** or **'designing-out'** crime is recommended through more security, **zero-tolerance policing** and increasing **surveillance** through, for example, CCTV – thereby increasing the risks of getting caught.

In criticism, it is argued that such policies merely **displace** crime because the wealthy can afford to live on secure estates protected by technology. Criminals may therefore concentrate on poorer areas. Marxists argue that crime is shaped by structural inequalities and capitalist ideology rather than being simply opportunistic.

Progress check

1 What did Durkheim mean when he said that crime is good for society?
2 What is the function of the law, according to Marxists?
3 What is opportunistic crime?
4 What controls prevent an older person committing crime?
5 Why do the benefits of crime outweigh the costs for some teenagers?
6 What does control theory recommend to cut crime?

1 It is functional in that certain types of deviance can bring about social change, alert us to major social problems and promote social solidarity through public outrage, etc.
2 To protect ruling-class interests such as wealth and private property and to distract from ruling-class crime by criminalising those with less power.
3 That which is unplanned and done on the spur of the moment.
4 Marriage and children, financial commitments such as a mortgage, a career, reputation, etc.
5 Because they lack controls in their lives.
6 Making punishment harsher, becoming a more security-conscious society, zero-tolerance policing and more camera surveillance.

8.5 Suicide

After studying this section you should be able to:

- *identify the sociological issues arising from the study of suicide*
- *outline and assess Durkheim's classic study of suicide*
- *describe and evaluate interpretivist theories of suicide*

LEARNING SUMMARY

Durkheim's 'Le Suicide'

AQA ▶ U6

The classic positivist study. See Chapter 1.

The classic sociological study of suicide that was carried out by **Emile Durkheim** in 1897 is based upon two central ideas.

- First, he believed that **individual action was shaped by social structure**. He therefore aimed to show that the 'supreme' individual act, i.e. suicide, was the product of social influences.

- Second, he believed that by studying patterns in suicide objectively and rigorously, sociology could prove itself to be **a scientific discipline**.

Durkheim examined official statistics in regard to suicide and observed three trends in suicide rates.

- First, **within single societies, the rate of suicide remains fairly constant over time**.

- Second, **suicide rates varied consistently between different societies**.

- Third, **the suicide rate varied between different groups within the same society**.

The comparative method is a type of experiment.

Durkheim therefore suggested that suicide rates were '**social facts**' – that is, they were **socially determined by the organisation of societies** (i.e. social structures).

Using the **comparative method of research**, Durkheim manipulated non-social and social variables in order to discover the cause of suicide. He eliminated non-social variables such as climate, heredity, alcoholism and the seasons. He examined psychological variables, e.g. he discovered a high rate of insanity amongst Jews but a low level of suicide. Consequently he dismissed mental illness as a 'cause' of suicide.

Note that all these types of suicide are influenced by the organisation of society, i.e. the social structure.

> After examining social variables, Durkheim concluded that '**suicide varies inversely with the degree of integration of the social group of which the individual forms a part**' and identified four types of suicide.
>
> **KEY POINT**

Types of suicide

> **Egoistic suicide** is the product of '**excessive individualism**' or egoism. The ties binding the individual to the social group are weak and so they experience **lack of integration into social life**. Durkheim suggested three social factors are responsible for the strengths or weaknesses of an individual's ties to a social group; **religious social controls, family life** and **political environment**.
>
> **KEY POINT**

- Durkheim noted that Catholics are less likely to commit suicide than Protestants. He argued that Catholics are more integrated into their communities because of the ritualistic character of their beliefs and practices whereas Protestants are not as integrated because their religion stresses '**free enquiry**' and therefore less social control.

- Second, Durkheim suggested that marriage and family life have an integrating effect upon individuals. Single or divorced people are more prone to 'egoism'.
- Finally, he argued that strong sentiments in terms of nationalism or patriotism that are present in the political environment can affect suicide rates. He noted that political upheaval and war promote integration and thus less suicide.

Altruistic suicide is the product of too much integration – the individual is too weak to resist the demands of the group, e.g. the Jonestown mass suicide in 1978. **Anomic suicide** is the product of the lack of regulation of the individual by society. In periods of economic depression or prosperity, people may be confused about goals and values as their circumstances radically change and become more likely to attempt suicide. Finally, **fatalistic suicide** is caused by over-regulation of the individual by society, e.g. suicide in prison.

Other functionalist theories of suicide

Halbwachs (1930) continued Durkheim's theme and suggested that **urbanisation** was the key variable in determining social integration because city life was characterised by **isolation** and **impersonal relationships**.

Criticisms of Durkheim have focused on the lack of reliability of official statistics on death in the period he was looking at and his failure to offer any guidance on how to recognise different types of suicide.

The interpretivist critique of Durkheim

AQA	U6
OCR	U2536

Remember interpretivists are anti-positivist. See Chapter 1.

Recently Durkheim's theory has been attacked by **interpretivist** sociologists who suggest that suicide rates 'do not exist as facts' but are **socially constructed** and thus **systematically biased**.

The cultural meaning of suicide

Douglas (1967) contends that suicide rates reflect the different cultural meanings attached to suicidal action in any particular society. Cultural interpretations of suicide influence the statistics. For example, Catholics regard suicide as 'morally wrong', as a cardinal sin. This interpretation may be more important than social integration and may influence the recognition and recording of suicide because relatives and friends cover the act up.

The social construction of suicide statistics

Atkinson (1978) also suggests that suicide rates are socially constructed. He argues that suicide statistics are the end product of a complex set of interactions and interpretations involving victims, doctors, friends and relatives of the deceased and, most importantly, coroners. Atkinson's research focused on coroners – legal officers who investigate suspicious deaths. He notes that a death is not a suicide until it is labelled as such by a coroner's court.

KEY POINT

The role of coroners

Coroners have to follow certain formal rules when investigating how a person died, e.g. a *postmortem* must be carried out and the coroner's officers will investigate the circumstances of the death – they will collect evidence. Coroners weigh up that evidence and must reach one of a number of legal verdicts available: natural causes, open verdict, accident, suicide or homicide. For a death to be recorded as a suicide it must be proved that the victim *intended* to die.

Atkinson shows that suicidal cues (evidence) are selected and interpreted by coroners as indicators of intent. **Primary cues**, e.g. suicide notes and the mode of death, come from the scene of death, whereas **secondary cues** are uncovered in the life history of the deceased. Primary cues in themselves are insufficient to prove intent. For example, suicide notes may not be left or may be destroyed whilst modes of death, e.g. overdoses, could be accidents. Therefore secondary cues are more important – the coroner will focus on the biography of the individual, seeking events, e.g. divorce, redundancy, mental illness, etc. which they regard as causing great unhappiness and despair.

Taylor investigated 32 deaths in which the mode and scene of death were the same, yet only 17 were labelled suicide because the family of the victim influenced the coroner's interpretation of the victim's state of mind.

The work of Steve Taylor

A structuration approach – see Chapter 1.

Taylor (1988) attempts to combine Durkheimian and Interpretivist approaches. Like Durkheim, Taylor suggests that social structure is important because it brings about levels of 'certainty' and 'uncertainty' in people's lives. For example, working-class people may experience more uncertainty than certainty because of unemployment, etc. In a patriarchal society, a career woman may face certain conflicts that do not exist for men, which may increase her sense of uncertainty. Stable lives, argues Taylor, arise from people's interpretations that they are experiencing a balance between certainty and uncertainty.

Taylor advances the view that **suicide is more likely in situations where the individual interprets their social situation as one of complete certainty or uncertainty**. In the former, people may feel that they know everything worth knowing or experiencing. The suicidal actions that result Taylor calls 'purposive'. Alternatively, some people may feel they know nothing worth knowing and attempt what Taylor calls 'ordeal suicides' – they don't know whether they want to live or die. Both sets of interpretations may be the product of some aspect of their experience of the way society is organised. Moreover, the suicidal response is only one possible alternative way of reacting to this experience.

Progress check

1 What was the main determinant of individual action, according to Durkheim?

2 What was the main influence on suicide rates, according to Durkheim?

3 What four types of suicide did Durkheim identify?

4 What caused egoistic suicide?

5 What does Durkheim neglect, according to Douglas?

6 Why does Atkinson conclude that suicide statistics are socially constructed?

7 What are primary and secondary cues?

8 What does Taylor suggest are the main influences on suicide?

8 The degree of certainty and uncertainty in people's lives. These may be shaped by social factors but ultimately the decision to commit suicide depends on how the individual interprets their social situation.
7 Primary cues are clues relating to the mode of death, the scene of death and the presence or absence of a suicide note. Secondary cues relate to key events in the life of the deceased which may have influenced the decision to commit suicide.
6 Because they are the end product of a complex set of interactions between coroners, victims and relatives of the victim.
5 The social meanings attached to suicide.
4 Lack of integration, i.e. too much individualism in a society.
3 Egoistic, altruistic, anomic and fatalistic.
2 The degree of social integration in a society.
1 The social structure or organisation of society.

Sample synoptic question and model answer

A synoptic question – you will be rewarded for linking to other topics especially theory and method.

Item A

Since the 1980s, victim surveys which ask samples of the population how many crimes they, or members of their households, have experienced over a fixed period of time and whether or not these have been reported, have increasingly been used. The most well-known of these surveys is the British Crime Survey. However, these types of survey do have some limitations. They are based on households and omit business and institutional victims. They only survey those aged 16 years and above. They are inevitably restricted to crimes which victims are aware of and miss out those which they cannot detect for themselves or have not defined as crime.

(Source: adapted from Crime and Society in Britain *(1998) by Hazel Croall, Longman, p. 27.)*

(a) Briefly discuss two social influences that might lead teenagers into delinquent behaviour. **(8 marks)**

Note stress on 'briefly' – don't overdo this response.

Cohen suggests in modern societies, achieved status is the primary goal of most young individuals. Young people who do not achieve it through conventional means, i.e. school or work, may experience status frustration and seek it collectively from their peer group by engaging in deviant or criminal activity.

Hirschi argues that older people commit less crime than teenagers because the possible cost of crime is too high for them, i.e. they may lose their job, home, family, reputation and freedom. Younger people are less likely to have these controls in their lives and so the possible benefits outweigh the costs.

(b) Examine some of the problems involved in using victim surveys to measure the extent and nature of crime. **(12 marks)**

This question focuses on methodological issues.

The main victim survey in the UK is the British Crime Survey (BCS). However, it has attracted some criticism especially in its assertion that people in the UK are only rarely likely to be victims of crimes. For example, the BCS suggested that the chances of an average home in the UK being burgled occurred only once every forty years. It also suggested that women and the elderly were unnecessarily anxious about being the victims of crime and concluded that the most likely victims of crime were young men.

The methodology and findings of the BCS were severely criticised by the Islington Crime Survey (ICS). This mainly focused on the inner city and found that the majority of people who took part in their survey had directly or indirectly experienced crime. Moreover, women and the elderly were actually at risk. As Jock Young points out, people who live in the inner city are not average people with average problems. The urban context throws up problems which are unique and relentless. The BCS was also criticised for ignoring sexual crime by the ICS and feminist researchers. The ICS through the employment of sensitive female interviewers found a large amount of unreported sexual crime.

Sample synoptic question and model answer (continued)

An essay question – you should aim for at least two sides.

Outline the theory before you evaluate it.

An alternative example which would have been truly synoptic could have focused on how teachers label children and create deviant subcultures in schools.

Evaluation – weaknesses.

(c) Evaluate the strengths and weaknesses of labelling theory as an explanation of deviant behaviour. (40 marks)

Labelling theorists such as Becker and Lemert argue that because of the diversity of different values in society, there can be never be a universally agreed definition of what constitutes 'normal' or 'deviant' behaviour. What is deviant for one person may not be deviant for another.

Deviance, therefore, is a matter of interpretation requiring not one but two activities: a group or individual must act in a particular fashion and another group or individual with different values and more power label the initial activity as deviant. Therefore the act only becomes deviant via interpretation or societal reaction. As Becker notes 'social groups create deviance by making the rules whose infraction constitutes deviance, and by applying those rules to particular people they label them as outsiders'. In other words, the powerful, by making the rules/laws, define what counts as deviance. For example, the middle class make rules for the working class, men make rules for women, etc.

Labelling theory has tended to focus on societal reaction to deviance. In particular, they have focused on the role of agents of social control, e.g. the police and media, who they suggest label on behalf of the powerful. Numerous studies of the police from a labelling perspective (e.g. Cicourel, Holdaway, etc.) indicate that stereotyping or labelling by some police may result in some groups (i.e the young and blacks) being over-proportionately represented in the criminal statistics. Studies of the media by Cohen, Young, etc. indicate that media societal reaction may result in groups such as gays being labelled folk devils (such as AIDS carriers, child molesters, etc.) and 'moral panics' being created around them.

Such societal reaction may have negative consequences for the self-concept of those labelled as deviant. The label may become a master status that has a number of consequences. First, it may produce a self-fulfilling prophecy. The labelled person may see themselves as deviant especially if, on a practical basis, they experience prejudice from society i.e. the 'ex-con' who experiences difficulty getting a job may be forced back into a life of crime. Second, the labelled individual may seek comfort, sympathy and normality within a subculture of similarly labelled people. Within this subculture 'deviant' behaviour is interpreted as 'normal' and this may compensate for the societal reaction. Such subcultures (e.g. gay subcultures) are usually cohesive and come complete with their own values and rules which may conflict with conventional society. Third, some subcultures may react to societal reaction by becoming more deviant.

Labelling theory has been extensively criticised. First, Ackers suggests that it places too much emphasis on societal reaction. Some actions, e.g. murder, child abuse, will always be deviant and therefore societal reaction is less important than the act. Second, labelling theory is accused of being too deterministic. Labelling theory may underestimate the degree of choice and consciousness that the deviant has – they know their actions are deviant and choose to act that way. Third, labelling has been accused of failing to explain the origins of deviance, i.e. why people commit the crime in the first place. Marxists, in particular, note that labelling theory neglects structural factors, especially social class and

Sample synoptic question and model answer *(continued)*

power. Marxists suggest that labelling is ideological – it is mainly concerned with the protection of the major priorities of capitalism, namely wealth, private property and profit.

Evaluation – weaknesses.

Left Realists such as Young and Lea have criticised labelling theory because certain powerless groups such as young blacks do commit more street crime. They argue that we need to understand how certain groups interpret their structural position in society, e.g. how young blacks interpret institutionalised racism as well as labelling by the agents of social control. Young and Lea suggest that young blacks may feel relatively deprived in relation to young whites and consequently marginalised. They may respond by turning to both legitimate and illegitimate subcultures. Young and Lea therefore acknowledge the influence of labelling theory and adapt it to account for the reality of inner-city crime.

Evaluation – strengths.

Despite the criticisms, labelling theory has made an important contribution to the sociology of deviance. It has shown that defining deviance is not a simple process. Second, it has highlighted the consequences of the labelling process. Third, it has shown that definitions of deviance originate in power differences. Consequently we now understand that deviance is not a fixed, unchanging and universal state.

Practice examination question

Outline and assess sociological explanations for the low recorded rates of white-collar and corporate crime. (60 marks)

Chapter 9

Stratification, social inequality and difference (AQA and OCR synoptic)

The following topics are covered in this chapter:

- *Stratification and social class*
- *Theories of social-class stratification*
- *Changes in the class structure*
- *Social mobility*
- *Ethnicity and inequality*
- *Gender and inequality*

9.1 Stratification and social class

After studying this section you should be able to:

- *identify and explain four different types of stratification*
- *describe the relationship between occupation and social class*
- *outline and assess different ways of measuring social class*

LEARNING SUMMARY

Types of stratification

AQA   U6
OCR   U2539

Remember this is a **synoptic** unit for both OCR and AQA.

> **KEY POINT**
>
> Social stratification refers to **the division of society into a pattern of layers or strata made up of a hierarchy of unequal social groups.** In other words, a society characterised by stratification will contain inequalities based upon factors such as wealth and income, occupation and status, social class, political power, religion, race, gender and age. One or two groups will dominate others.
>
> Sociologists have identified **four types of stratification** system which have existed throughout history, some of which are still around today.

The caste system

Although officially banned in India today, this Hindu system of stratification is still enormously influential. People in caste societies occupy **ascribed roles** based upon religious purity. The caste system is a **closed society** – people are born into **castes** and cannot move out of them during the course of their lives.

The feudal system

This was found in medieval Europe and was a hierarchical system based on ownership of land, with the king at the top and peasants at the bottom. Feudal societies, too, were mainly **closed societies** – people's positions were largely **ascribed** and it was rare for people to be upwardly mobile.

Apartheid

This system, which existed from the early 1960s to the late 1980s in South Africa, categorised society into layers on the basis of **race**.

Social class

The main type of stratification in the UK. Know it well!

> **KEY POINT**
>
> This is mainly found in modern industrial societies like the UK. Social classes are **groups of people who share a similar economic position such as occupation, income and ownership of wealth**. They also probably have similar levels of education, status and lifestyle (i.e. living standards) and power.

Class systems are different to the previous systems in the following respects.

- They are not based on religion or law or race but on **economic factors** such as job, money, etc.
- There is **no clear distinction between classes** – it is difficult to say where the working class finishes and the middle class begins.
- All members of society whether working or middle or upper classes have **equal rights**.
- There are **no legal restrictions on marriage** between the classes.
- Social-class societies are **open societies** – people can experience downward or upward **social mobility**, i.e. you can move up or down the class structure through jobs, the acquisition of wealth or marriage.
- Such systems are usually **meritocratic** – that is **people are not born into ascribed roles**. We are encouraged to better ourselves through **achievement** at school, e.g. qualifications, and at work through working hard and gaining promotion.

Occupation is the most common indicator of social class used by governments, by advertising agencies when they are doing market research and by sociologists when they are doing social surveys. This information is easy to obtain and it is generally a good guide to people's skills and qualifications, their income, their futures and their present standard of living. Occupation also leads to **status** in modern society – most people judge other people's and their own social standing by the jobs they do.

Measuring social class

AQA   U6
OCR   U2539

There are a number of ways of categorising people into social classes in the UK but the best known and most widely used way until 2000 was the **Registrar General's Scale**. This divided the population into the following five social classes.

- **Class I: Professional**, e.g. accountants, doctors, solicitors, etc.
- **Class II: Intermediate**, e.g. teachers, managers, pilots, farmers, etc.
- **Class III: Skilled Non Manual**, e.g. office workers, shop assistants, etc.
  (All of the above are **middle-class occupations**; those who work in these categories are often called **white-collar workers**.)
- **Class III: Skilled Manual**, e.g. electricians, plumbers, factory foremen, etc.
- **Class IV: Semi-skilled Manual**, e.g. agricultural workers, postal workers, etc.
- **Class V: Unskilled Manual**, e.g. road-sweepers, labourers, refuse collectors, etc.
  (The last three categories are generally regarded as the **working classes** and are often called **blue-collar workers**.)

There are problems in using occupation to determine social class as illustrated by the following.

- If we use occupation we **exclude the wealthy upper class** who own property and have a great deal of power but who often don't have jobs because they live off rents and stocks and shares.

- **Groups outside paid employment are excluded**, such as housewives and the never-employed unemployed.
- Classifying unemployed people on the basis of their last job assumes that they continue to enjoy the same income, status, lifestyle, etc. as they had before they became unemployed. This is unlikely to be the case.
- The RG scale was based on the job of the head of the household – this was generally assumed to be the man. Married women therefore were classified on the basis of their husbands' occupation rather than their own. This is obviously **sexist** and dated considering the number of women who now work and who hold professional positions.
- The focus on the head of the household neglected those families in which both partners are important in bringing home a wage (**dual-career families**). For example, their joint incomes could give them the lifestyle of a higher social class.
- In some families, both parents may be breadwinners. However, although the female may have a higher status and higher paid job than the male, she will be classed in the husband's lower occupational class. Some sociologists therefore suggested that the RG scale was dated because it did not consider these **cross-class** families.
- There are **major differences between occupations within the social classes**, e.g. in terms of income. For example, Social Class I includes doctors but this group includes surgeons who are paid vast sums and junior doctors who are poorly paid. Teachers are in Social Class II but this class also includes Members of Parliament!

The new Socio-economic Classification (NS-SEC)

> It is extremely important that you focus on this change.

In the year 2000, the RG scale was replaced by the **National Statistics – Socio-economic Classification (NS-SEC)** devised by **John Goldthorpe**. The RG's scale has been abandoned because it failed to reflect the massive decline in manufacturing, the huge increase in service industries (finance and retail) and the huge shift in the proportion of women in the workforce.

The NS-SEC is based on data from the Labour Force Survey on the employment conditions of over 65 000 individuals across 371 occupations. It differs from the RG scale in the following respects.

- It is no longer based purely on skill like the RG's scale. Rather it is based on (a) **employment relations** – whether people are employers, self-employed, employed, whether they exercise authority, etc. and (b) **market conditions** – salary scales, promotion prospects, sick pay, how much control people have over hours worked or how work is done, etc.
- It recognises **eight** social classes rather than five, including the long-term unemployed or the never-worked.
- This classification system no longer divides workers along manual and non-manual lines. Each category contains both manual and non-manual workers.
- Class 8 (i.e. the never-worked) might be termed the '**underclass**'. The RG's scale suffered from the weakness of not having a category that effectively accounted for this group.
- Occupations such as check-out assistants and sales assistants who used to be in Class 3, NM have been dropped to Class 6 because of their relatively poor conditions of employment, i.e. their market situation has deteriorated in terms of pay, job security, autonomy, etc. Teachers, on the other hand, have been promoted from Social Class 2, i.e. lower professionals to Class 1, higher professionals because their market position has improved in terms of pay, etc.

- The **self-employed** are recognised as a separate category.
- **Women are recognised as a distinct group of wage-earners** and no longer categorised according to the occupation of their husbands or fathers.

A number of potential **weaknesses** have been identified with regard to the NS-SEC.

- It is still based primarily on occupation. This may differ from what people understand by the term 'social class' and especially people's **subjective** interpretation of their own class position.
- The NS-SEC has taken into consideration **changing class boundaries,** e.g. the fact that the social position of clerical workers has declined. However, there are still significant differences within categories between occupations. For example, do teachers really share the same market position as lawyers and doctors? This classification tells us little about the huge differences within occupations – consider a GP's or junior doctor's salary with that of a consultant, or a solicitor with a barrister or judge.
- It still fails to account for those wealthy enough not to have to work.

Progress check

1 How did the Registrar-General's scale classify the occupations of teacher and refuse collector?

2 Why do you think feminists were very critical of the RG scale?

3 Why do you think Marxists were very critical of the RG scale?

4 What is a cross-class family?

5 What is the NS-SEC classification based on?

6 Identify two groups not included in the RG scale but included in the NS-SEC scale.

6 The self-employed and the underclass.
5 The employment relations and market conditions of jobs.
4 A family in which there are two breadwinners who have jobs that are classified in different classes.
3 It doesn't include the upper class who live off their wealth.
2 Because it was based on head of household and assumed that this was the male. Women were therefore classified according to their husband's or father's jobs.
1 As Social Class 2 and 5 respectively.

9.2 Theories of social-class stratification

After studying this section you should be able to:

- *outline and evaluate theories of stratification*
- *identify how social class relates to social order, conflict and status*

Functionalism

AQA	U6
OCR	U2539

Functionalists view stratification positively.

Davis and Moore argue that stratification makes a contribution to social order – therefore, **class inequality is beneficial, positive and necessary.** All societies have to ensure that their most functionally important, i.e. unique, positions are filled with people who are talented and efficient. Talent and skill, however, are in short supply and top jobs require an intensive amount of training and time to acquire the necessary expertise. Educational qualifications and the stratification system function **to allocate all individuals to an occupational role that suits their abilities.** Stratification encourages all members of society to work to the best of their ability because class societies are **meritocracies** – high rewards in the form of income and status are guaranteed in order to motivate gifted people to make the necessary sacrifices in terms of education and training. Inequality also motivates, e.g. those at the top will wish to retain their advantages whilst those placed elsewhere will wish to improve on their position.

Evaluation of functionalism

Davis and Moore suggest that unequal rewards are the product of consensus. However, there exists a substantial level of resentment about the unequal distribution of income and wealth as illustrated by on-going controversies over 'fat-cat' levels of pay. Moreover, unequal rewards may be the product of inequalities in power. Some groups may be able to use economic and political power to increase their rewards against the will of the people.

High rewards also go to people who play no functionally important roles such as film and rock stars. Lots of occupations can be seen to be functionally essential to the smooth running of society but are not highly rewarded, e.g. nurses – although Davis and Moore would argue that the type of people who become nurses are not in short supply. The **dysfunctions of stratification** are neglected by Davis and Moore. For example, **poverty** is a major problem for people and negatively impacts on mortality, health, education and family life.

Marxism

AQA	U6
OCR	U2539

Marxists view stratification negatively.

Marx argued that **history is the history of class struggle.** Apart from primitive communism which existed in early hunting and gathering society, all stages of history, e.g. ancient slavery, feudalism and capitalism, have been characterised by class societies. **Social class is essentially the product of the mode of production of a society.** The mode of production of capitalist societies is **industrial.** In feudal societies, it was agricultural.

The mode of production is made up of the relationship between **the means of production** and **the social relations of production.**

- The means of production refers to resources such as land, factories, machinery, raw materials, etc. which are owned by the **capitalist class or bourgeoisie.** This group is in an extremely powerful and privileged position.

The **workers or proletariat** do not own productive property. Their only asset is their **labour power**.

- The social relations of production refer to the economic relationship between the bourgeoisie and proletariat as the latter hires out its labour power to the former. Inequality, exploitation and conflict result from the fact that it is in the interests of the capitalist class to keep wages low in order to increase profits. Moreover, the value of the worker's labour-power is worth a good deal more than the wage paid by the employer for it. **Marxists therefore see this relationship as deeply unequal, exploitative and the cause of class conflict.**

Marx argued that capitalism's pursuit of profit means that workers lose control over the work process as new technology is introduced. However, workers very rarely see themselves as exploited because they are suffering from **false class-consciousness** – they have been socialised by **ideological apparatuses** such as education and the media into believing that their position at the lower end of the socio-economic hierarchy is deserved and therefore natural.

Evaluation of Marxism

Marx was **an economic determinist or reductionist** in that all major ideas are seen to be the product of the economic relationship between the bourgeoisie and proletariat. However, conflicts resulting from **nationalism, ethnicity and gender** cannot be explained adequately in economic terms. Marx made certain predictions (e.g. that the working class would experience so much poverty and misery that they overthrow the capitalist class, that the middle class would disappear, that communism would replace capitalism, etc.) which have not come true. The living standards of the working class have risen, the middle classes have grown and communism was rejected in Eastern Europe. Western class-societies may have problems such as poverty and homelessness but they have a reasonably good record in terms of democracy and trade union rights.

Max Weber

| AQA | U6 |
| OCR | U2539 |

Weber recognised that social class had a profound effect on people's life chances (i.e. their chances of getting on in terms of jobs, health, etc.) but argued that **status** was also an important source of power. Marx defined social class in terms of productive property. However, Weber defined it differently in terms of **market position**, which is made up of income, skills and qualifications. On this basis, he argued that within social classes there exists a range of life chances.

Weber also argued that **status inequality derives from class inequality**, i.e. people who occupy high occupational roles generally have high social status. However, it can also derive from other sources of power such as **gender, race, religion**, etc. Weber noted that status was also linked to **consumption styles** (i.e. how people spend their money). For example, some people derive status from **conspicuous consumption**, i.e. being seen to buy expensive designer products. This idea has led to the **post-modernist** idea that in the 21st century consumption style rather than social class will structure people's identity.

Evaluation of Weber

Marxists argue that Weber was too concerned with identifying trivial market details and neglected the basic split between capitalists and workers. Marxists argue that class and status are strongly linked, e.g. the capitalist class not only has wealth but also high status and political power. Weber recognises that these overlap but suggests that a person can have wealth but little status, e.g. a lottery winner.

9.3 Changes in the class structure

After studying this section you should be able to:

- *identify, explain and evaluate key changes in the class structure*
- *describe and assess the impact of social and economic change on class composition*
- *evaluate the validity of concepts such as 'embourgeoisement' and proletarianisation*
- *outline and assess the underclass thesis*

The upper class

| AQA | U6 |
| OCR | U2539 |

It is important to use contemporary statistics and studies to illustrate changes in the class structure.

John Scott argues that the upper class is a **'unified property class'** which owns and controls major sections of the manufacturing, financial (e.g. banks) and retail (e.g. supermarkets) sectors. Moreover, a significant proportion of this group is made up of the **traditional 'landed gentry' and aristocracy** who have 'merged' with the **industrial rich** (sometimes called the 'nouveau' rich) via investment and marriage. This upper class is still very wealthy. **The top 1% still own about one-third of all wealth in the UK**. Moreover, much of their previous wealth has merely been transferred to the top 5% via trust funds. Inheritance is responsible for some two-thirds of inequality in the distribution of wealth.

The upper class practises **self-recruitment** and **'social closure'** i.e. wealth and power is kept within the class) via:

- marriage between wealthy families
- an old-boy network based upon public school and Oxbridge links
- interlocking directorships (upper-class individuals will sit on the boards of several companies)
- membership of exclusive gentlemen's clubs.

Adonis and Pollard (1998) suggest that the upper class is in the process of assimilating a new group which they call the **'super class'**. This group is based on people in the old professions (especially law) who have made their fortunes in the City, accountants and managers of investment funds and directors of the former public utilities (e.g. water, gas, electricity, British Rail, etc.) who earn astronomical salaries.

This super class tend to **intermarry** and therefore earn combined super-salaries. They can be distinguished from the rest of society by their **consumption patterns**, which revolve around nannies and servants, second homes, exotic holidays, private health and pension schemes and private education for their children. Most of this super class live in London and the south-east.

The middle classes in modern Britain

| AQA | U6 |
| OCR | U2539 |

In 1911 80% of workers were in manual occupations (i.e. working-class positions). This number fell to 52% in 1981 and to 32.7% in 1991. In the last ten years, **non-manual workers** (i.e. traditionally seen as the middle class) **have become the majority occupational group in the workforce**. Savage (1995) notes that in 1991 29.4% of the workforce worked in the professions and management, 10.7% were self-employed and 27.2% were routine white-collar workers. In other words, **67.3% of the working population could be considered as part of the middle class. As Savage notes, there are now more university lecturers than coal miners.** Primary industries and manufacturing have gone into decline because of world-wide recession and globalisation – the same raw materials and goods can be produced cheaper in the Third World.

The boundary problem

Sociologists tend not to agree on which occupational groups qualify to be classified as 'middle class'. This is the so-called **'boundary problem'**. Traditionally, differentiating between the middle class and working class was a simple task involving distinguishing between white-collar or non-manual workers on the one hand and blue-collar or manual workers on the other. Generally, the former enjoyed better working conditions in terms of pay, holidays, promotion possibilities, etc. Today, however, this distinction is not so clear-cut.

> **Savage (1992)** argues that it is important to see that **the middle class is now fragmented** and can be seen in terms of **'class fractions'**. He identifies six class fractions – higher and lower professionals, higher and middle managers, the petite bourgeoisie and routine white-collar workers.
>
> **KEY POINT**

The self-employed

Middle-class fractions.

Between 1981 and 1991, the number of **self-employed or 'petit-bourgeoisie'** rose from 6.7% of the workforce to over 10%. Research by **Fielding (1995)** examined what the self-employed in 1981 were doing in 1991. Fielding showed that two-thirds of his sample were a relatively stable and secure part of the workforce in that they remained self-employed over this ten-year period. The character of the self-employed has changed in some respects too. The number of managers who prefer to work for themselves, i.e. as consultants, rose considerably in the 1980s especially in the finance and computer industries

Professionals

Savage et al. argue that **higher and lower professionals** mainly recruit internally, i.e. the sons and daughters of professionals are likely to end up as professionals themselves. The position of professional workers is based on the possession of educational qualifications. Savage argues that professionals possess **economic capital** (i.e. a very good standard of living, savings, etc.) and **cultural capital** (e.g. they see the worth of education and other cultural assets such as taste in high culture) which they pass on to their children. Moreover, professionals have strong **occupational associations** that protect and actively pursue their interests (e.g. the Law Society, the British Medical Association) although the lower down the professional ladder, the weaker these associations/unions become (e.g. teachers). The result of such groups actively pursuing the interests of professionals is high rewards, status and job security. Savage concludes that professionals are aware of their common interests and quite willing to take **collectivistic** action to protect those interests. In this sense, then, professionals have a greater sense of **class identity** than any other middle-class group.

Managers

Savage suggests that many managers have been upwardly mobile from the routine white-collar sector or the skilled working-class and often they lack qualifications such as degrees. Many will have worked their up through an organisation. Their social position, therefore, is likely to be the result of **experience and reputation** rather than qualifications.

Savage argues that **job security differentiates professionals from managers** – managers are less likely to have it and are constantly under threat from **recession, mergers, downsizing**, etc. Middle managers, e.g. bank managers, may find themselves unemployed, downwardly mobile into the routine white-collar sector or becoming self-employed.

Routine white-collar workers and proletarianisation

Marxists such as **Harry Braverman** argue that routine white-collar workers are no longer middle class. Braverman argues that they have been subjected to a process of **proletarianisation**. This means that they have lost the social and economic advantages that they enjoyed over manual workers such as superior pay and working conditions. Braverman argues that, in the last twenty years, employers have used **technology**, especially computers, to break down complex white-collar skills such as book-keeping into simplistic routine tasks. This process known as **de-skilling** is an attempt to increase output, maximise efficiency and reduce costs. Control over the work process has therefore been removed from many non-manual workers. These developments have been accompanied by the parallel development of **feminising** the routine white-collar workforce especially in the financial sector, because female workers are generally cheap to employ and are seen by employers as more adaptable and amenable to this type of work.

> Braverman therefore concludes that de-skilling means that occupations that were once middle class are today in all respects indistinguishable from those of manual workers.

KEY POINT

The working class

AQA ▷ U6
OCR ▷ U2539

Lockwood's (1966) research found that many workers, especially in industrial areas, subscribed to a value system he called **'proletarian traditionalist'**. Workers felt a strong sense of loyalty to each other because of shared work experience. They had a keen sense of class solidarity and consciousness and tended to see society in terms of conflict, in terms of 'them versus us'.

The embourgeoisement thesis

It was argued in the 1960s by **Zweig** that a section of the working class – skilled manual workers had adopted the economic and cultural lifestyle of the middle class. This argument was known as the **'embourgeoisement thesis'** because it insisted that skilled workers had developed bourgeois values and were supportive of the Conservative Party. However, this thesis was investigated by **Goldthorpe and Lockwood's Affluent Worker study** in the late 1960s. They found little evidence to support Zweig's assertion because 77% of their sample voted Labour, although they did argue that there were signs of **'convergence'** between working-class and middle-class lifestyles.

Goldthorpe and Lockwood did, however, suggest that **the economic basis for class identity and solidarity was weakening** and identified the emergence of the **'privatised instrumentalist'** (sometimes called **'instrumental collectivist'**) worker who saw **work as a means to an end rather than as a source of identity**. These affluent workers were more home-centred than traditional working-class groups and were less likely to subscribe to the notion of working-class community and 'them versus us' attitudes. They did not join trade unions or vote Labour because of a keen sense of class identity. If they took any form of collectivistic action, it was in pursuit of higher pay or to protect living standards relative to other groups of workers who they perceived as 'better-off'.

The underclass

There are **two versions** of this theory – one which blames the victim and one which blames society.

The **victim-blaming version** is associated with the New Right and sociologists such as **Murray and Saunders**. It is suggested that the underclass is a distinct group that exists in the inner city and on council estates which subscribes to a 'way of life' or culture made up of deviant values and norms. It is argued that such values include being work-shy, being welfare-dependent, lacking commitment to family life and engaging in criminality. New Right sociologists argue that this value system differs sufficiently significantly from the mainstream working class for this group to constitute **a separate and distinct social grouping**. Moreover, this underclass is reproduced generation by generation as parents socialise their children into this culture. The Welfare State is seen as perpetuating such a system because knowledge that benefits are available demotivates people in their search for work.

In contrast, **the structural view of the underclass** stresses that structural obstacles, beyond the control of individuals, are responsible for their poverty and encourages fatalism and dependency. For example, many people are long-term unemployed because of **recession** or the fact that goods can be produced cheaper in the Third World. Groups such as ethnic minorities may be denied access to jobs and decent housing because of **racism**. Single mothers may find it impossible to return to work because of a **lack of free child-care**. This approach to the underclass therefore argues that poverty needs to be seriously tackled if the underclass is not to be **scapegoated** for its position at the bottom of the socio-economic hierarchy.

Post-modernism and class

An important set of ideas.

In the 1990s, **post-modernist sociologists** have argued that class has ceased to be the prime determinant of identity. It is suggested that societies are now organised around **consumption rather than production**. Consequently people now identify themselves in terms of what they consume rather than in terms of social-class position. **Class identity has therefore fragmented into numerous separate and individualised identities**.

Marshall's research, however, suggests that post-modernist ideas may be exaggerated. Surveys indicate that social class is still a significant source of identity for many. Members of a range of classes are aware of class differences and are happy to identify themselves using class categories. Finally, post-modernists conveniently ignore the view that consumption depends on having a job and levels of income. For example, poverty is going to inhibit any desire to pursue a post-modern lifestyle. In other words, consumption and social class are closely related.

The death of class?

Key points from AS

• **Poverty as a dimension of inequality**
Revise AS pages 111–117

Look at the chapters on health, welfare and social policy and education to illustrate the view that social class is still very important.

In recent years, politicians have been fond of suggesting that social class is dead or in decline. For example, in 1999 Tony Blair claimed that **'we are all middle class now'**. However, the evidence does not support such an assertion. Social-class inequalities can clearly be seen in a number of areas such as **morbidity, mortality, education and wealth**. Moreover, such inequalities are widening rather than narrowing. **Poverty**, too, continues to be a major problem, e.g. child poverty has trebled in the past twenty years.

Progress check

1 How does the upper class practise social closure?
2 What is the super class?
3 What is the boundary problem?
4 What does Savage conclude about the middle class?
5 What does Braverman conclude about routine white-collar workers?
6 What is embourgeoisement?
7 What do the New Right and structural theories respectively blame for the emergence of an underclass?

1 By intermarriage, an old-boy network based on common educational experience and membership of clubs.
2 A new social grouping made up of highly paid professionals and managers.
3 The sociological problem of allocating occupational groups to specific social classes.
4 That it has fragmented into a number of class fractions.
5 They have experienced proletarianisation due to de-skilling and become part of the working class.
6 The idea that skilled manual workers are adopting middle-class lifestyles and attitudes.
7 An over-generous Welfare State and structural constraints such as economic recession, respectively.

9.4 Social mobility

After studying this section you should be able to:

- *identify and outline the nature and extent of patterns of mobility*
- *assess the significance and implications of patterns of mobility for social-class composition*

Defining social mobility

AQA   U6

> Social mobility studies provide evidence for sociologist to assess whether the UK is a meritocratic society.

Social mobility refers to **the movement of individuals between social classes.** Such movement can be either upward or downward. Sociologists distinguish between **inter-generational mobility** (movement between generations, e.g. father and son) and **intra-generational mobility** (movement between jobs within the lifetime of an individual, e.g. starting on the shop-floor and working up to company director).

- **Functionalist and New Right** thinkers believe that social-mobility studies are important because they support their belief that the UK is an open society or meritocracy.

- **Weberians** argue that social-mobility studies are important in order to test theories such as embourgeoisement and proletarianisation.

- **Marxists** argue that social-mobility studies are useful in exposing the 'myth of meritocracy'.

The Oxford Mobility Study

The Oxford (Nuffield) Mobility Study (OMS) conducted in 1972 and associated with the sociologists Goldthorpe and Heath, carried out 10 000 interviews with men aged between 20 and 64 years of age. Goldthorpe allocated these men to three broad classes (the service class, the intermediate class and the working class) on the basis of **market situation** (e.g. salary, fringe benefits, promotion prospects, job security, etc.) and **work situation** (e.g. power, control, autonomy, etc.). Goldthorpe's research uncovered three major findings.

- The OMS found that only a small minority of the service class in 1972 had been born into that class. Most of the service class in 1972 was recruited from either the intermediate or working class.

- The OMS found high rates of '**absolute mobility**'. This means the total mobility that takes place within a society. Comparing sons with fathers in their sample, the OMS discovered much greater opportunities of being upwardly mobile into the service class in the 1950s and 1960s. However, as Goldthorpe pointed out, this was not necessarily the product of meritocracy. Rather Goldthorpe identified three alternative reasons for this profound change.

  - **The service class had almost doubled in numbers because of changes in the job market created by post-war economic expansion in areas such as the Welfare State** – which led to a greater demand for professionals and bureaucrats in the fields of education, welfare and health. Moreover, the nature of the economy changed and the financial sector, in particular, had expanded in the 1950s at the expense of heavy industry.

  - **The fertility rates of the service class were too low to cope with the growth of service-sector jobs.** This sector therefore had no choice but to recruit from other social classes.

  - **The introduction of free secondary education in 1944** made this recruitment easier because for the first time people from other social classes, especially the working class, had access to educational qualifications.

- However, the OMS also challenged the view that this evidence indicates meritocracy by examining rates of '**relative mobility**'. This refers to comparisons of mobility between different social groups. The OMS data indicated that some social groups were more likely than others to fill the top service jobs. Analysis of the OMS data revealed the **1.2.4. Rule of Relative Hope** which suggests that for every working-class male who reaches the service class, two males from the intermediate class achieve the same goal, whilst four sons of the service class would return to the class of their fathers. In other words, the service class was able to provide its sons with more advantages than other classes.

> The OMS does not support the view that the UK is a meritocracy.

Other studies of social mobility

Social mobility studies in the 1980s confirm the pessimistic conclusions of the OMS. **The Scottish Mobility Study (SMS)** conducted by **Payne (1987)** noted that the potential for social mobility was dependent upon age and region. For example, working-class young people working in urban areas in the south of England were more likely to experience upward mobility compared with those in the north and Scotland. Moreover, living and working in urban areas generally led to more opportunities than living and working in rural areas. **The Essex University Mobility Study (EUMS)** led by **Marshall (1984)** found that someone starting in the service class rather than the working class had a **seven** times greater chance of ending up in the service class. The figure increased to thirteen for women. One explanation for these continuing disparities is that the expansion of service-class jobs has slowed down and even ended. This is supported by recent upward trends in middle-class unemployment levels.

> The SMS and EUMS do not support the view that the UK is a meritocracy.

The Saunders critique

The New Right sociologist, **Peter Saunders**, argues that all mobility studies acknowledge improvements in absolute levels of mobility. He argues that this is convincing evidence that capitalism has opened up new opportunities for advancement and brought benefits to the working class. Saunders argues that sociologists like Marshall ignore the possibility that differences in relative mobility between social classes may the result of **natural inequalities, i.e. genetic** or **hereditary factors**. Successful middle-class parents pass on these genetic advantages to their offspring and this is reinforced by superior middle-class parenting skills.

> Saunders argues that the OMS and EUMS studies are politically biased.

Social-mobility studies of women

The evidence suggests **women experience less upward mobility than men**. The **EUMS** found that even when their male and female samples had the same qualifications, women were not as upwardly mobile as men. **The Open University People in Society Survey (OUPSS)** conducted in 1987 concluded that **women were more likely to be downwardly mobile compared with men because of career interruptions** (e.g. pregnancy, child-care, being the secondary breadwinner). Other social factors such as divorce and the likelihood of being head of a single-parent family also impede upward mobility. When women did experience upward mobility, it was limited to travelling from skilled manual to skilled non-manual.

Progress check

1 Define what is meant by inter-generational and intra-generational mobility.

2 What is meant by absolute mobility?

3 Identify three reasons why absolute mobility increased up to the 1980s.

4 What is relative mobility?

5 What is the 1.2.4 Rule of Relative Hope?

6 How does the EUMS confirm the findings of the OMS?

7 What two factors does Saunders use to explain middle-class advantages in mobility?

7 Genetic advantages and superior child-rearing.
6 The chances of working-class children getting top jobs has narrowed even further.
5 Data that reveals that the children of professionals have more opportunity of becoming professionals themselves than working-class children.
4 Mobility as compared between different social classes.
3 The increase in the size of the service class, the failure of the service-class fertility rate to cope with this increase and a more qualified population.
2 The total mobility that takes place within a society.
1 Inter-generational means between generations whilst intra-generational means within one's lifetime.

9.5 Ethnicity and inequality

After studying this section you should be able to:

● *identify specific differences in life-chances according to ethnic-minority background*
● *outline and assess sociological explanations of the relationship between ethnicity and inequality*

Definitions of race and ethnicity

AQA	U6
OCR	U2539

> The term 'ethnic minority' should be used with care. Don't use it as an all-embracing term implying that all ethnic minority groups have the same experience. They don't!

The term '**race**' refers to the classification of human beings into different biological groups on the basis of physical characteristics such as skin colour. '**Ethnicity**' refers to the **cultural and social features of particular groups** such as language, shared history, religion and cultural traditions. Usually the term 'ethnicity' is used in conjunction with comparatively small and powerless minorities who subscribe to significantly different customs and beliefs from a majority culture, which they live alongside.

There is a good deal of evidence that ethnic-minority groups in the UK are subjected to racism. **Racism** refers to a combination of discriminatory practices, unequal relations and power and prejudice. **Institutional racism** is the idea that racist assumptions are built into the rules and routines of Britain's social institutions, thus neglecting the specific needs of ethnic minorities. Recently both the Home Office and the London Metropolitan Police have separately admitted that their organisations are institutionally racist. This type of racism is taken for granted and habitual – in other words, it has become so institutionalised, it is not recognised as racism, e.g. in the police force, the practice of automatically assuming that black youth are suspicious or criminal.

Prejudice refers to a type of negative thinking that relies heavily on stereotypes which are usually factually incorrect, exaggerated and distorted. **Discrimination** is prejudice put into practice in regard to jobs, housing, racial attacks and perhaps even policing.

Ethnicity, workplace inequality and discrimination

Ethnic minorities are disadvantaged compared with the ethnic-majority population but there are also important differences between the various minorities.

Unemployment rates for white men were 8% in 1995 compared with 18% for Pakistani/Bangladeshi men and 21% for black men (Afro-Caribbean). Unemployment is particularly severe for young ethnic-minority people. In the late 1980s, unemployment among young whites aged 16–24 was 12% but 25% for Afro-Caribbean youth and 27% for Pakistani/Bangladeshi youth.

White males are twice as likely as Afro-Caribbeans and Pakistani/Bangladeshi males to hold down professional and managerial jobs, although Indian and Chinese participation – levels in these types of jobs is only 2% behind whites. Only 52% of the white workforce in 1988–90 worked in manual jobs compared with 68% of Afro-Caribbeans, 71% of Pakistanis and 75% of Bangladeshis. Manual jobs that are available to ethnic minorities are often dirty, poorly paid and involve unsociable hours, e.g. shift-work. Ethnic minorities also generally earn low incomes because of their higher rates of unemployment and their likelihood of occupying semi-skilled and unskilled manual work.

Theoretical explanations for ethnic inequalities in employment

AQA   U6
OCR   U2539

Weberian explanations

Parkin argues that ethnic inequalities stem from **status inequality** which Weberian sociologists see as being just as influential as social class. Status and power are in the hands of the majority ethnic group, therefore, making it difficult for ethnic-minority groups to compete equally for jobs, housing, etc.

Focus on racism.

The **'dual labour market'** theory of **Barron and Norris** suggests that there are two labour markets – the **primary sector** characterised by secure, well-paid jobs with long-term promotion prospects dominated by white men, and the **secondary sector**, characterised by low-paid, unskilled and insecure jobs. Barron and Norris point out that black people are more likely to be found in the secondary sector. They are less likely to gain primary-sector employment because employers may subscribe to racist beliefs about the unsuitability of black people and practise discrimination against them when applying for jobs or deny them responsibility and promotion.

Some Weberians, especially **Rex and Tomlinson**, argue that ethnic-minority experience of both class and status inequality can lead to poverty – which is made more severe by racism. Consequently, a **black underclass** may exist which lacks any power to change its situation and which feels alienated and frustrated. This sometimes results in **inner-city riots**.

Marxist explanations

Marxists are adamant that **black people are part of the exploited working class** and they generally see status inequality as less important than class inequality. They argue that racism is a **capitalist ideology** aimed at encouraging white workers to perceive black workers as a threat to their jobs. Marxists therefore see racism as a **'divide and rule'** tactic. Black people can also be **scapegoated** for unemployment (e.g. beliefs like 'they've come over here to take our jobs') or inner-city decline (e.g. 'this was a nice neighbourhood before they moved in').

Focuses on how racism benefits capitalism.

Criticisms of Marxism

It is difficult to prove that racism is a capitalist ideology. If racism is of benefit to capitalism, this is probably an accidental by-product rather than a deliberately constructed ideology.

Robert Miles

Miles argues that we should see ethnic minorities as members of **'racialised class fractions'**, meaning that there are significant cultural differences between them and the white working-class. This may result in them stressing aspects of their ethnic identity. For example, young Afro-Caribbeans may stress black power through membership of the Rastafarian sect or by stressing elements of black history. Asians may stress family ties and community. The result of this may be little contact between black, Asian and white working-class communities which may encourage greater suspicion and mutual hostility.

Acknowledges differences in experience of ethnic minority groups.

Miles also notes that some ethnic minorities who are members of the middle class may see their interests lying with capitalism. Their ethnic culture, e.g. the Asian emphasis on entrepreneurship, enterprise and mutual support, may be advantageous in achieving business success. However, Miles points out that racism probably means that the white middle-class will never accept that Asian professionals have the same status as them.

Progress check

1 What is the difference between race and ethnicity?

2 Define what is meant by institutional racism.

3 Which two ethnic-minority groups are relatively successful in gaining access to professional and managerial jobs?

4 What do Weberians see as the main cause of ethnic inequalities generally?

5 Why do Marxists see racism as an ideology that benefits capitalism?

6 What does Miles mean when he says black people exist as a racialised class fraction within the working class?

1 Race refers to physical differences whilst ethnicity refers to cultural differences.
2 Racist assumptions that are built into the rules and routines of institutions in such a way that racist practices go unrecognised as such.
3 Indians and Chinese.
4 Status inequality in the form of racism.
5 It divides and rules the working class white working class grievances away from employers to black people.
6 They are objectively part of the working class but will never be accepted as such by the white working-class. They therefore develop alternative ethnic identities.

9.6 Gender and inequality

After studying this section you should be able to:

- *identify specific differences in life-chances according to gender*
- *outline and assess sociological explanations of the relationship between gender and inequality*

LEARNING SUMMARY

Gender inequalities in employment

AQA U6
OCR U2539

Since the 1950s there has been a trend towards the **'feminisation' of the labour force.** For example, between 1969 and 1989 the number of female workers in the UK rose by 2.25 million (whereas males rose by only 0.5 million).

Labour market segmentation

Sociologists have noted that the labour market is both **horizontally** and **vertically** segregated in terms of gender.

- **Horizontal segregation** refers to the sectors in which people work. A survey by the **Equal Opportunities Commission (EOC) in 1996** concluded that women in the public sector were mainly employed in health and education, especially teaching. For example, nursing and primary-school teaching is almost exclusively female. In the private sector women are over-concentrated in clerical, administrative, retail and personal services such as catering, whereas men are mainly found in the skilled manual and upper professional sectors.

- **Vertical segregation** refers to levels of jobs and pay. Women tend to be concentrated at the **lower levels of employment in terms of skill and consequently status.** They are more likely than men to be employed in **part-time work** and in temporary or casual work. Even when women gain access to the upper professional or management sector, they are likely to encounter a 'glass ceiling'. For example, in 1991, 69% of managers and 83% of professionals were male.

There exists a **gender pay-gap**. In 1998 the EOC noted that the average gross weekly pay of all women was only 72.5% of men's earnings. **The EOC estimate that the average pay-gap has remained steady at 20%.**

Theoretical explanations of gender stratification and inequality

AQA ▷ U6
OCR ▷ U2539

▷ Focuses on male domination of labour market.

The **'dual labour market'** theory of **Barron and Norris** suggests that women are more likely than men to be found in the **secondary labour-market** because employers subscribe to stereotypical beliefs about the unsuitability of women. Promotion streams are organised in ways that match the life experiences of men better than women because employers demand continuous service. The legal and political framework supporting women is weak. Both the Equal Pay Act and Sex Discrimination Act are feeble laws, which fail to protect women's employment rights.

Neo-Weberian sociologists like Barron and Norris are saying that women are experiencing **status inequality** because of **patriarchy**. The patriarchal nature of society makes discrimination against women at work both 'natural' and possible. Better qualifications and increased ambition for women may not therefore automatically dismantle gender divisions in employment. Women with the same qualifications as men will continue to be disadvantaged as long as these two labour markets continue to exist and are underpinned with patriarchal assumptions about the role of women.

However, in criticism, **Bradley** points out that Barron and Norris fail to explain inequalities in the same sector. For example, teaching is not a secondary-labour-market job yet women are less likely than men to gain high-status jobs in this profession.

Liberal feminism

▷ Focuses on agencies of socialisation.

Liberal feminists argue that gender roles are largely socially constructed through the socialisation process, primarily in the family, but also through such secondary agencies as the education system and the mass media. In other words, **gender-role socialisation** is responsible for reproducing a sexual division of labour in which masculinity is largely seen as dominant and femininity as subordinate.

Liberal feminist research in the 1970s, in particular, focused on how the dominant images of females disseminated by such agencies as the family, education, and mass media stressed marriage as a priority and education and careers as secondary. In the 1990s, liberal feminists have suggested that these processes are coming to an end. **Sue Sharpe's** work on the attitudes of teenage girls suggests that education and careers are now a priority for young women, whilst females have also enjoyed great educational success in recent years.

Another liberal feminist, **Ann Oakley**, argues that the main reason for the subordination of women in the labour market is the **dominance of the mother–housewife role for women**.

In criticism, **Sylvia Walby (1990)** suggests that although there is evidence that masculinity and femininity are socially constructed, liberal feminism does not explain why this leads to men dominating and women being oppressed. Second, it implies that people passively accept their gender identities and underestimates the **degree of resistance** of women. Third, it fails to acknowledge that women's experiences differ according to social class and race.

Marxist–feminism

Focuses on capitalism.

Marxist-feminists suggest that **capitalist ideologies locate women in the home.** The idea that married women have less right to a job than men is common among management, unions and women themselves. Women make up a **reserve army of labour** which is hired when the economy is booming. Therefore when women are made unemployed such ideology operates to suggest that 'women have gone back to their proper jobs'.

The reserve army of labour theory has been criticised because it does not explain why male and female labour is put to different uses. In other words, it fails to explain why there are men's jobs and women's jobs. Moreover, if women are cheaper than men, surely capitalists would get rid of the more expensive men. In other words, men's jobs would be more insecure.

Triple-systems theory

Excellent definition of patriarchy – adopt it!

> **KEY POINT**
>
> **Sylvia Walby's 'triple systems theory'** develops the concept of patriarchy to explain gender stratification. She suggests that patriarchy has three elements to it:
>
> - **subordination** – patriarchal institutions like the family, media and education inevitably produce unequal relations between men and women
> - **oppression** – women experience sexism because men discriminate against them on the basis of unfounded stereotypes or ideology
> - **exploitation** – men exploit women's skills and labour without rewarding them sufficiently, e.g. in the home.

Walby argues that **patriarchy interacts with capitalism and racism to produce gender stratification.** This results in the subordination, exploitation and oppression of women in the family, at work, in sexual relations (e.g. the sexual double standard) and in culture systems (e.g. the mass media represents women either as sex objects, as appendages of men or as mothers). The state, too, acts in the interests of men rather than women, e.g. in terms of taxation and welfare rules, the weakness of laws protecting women at work, etc. However, Walby does acknowledge that inequalities between men and women vary over time and in intensity. For example, young women are now achieving better educational qualifications than young men.

Rational-choice theory

Hakim suggests patriarchy is not to blame.

Catherine Hakim is extremely critical of all the previous feminist positions. She argues that feminist theories of patriarchy are both inaccurate and misleading. She argues that women are not victims of unfair employment practices. Rather they make **rational choices** in terms of the type of work they do, e.g. they choose part-time work in order to manage child-care and housework because they choose to put child-care first. She argues that a lack of available and affordable child-care is not a major barrier to women getting jobs because mothers prioritise childrearing over employment. In other words, women are not as committed to careers as men.

Hakim's own work has provoked criticism. For example, **Ginn and Arber** point out that all too often it is employer attitudes rather than women's attitudes that confine women to the secondary labour-market.

Progress check

1 Explain the meaning of horizontal segregation.

2 Give two examples of vertical segregation.

3 What is meant by the 'glass ceiling'?

4 Give two reasons why women are more likely to occupy the secondary labour market.

5 Define patriarchy.

6 What do Liberal feminists blame for gender inequalities?

7 What do Marxist feminists blame for gender inequalities?

8 Why does gender inequality exist, according to Hakim?

8 Because women make rational choices to forego their careers and bring up children.

7 Capitalism and patriarchy.

6 Any from: patriarchy; institutionalisation of the mother–housewife role; gender role socialisation.

5 A male-dominated society in which women are subordinated, exploited and oppressed by men.

4 Any two from: employers are prejudiced against women; the laws protecting women workers are weak; the mother–housewife role interrupts women's careers; etc.

3 It refers to the idea that well-qualified women are capable of top jobs but the male occupational culture and gatekeepers prevent female access to them.

2 Pay differentials and the fact that women are found mainly in part-time work.

1 It refers to the trend of women finding themselves in different employment sectors to men.

Sample synoptic question and model answer

An AQA synoptic question.

Item A

In modern industrial societies like Britain, social class forms one of the main ways in which society is stratified. However, definitions of social class are not straightforward and there are disagreements on how to measure it.

There are many characteristics which individuals possess that may form the basis of an identification or grouping in society. In modern industrial societies, ethnicity is a form of stratification which is increasingly important. Others take the view that what unites all women – their situation of disadvantage compared to men – is more important than the differences in income or circumstances that might divide them.

(Adapted from Sociology for A Level: A skills-based approach *(1997) by Tony Lawson, Collins Educational, pages 129–133.)*

Always read a question properly – note the focus on 'apart from social class'.

(a) Briefly discuss the different types of stratification found in modern societies apart from social class. **(8 marks)**

Gender is an important form of stratification in modern societies according to feminists. They see modern societies as patriarchal in that men dominate, exploit and oppress women at work and in the family. This latter institution is seen as the major cause and site of women's oppression because both men and women are socialised into gender roles which stress male dominance and female subordination. Examples of gender stratification can clearly be seen in the field of employment.

Another important type of stratification is ethnicity. If we look at employment and unemployment we can see great inequalities between Afro-Caribbeans and the white population. There is plenty of empirical evidence that suggests that this may be partly due to employer racism and the institutional racism recently acknowledged by a range of social institutions.

A synoptic question in that it focuses on the reliability and validity of how sociologists measure social class.

(b) Examine the extent to which classifications of occupations are useful as measurements of social class. **(12 marks)**

Until 2000 social class was measured using the Registrar-General's (RG) classification of occupations which divided jobs into five major social classes. However, this system which was in place for over 80 years, was criticised because it failed to include certain key groups who lacked paid work but who were very much part of the class system. These included the wealthy who lived off their inheritance, rents, etc., the never-employed unemployed and housewives. Moreover, the RG scale was based on the job of the head of the household and this was always assumed to be the male. The fact that families relied just as much on the wife's income was ignored as, too, were cross-class families in which wives were in higher status and paid jobs than their husbands.

In the year 2000 the RG scale has been replaced by the socio-economic classification (NS-SEC) which is still based on jobs but categorises them into eight categories on the basis of 'employment relations' (i.e. status of job, exercise of authority, etc.) and 'market conditions' (i.e. salary, promotion prospects, control over work, etc.). The self-employed and the never-employed unemployed are now included although there is still no sign of the wealthy. Women are now recognised as a group of earners in their own right. However, it is still not a precise measurement of social class. It tells us little about the huge differences in occupations in the same category, e.g. consultants and junior doctors differ in a number of respects but are placed in the same category.

Sample synoptic question and model answer *(continued)*

An essay question – you should aim for at least two sides.

Introduction identifies view, i.e. Hakim.

Outline of Hakim's view.

Evaluation of Hakim.

Alternatives to Hakim.

Conclusion – summarises key arguments covered.

(c) Assess the view that gender inequalities are the result of women making rational choices about their futures rather than patriarchy.   (40 marks)

The above view is that of Catherine Hakim who has entered into a controversial debate with feminist sociologists as to the cause of the horizontal and vertical forms of gender inequality that are evident in employment.

Hakim argues that patriarchy is not the cause of gender inequality in employment. She argues that the real cause lies in women making rational choices about work and family life. For example, she suggests that women's commitment to work and careers is not equal to men's and lack of child-care is not the main barrier to women's employment. She, instead, argues that many women choose to put children and family first. This is because many women are happy with the traditional sexual division of labour. Consequently they are happy to enter work on a part-time or flexible basis and to spend less time in full-time paid work as men do. In fact, Hakim argues that the great movement of women into economic life which feminism is very keen to emphasise is a myth because most of the jobs women do are part-time.

Feminists argue that Hakim puts too much emphasis on women's attitudes and commitment to paid work. She is accused of neglecting patriarchal and family ideology which 'persuades' mothers to stay at home by making them feel guilty about working and allegedly neglecting their children. Moreover, she ignores the structural barriers in place in the male-dominated world of work.

Such structural barriers are highlighted by the dual labour-market theory which suggests that work is made up of a primary market dominated by men on good pay experiencing training and promotion opportunities and a secondary market dominated by females made up of low-paid, part-time work. Barron and Norris argue that this segregation is the result of employer attitudes that see women as less reliable than men because of their family commitments. Gatekeepers, i.e. managers and personnel officers who control entry to the primary labour market, are often men who subscribe to patriarchal ideas about women's roles.

Marxist-feminists argue that gender inequality is directly related to the organisation of capitalism. Capitalism's need for a fit and healthy workforce and future labour force means that it transmits a patriarchal ideology that stresses that the mother-housewife role should be the primary concern of women. In other words, capitalism not only exploits its male workforce but it also exploits the domestic labour of women.

In conclusion, however, Hakim argues that we need to stop presenting women as victims of patriarchy and capitalism. She argues that women's roles both within the home and at work are not shaped by social forces beyond their control. Women, she says, are not an 'undifferentiated mass' of mindless zombies. Rather, she says that women are active as social actors in rationally choosing their own destiny. Feminists beg to differ with this view and, although they recognise that women are social actors exercising choices, they argue that these choices are severely constrained by a social structure and ideology largely shaped by patriarchy and capitalism.

Practice synoptic examination question

Item A

Andrew Adonis and Stephen Pollard argue that social class is very much in evidence in the late 1990s and is being bolstered by the emergence of a new social class in Britain. They point to evidence of an emerging professional and managerial élite, a new 'Super Class', separating off from other professionals and managers who are lower paid and mainly in the public sector. Glimpses of the new Super Class have come through newspaper coverage of the fat-cats of business and industry whose earnings have been portrayed as outrageous. But according to Adonis and Pollard, these are just the tip of the iceberg. There are many, many more top earners operating at the higher echelons of the financial services industry mainly located in the City of London and in the private-sector professions. This is where the new Super Class is coming from.

(Source: adapted from Sociology Update, (1998) *by Martyn Denscombe, Olympus Books, p.90.)*

Item B

Social Class from British General Election surveys, by respondent

		1964 %	1992 %
I	Higher salariat	7.0	11.6
II	Lower salariat	12.3	16.3
III	Routine clerical	16.5	24.2
IV	Petty Bourgeoisie	6.6	7.1
V	Foremen and technicians	7.6	4.8
VI	Skilled manual	17.8	10.9
VII	Unskilled manual	32.4	25.1

(Source: A. Heath, Nuffield College, Oxford University quoted in Sociology Update (1998).*)*

(a) Using the information in Item A, briefly outline in your own words what is meant by the term 'super class'. (10 marks)

(b) Summarise the patterns shown by the data in the table in Item B. (10 marks)

(c) Identify the problems facing sociologists trying to research social class. (18 marks)

(d) Using your sociological knowledge from any one area of social life with which you are familiar, show how 'social class is very much in evidence in the late 1990s'. (30 marks)

(e) Outline and assess any one sociological explanation of class inequality. (52 marks)

Practice examination answers

Chapter 1 Theory and method

This is a typical AQA question.

1 (a) Any from: Only 45 women were interviewed. The women in the survey were mainly professional women who may not be representative of working women in general. There is no indication in the data that a range of different types of women, e.g. working class, members of ethnic minorities, etc. were sampled.

(b) 'Women who choose childlessness are rejecting parenting because they see having children as both socially and financially disruptive.'

(c) In terms of strengths, you might have focused on: the comparative approach; the way the schoolchildren were randomly sampled; the representativeness of the sample, especially the equal sex-ratio; interviews with offenders in their home to decrease the threat factor and anonymity of the questionnaires.

In terms of weaknesses, you might have focused on: the offenders might think the research was official and feel threatened by it, refuse to co-operate with it, etc. – responses may therefore not reflect the truth; despite anonymity, the questionnaires were still supervised by teachers and in reaction, some pupils may not have co-operated fully; experience of self-reports tell us that adolescent boys have a tendency to exaggerate, lie, not take surveys seriously, etc.

(d) Possibilities for this hypothesis are: (i) Structured interviews with the parents of a sample of delinquents. The interview schedule should attempt to operationalise the concepts of socialisation, discipline and social control in such a way that it is not judgmental of the parents. The parents could be interviewed together, although a more interesting variation might be to interview them separately and compare data to get a gendered version of their child's upbringing. (ii) Examine secondary data in the form of social-work records (official documents) prepared for the juvenile court. These are derived from a range of sources: school reports, interviews with teachers, people in the community, police, etc. They may give us an official picture of the parenting situation.

2 • Begin by defining what is meant by a structural theory (i.e. human behaviour is strongly influenced by, and even shaped by, the structure or social organisation of society) and by social action theory (i.e. human behaviour is not shaped by social structure but by interaction and interpretation – people choose to behave the way they do).

• Outline structuralist ideas in general but use both functionalism and Marxism to illustrate. This can be done by reference to general functionalist theory (i.e. human behaviour is the result of value consensus) or general Marxist theory (i.e. working-class behaviour is the product of ideology and the class inequality that characterises the infrastructure). Other topics could be used to illustrate the functionalist and Marxist argument, e.g. education or religion would be good choices.

• Outline the general principles of social action theory, i.e. people have consciousness, they can choose to act in certain ways, etc. Think about using interactionist theories of classroom interaction to illustrate. Show teachers may label pupils and how these are transmitted to pupils and interpreted in various ways. These interactions and interpretations may result in a self-fulfilling prophecy, pupil resistance or pupils learning to interact with teachers in such a way that they negotiate their way through school without attracting too much teacher attention.

• The question says 'assess' – structuralist theory is accused of ignoring day-to-day social action in favour of macro relationships between institutions like the educational system and the economy. It is also a little over-deterministic in its insistence that people are shaped by society and fails to consider that people may shape society and its institutions. Social action theory neglects larger issues such as social class, gender and race.

• Finish off by outlining Giddens' structuration theory which combines both structuralist and social action approaches.

Chapter 2 Power and politics

This is a typical OCR question.
Note the focus on *outline* (you must describe the view) and *assess* (you must criticise it).

• Begin by clearly defining what is meant by 'new social movements' (NSMs). A good way to do this in an introduction might be to compare it with a definition of either a 'pressure group' and/or an 'old social movement'.

• Elaborate on your definition by describing the characteristics of NSMs, i.e. loose-knit, informal, non-hierarchical, participatory, etc. Finish this section with some illustration of examples of NSMs in different fields, e.g. environmentalism/Greenpeace, animal rights/Animal Liberation Front, etc.

• Focus on the use of direct action as an NSM tactic. Examples: Greenpeace's Rainbow Warrior, the destruction of genetically modified crops, etc.

• Outline theories of NSMs – attempt to link these to specific key words in the essay title. For example, Marcuse focuses on the cultural order when he sees NSMs as challenging mass culture and alienation. Touraine sees NSMs as challenging the overly bureaucratic and rational economic and political order.

• Critique: two possible sources: (i) Marxism – the influence of NSMs is exaggerated because social-class divisions are still more important than identity inequalities. People still see their class identity as very important and consequently are more concerned with class divisions and inequalities. (ii) Post-modernism – sees NSMs very positively because they are a symbol of diversity but acknowledges the potential conflict that might arise from irrational and emotional competition between different identities.

Chapter 3 Religion

This is a typical AQA question.

(a) There are some major events in life that can cause great crisis, anxiety and disruption. These include the birth of a child, the onset of puberty, marriage and especially death. All of these events are accompanied by ceremonies that help members of society re-adjust to changed circumstances. The funeral is a symbolic activity which celebrates the dead person as a member of a social group. It also gives people the opportunity to show group support for bereaved relatives. It binds the bereaved together as a social group. It marks the end of official mourning when the bereaved are expected to re-take their place in society.

(b) It was Weber's belief that scientific rationalism was replacing religion as the main explanation for questions which were once answered by religion. Wilson argued that people have become increasingly 'disenchanted' with religion and have more faith in science today. However, his critics argue that he may be over-emphasising the influence of rationality because there is evidence that people prefer 'religious' explanations for random events like early death and people still believe in horoscopes, luck, fate, etc. Social-attitude surveys show that a majority of people believe in God.

(c) Your introduction should begin by clearly defining sects and cults – describe their characteristics and give examples.

- Elaborate by examining the key arguments relating to 'the anxieties created by profound social change':
  - Wilson on sects appearing as a reaction to the anxieties caused by early industrialisation and urbanisation
  - Wallis and Bellah on the rejection by young people of the materialist values associated with capitalism at the end of the 1960s and the subsequent popularity of hippy and Eastern mystical sects and cults
  - the appearance of millennium cults at the end of the 20th century obviously worried about what 2000 would bring – link to suicide, e.g. Heaven's Gate, The Solar Temple, etc.
- Look at other possible explanations as a form of evaluation, especially ideas revolving around deprivation – economic, social, organismic, ethical and psychic. Some of these may be related to social change. Also mention disillusionment with the established church – Nelson argues that sects and cults indicate that young people in particular are turned off by established religions – sects, etc. are a rejection of traditional rituals and symbolic of the search for a new type of spirituality, etc.

Chapter 4 World sociology

This is a typical AQA question.

(a) Western countries have not given aid to the Third World as generously as they promised the United Nations they would. Very little aid to the developing world directly benefits the poor because most new aid goes to paying off the interest on previous loans. As a result, some countries are going bankrupt. Some countries seem to get aid by simply giving the USA political support in times of war.

(b) A very straightforward question. Briefly outline some trends in debt but spend most of this response on the effects of debt dependency – such as money which would be better spent on education, health, clean water supplies, etc. being spent on servicing debt interest. Also describe how easy it is to manipulate the internal politics of a country if it is in debt – for example, the USA was able to use debt dependency to gain UN support from countries such as Kenya and Pakistan during the Gulf War.

(c) Your introduction should focus on facts of gender inequality in the developing world, e.g. relating to jobs women do, illiteracy, life expectancy, reproductive rights, health, etc.

- Elaboration – think about what modernisation theory might blame, i.e. internal obstacles; patriarchal cultures and religions that ascribe women to the home. Solutions are education for women, family-planning programmes, etc.
- Elaboration – think about what Marxists would blame, i.e. external factors – colonialism exported traditional values about men and women from West, aid agencies discriminate in favour of males whilst multinationals exploit women's labour. Solution – socialism
- Evaluation – women are just as exploited in socialist and developed societies. In Western societies, women experience gender inequality especially in terms of pay and domestic responsibilities, patriarchy is a global fact, etc.

Chapter 5 Education

This is a typical OCR question.

Your introduction should focus on two facts:

- males have always been the disadvantaged sex in education but
- it was always assumed that females were more disadvantaged.

Boys have always failed but it was not regarded as a major social problem because there were plenty of jobs available for these 'failures' to do. Females have actually done quite well at school but were less likely to go on to university and if they did it was always into stereotypically female subjects. It was outside school that gender inequalities were very pronounced – especially in pay. However, a number of female-centred initiatives have led to girls out-performing boys at virtually every level.

Therefore you should focus on three broad explanations for boys' underachievement.

- It is the fault of teachers – who have allowed a culture of male underachievement to thrive.

Chapter 5 Education

- Learning is associated with a culture of femininity (e.g. mothers, female primary-school teachers) which boys reject as they get older.
- The crisis of masculinity has led to anti-school subcultures because boys can see that male jobs are in decline and therefore they don't see the point of qualifications.

In your evaluation cover the following:

- Middle-class boys and some ethnic-minority boys (especially Indians) do very well, whilst working-class girls and some ethnic-minority girls (especially Pakistani and Bangladeshi) do poorly.
- Therefore social class and race may be more influential than gender.

Chapter 6 Health

This is a typical OCR question.

Your introduction should clearly focus on the notion of class inequalities. Three specific types of illustration relating to inequalities should be used.

- Morbidity – show differences between Social Class I and Social Class V in relation to the types of illness and disease they experience.
- Mortality – illustrate how these differ especially in regard to infant mortality.
- Recent trends – these indicate that the gap in morbidity and mortality between Social Class V and the rest has actually increased, (despite the NHS) since 1980.

Elaboration should focus on a range of explanations. You should use studies to illustrate:

- Cultural – blames the behavioural habits and values of the victim or the culture of the victim.
- Material – blames the living conditions especially poverty, low income, etc.

- Administrative – blames the allocation and distribution of NHS resources and services, the Conservative re-organisation of the NHS plus the fact that the middle class have access to the private sector.
- Structural – Marxists blame the organisation of capitalism.
- Feminist – blames gender-role socialisation and working-class definitions of masculinity in a patriarchal society.
- The third way – combination of cultural, material, administrative and structural explanations. NHS policy now encourages people to take more responsibility for their health and welfare whilst acknowledging that the state has an obligation to deal with problems beyond the individual's power and control.

Evaluation might acknowledge gender and ethnic inequalities which probably interact with social class. Those at the very bottom of the socio-economic hierarchy, i.e. ethnic-minority groups may suffer greater stresses than working-class whites (e.g. racial prejudice and racial attacks) which means that their health might be significantly worse than that of the white working-class.

Chapter 7 Social policy and welfare

This is a typical OCR question.

Your introduction needs to define what is meant by 'the post-war consensus' in regard to the Welfare State. Moreover, when did it break up? – Mrs Thatcher took office in 1979 and set about reforming the welfare system.

You also need to define what 'universal welfare services and benefits' mean. Child benefit is an example of a universal benefit – meaning it is paid to all mothers. However, welfare in the UK has always been made up of a combination of universal and selective (i.e. means-tested) benefits. What you need to work out is whether there was a decline in universal benefits and a rise in means-tested services or benefits.

Elaboration: Outline the ideology of Mrs Thatcher, i.e. the New Right, in regard to the Welfare State. You should particular highlight:

- the role of market forces,
- rolling back the frontiers of the state and
- privatisation.

The question focuses on benefits and services so focus your response on social security. Outline the changes made to the benefit system. For example, highlight:

- the freezing of child benefit (universal benefit)
- fears about the costs of pensions (universal benefit) – huge campaign, carried on by Labour in 1998, to encourage people to invest in private-pension schemes

- simplification of unemployment benefit (universal) but clauses attached to deny benefit if perceived not to be looking seriously for a job or if a training course is turned down
- income support/Job Seekers Allowance (means-tested). This benefit (which usually supplements a pension and unemployment/disability benefit) has always been means-tested. Housing benefit was significantly reduced after 1986. Income support for 16- and 17-year-olds was abolished
- introduction of a Social Fund (means-tested). Previously grants given for one-off major items such as a cooker or school uniform for a child. Social Fund involves loans which must be paid back
- privatisation of services – give examples
- incentives to opt into private welfare and health schemes were introduced.

Outline Labour policy on social security. You will hopefully notice that they have not significantly altered Conservative reforms but have adopted a so-called third way which stresses helping the 'socially excluded'. However you should outline the 'New Deal' and how this has led to 'welfare to work' schemes and the 'working families tax credit'. Note, too, Labour's support of private stake-holder pensions.

Conclusion – means-tested benefits have increased but universal benefits remain in place.

Chapter 8 Crime and deviance

This is a typical OCR question.

- Introduction – set the scene. You will need to clearly define white-collar and corporate crime with examples and clearly state that middle-class and upper-class individuals and companies commit this type of crime.

- Elaboration –

  - The official criminal statistics (OCS) show that most recorded and reported crime is committed by working-class individuals. However, critics of the OCS note that these are socially constructed – they are the end product of policing and judicial practices which are systematically biased against working-class individuals. You should focus in particular on the radical critique of the OCS – this argues that white-collar crimes are selectively policed, under-punished and not defined as 'serious crimes' by the law and its agents.

  - Outline the reasons for this by describing the Marxist theory of crime and social control – the law and the OCS are an ideological attempt to criminalise the working class in order to distract society from class inequality and the mismanagement of capitalism.

  - Evaluate the Marxist perspective by outlining the work of Hazel Croall on white-collar crime and the practical reasons why such crimes go unreported, undetected and under-punished. Left Realists acknowledge white-collar crime but point out that it is working-class and black street crime and burglary that cause real fear in communities, not white-collar crime.

Chapter 9 Stratification, social inequality and difference

This is a typical OCR synoptic question.

(a) The super class is a group of professionals and managers mainly working in the City of London who are earning fantastic 'fat-cat' salaries. Their earnings have made them so wealthy that they have little in common with lower paid professionals and managers, mainly found in the public sector who traditionally make up the middle class. The super class has more in common with the upper class.

(b) Between 1964 and 1992 the employment sectors that have been traditionally seen as 'working class', i.e. foremen and technicians, skilled manual and unskilled manual, have fallen from 57.8% of the working population to 40.8%. In the same period there has been a rise in the number of middle-class jobs, from 42.4% in 1964 to 59.2%. Therefore, working-class jobs are now in the minority. However, some Marxist sociologists argue that routine clerical workers who have traditionally been categorised as middle class, have undergone proletarianisation and are now part of the working class. If this is so, then the majority of jobs are still working class.

(c) There are three broad problems faced by sociologists researching social class which need to be discussed.

  - *Defining and, consequently, measuring the concept.* You should examine the problems involved with the Registrar-General's classification of jobs into social classes. This was replaced in 2000 by the NS-SEC. Briefly describe how it differs and discuss one or two potential problems.

  - *The 'boundary' problem.* You need to focus on changes in the economy (as illustrated by Item B) and show that class categories are no longer straightforward. Brief references could be made to the super class (as in Item A), embourgeoisement, proletarianisation and the underclass.

  - There is often a difference between *objective measurements* of social class and people's *subjective interpretation* of their class position.

(d) Areas of social life might include:

  - the distribution of income, wealth and poverty
  - education
  - health, i.e. morbidity and mortality.

Outline examples of class inequalities from one of these areas.

(e) The focus is on class inequality so outline the Marxist theory of stratification paying particular attention to the following concepts:

  - mode of production
  - social relations of production
  - means of production
  - bourgeoisie
  - proletariat
  - labour power
  - surplus value
  - exploitation
  - infrastructure
  - superstructure
  - ideology
  - false class-consciousness.

Don't forget to evaluate this by:

- briefly outlining Weber's ideas about other sources of inequality
- briefly describing the functionalist idea that inequality is inevitable and beneficial (functional) to society, and
- pointing out that Marx's predictions (i.e. the middle class would disappear and the working class would eventually recognise their exploitation and overthrow the ruling class) did not happen.

However, Marxism has provided sociology with an effective and convincing analysis of how economic relationships can lead to social and economic inequalities.

You could have answered this question by examining the Marxist or functionalist perspectives. I chose Marxism because it is concerned purely with class inequality.

Index